MW01244730

EX AUDITU

An International Journal for the Theological Interpretation of Scripture

VOL. 30   **2014**

Ex Auditu is published annually by Pickwick Publications, an imprint of
Wipf and Stock Publishers, 199 West 8th Avenue, Suite 3, Eugene, Oregon 97401, USA

SUBSCRIPTIONS

Individuals:
U.S.A. and all other countries (in U.S. funds): $20.00
Students: $12.00

Institutions:
U.S.A. and all other countries (in U.S. funds): $30.00

This periodical is indexed in the ATLA Religion Database, published by the American
Theological Library Association, 300 S. Wacker Dr., Suite 2100, Chicago, IL 60606, Email:
atla@atla.com, www: http://www.atla.com/; *Internationale Zeitschriftenshau für Bibelwissen-
schaft; Religious and Theological Abstracts;* and *Old Testament Abstracts.*

Please address all subscription correspondence
and change of address information to Wipf and Stock Publishers.

ISSN: 0083-005-3
ISBN: 978-1-4982-2438-3

EX AUDITU

An International Journal for the Theological Interpretation of Scripture

Klyne R. Snodgrass, Editor
Stephen J. Chester, Associate Editor
D. Christopher Spinks, Associate Editor

North Park Theological Seminary
3225 West Foster Avenue
Chicago, Illinois 60625-4987
USA

Tel: (773) 244-6243
Fax: (773) 244-6244
email: ksnodgrass@northpark.edu
Web site: http://wipfandstock.com/catalog/
  journal/view/id/12/

EDITORIAL BOARD

Terence E. Fretheim, Luther Seminary,
  St. Paul, MN
Richard B. Hays, The Divinity School,
  Duke University, Durham, NC
Jon R. Stock, Wipf & Stock Publishers,
  Eugene, OR
Miroslav Volf, Yale Divinity School,
  New Haven, CT
John Wipf, Wipf & Stock Publishers,
  Eugene, OR

THE EDITORIAL BOARD MEMBERS AND CONSULTANTS represent various disciplines and denominations. Theological interpretation of Scripture is a task to be taken seriously by scholars who are committed to the Christian faith and tradition. However, as one editorial consultant stated: "Let people gradually get used to the idea that a sane hermeneutics is both oriented in advance toward agreement/consent and is simultaneously exigent, discriminating, critical."

CONTENTS

Contents

ANNOUNCEMENT OF THE 2015 SYMPOSIUM

North Park Theological Seminary in Chicago, Illinois, is pleased to announce that the thirty-first Symposium on the Theological Interpretation of Scripture will take place September 24–26, 2015. The symposium will start at 7:00 p.m. on September 24 in Nyvall Hall and will extend through a Saturday afternoon worship service on September 26. The theme in 2015 will be Race and Racism. The following persons have agreed to make presentations:

Ray Aldred, Theology, Ambrose Seminary/Ambrose University
Lewis O. Brogdon, New Testament, Claflin University
Bo Lim, Old Testament, Seattle Pacific University
Nestor Medina, Theology, Regent University
Emerson Powery, New Testament, Messiah College
Love Sechrest, New Testament, Fuller Theological Seminary
Lisa Sung, Theology, Trinity Evangelical Divinity School
Soong-Chan Rah, Preaching, North Park Theological Seminary
Kyle Small, Church Leadership, Western Theological Seminary

Persons interested in attending the sessions should write before September 1 to:

Ms. Guylla Brown
North Park Theological Seminary
3225 W. Foster Avenue
Chicago, Illinois 60625

Meals may be taken at North Park and assistance can be provided in finding nearby lodging.

ABBREVIATIONS

All abbreviations are as specified in Patrick H. Alexander et al., eds., *The SBL Handbook of Style* (Peabody, MA: Hendrickson, 1999). Bibliographical details and any abbreviations not listed here can be found there.

AB	Anchor Bible
BibSac	*Bibliotheca Sacra*
BBR	*Bulletin for Biblical Research*
BCOTWP	Baker Commentary on the Old Testament Wisdom and Psalms
CD	*Church Dogmatics* (Karl Barth's)
HUCA	*Hebrew Union College Annual*
LHB/OTS	Library of Hebrew Bible/Old Testament Series
NASB	New American Standard Bible
NIV	New International Version
NIVAC	New International Version Application Commentary
NLT	New Living Translation
TNIV	Today's New International Version
TynBul	*Tyndale Bulletin*
VTSup	Vetus Testamentum Supplements
WBC	Word Biblical Commentary

INTRODUCTION

Encounter with God is surely what any human should seek, and surely any biblical approach to the topic will always underscore the divine initiative. After that, all bets are off. Do humans have to respond, can they respond, and, if they can, how should they respond? The church's history has seen numerous debates on the topic, and key issues are at stake. Just how fallen is the human race? Is depravity so fierce that any thought of response is precluded? Is the human will so bound in sin that freedom to act does not exist? If the race is so fallen that response is precluded, is there either dignity or responsibility still left for humans? The biblical texts urge response, and if humans are not engaged in acting, nothing observable happens in the human sphere. What are humans supposed to do? How is obedience achieved, assuming obedience is indeed important. The biblical texts do not sort out the relation of divine initiative and human response, and despite discussions in church history, not much focus is given to this topic in current theological discussions.

A Swedish friend says, "With theology you always have to pay," meaning, if you put too much down on one aspect of theology, you do not have enough left for other aspects. Any discussion of encounter with God and human response treats anthropology, hamartiology, sovereignty of God and the freedom of humanity, and the relation of community and individual, all evident in the essays. As at least two essays imply, Jews do not have a problem with this topic and seem generally not to bifurcate themes like divine initiative and human responsibility the way some Christians tend to. Further, much of Scripture orbits around divine initiative and human response, as, for example, Luke 14 and 15 demonstrate.

Perhaps the problem is that we do not have a sufficiently robust anthropology. Human action, choice, and responsibility are crucial, but we humans do not act in a vacuum by ourselves. Even our acting is an engagement with the Holy Spirit, and a more biblical view is the awareness that we do not exist apart from God and that in all we do we have to do with God. Any action we take is in response to God and involves God, but our own involvement is still very much a factor. If this is true, perhaps we should have focused on *how* humans engage with God. We have no illusion that we have solved the problems in this debate, but hopefully the essays will stimulate thought and encourage discussion.

At the symposium twice as much time is given to discussion of the papers as to their delivery, and the journal cannot reproduce the character of those discussions, which are always stimulating and enriching. People in attendance at the symposium include an interesting mix of faculty types, pastors, church leaders, students, and lay people. We are grateful to all who participated. Appreciation is especially expressed once again to all the presenters and respondents who made a significant investment in the life of North Park. Special gratitude is expressed to Jay Phelan for stepping in to offer a paper after a presenter withdrew late in the game. The friendship of all the people involved is a gift we value deeply. The authors of papers were given a chance to edit their contributions after the symposium, but the responses are essentially as they were presented. As is obvious, the views expressed are those of the authors and not necessarily those of the journal or of North Park. Special gratitude is expressed to Anne Jorgensen and Peter Schwich, students at North Park, for their work on the bibliography and especially to Guylla Brown from North Park's staff, without whom the symposium would be impossible. Anyone who has been to the symposium knows that is true every year.

Since this is the thirtieth issue of *Ex Auditu*, some comment is in order concerning the history of the symposia and the journal. The first three symposia and their publication were connected to Princeton Theological Seminary (1985–1987) as the Frederic Neumann Symposium, which was started largely because of the work of Dikran Hadidian, Ben Meyer, and Peter Stuhlmacher and their conviction that not enough attention was being given to theological interpretation of Scripture. Thomas Gillespie was editor of the journal, and Dikran Hadidian, who owned Pickwick Publications, did the publishing. The next two issues of the journal did not really have a home, but Pickwick remained the publisher. Robert Guelich became the editor, and shortly thereafter he inquired about North Park's interest in hosting the symposia, to which an affirmative answer was quickly given. From 1990 and volume six of the journal North Park has hosted the symposia. Unfortunately, shortly after that first symposium at North Park Guelich died. Don Miller served as interim editor for one year, and then Hadidian asked me to edit the journal. Later Pickwick Publications was sold to Wipf and Stock, and since 2004 Wipf and Stock has published the journal. Gratitude is expressed to the good people there for all their assistance and cooperation. Their involvement with us is a delight.

The symposia and journal have always had the goal of doing theological interpretation of Scripture for the church. The academy too easily ends up in its own discussions—at times disconnected from life, and the church too frequently is naïve about the contours and significance of its own theological foundation. Scripture is often examined with little concern for theology, and conversely some theological discussions forget the necessity of rootedness in Scripture. When *Ex Auditu* began, few others were focused on doing theological interpretation of Scripture, but a movement started. Today there is a burgeoning trend toward theological interpretation, with commentaries, sessions at AAR/SBL, and other journals engaged in the task.

North Park's symposia are always interdisciplinary and interconfessional, with the only requirement of presenters being a commitment both to the church and to Scripture. I confess that at times it has been difficult to get presenters to stay with the goal and on topic. Still, the agenda of the symposia and the journal is precisely what is needed of Christian academics and what is needed for the church. The symposia have always attracted some of the most important people doing theology, there has always been a variety in outlook and procedure, and many truly significant articles have been published. Over the twenty-five years I have been editor the symposia have treated a variety of aspects of Christian theology such as Christology, the authority of Scripture, atonement, and conversion. We have also treated issues related more to practice such as worship, spiritual formation, and money and possessions. The amount of time given to conversation of each paper is almost without parallel. For me personally the conversations and the resulting friendships are among the most significant and enjoyable aspects of this enterprise, and I thank all those who have been involved.

Theological interpretation of Scripture is an ongoing task, the apex of what Christian Scripture is about, and I can only hope that future symposia and the volumes of the journal make a decided mark in the work of the church and the lives of Christians.

Klyne Snodgrass
Paul W. Brandel Professor of New Testament Studies
North Park Theological Seminary

THE LONG SHADOW OF AUGUSTINE

John E. Phelan Jr.

In his programmatic essay "Discipline and Hope" Wendell Berry indicts American education for being "not a long-term investment in young minds and in the life of the community, but a short-term investment in the economy. We want to be able to tell," he continues, "how many dollars an education is worth and how soon it will be able to pay." He argues this has had a dire impact on the discipline of teaching: "It produces a race of learned mincers, whose propriety and pride is to keep their minds inside their 'fields,' as if human thoughts were a kind of livestock to be kept out of the woods and off the roads."[1] By definition the work of doing theological reflection for the church is multi-disciplinary. By necessity it involves us in wandering out of our "fields." A NT scholar examining a text cannot ignore how that text has been read for the last two thousand years. A theologian reading a NT text cannot ignore the historical, social, and cultural context of the original writers. Church historians, of course, can criticize both of them! We all, to a certain extent, must venture, at least on occasion, out of our "fields."

Having said this, with due respect to Berry's complaint and the essential character of doing theological reflection for the church, I must admit that with this paper I have wandered rather far out of my "field." By training I am a NT scholar, although my interests have always been wide—perhaps too wide. Be that as it may, I am wandering knowingly into the dense woods of patristics and particularly the tangled thickets of Augustine of Hippo.

Few people have influenced the West and the Western church more than this great North African. Perhaps no one had greater influence on the conundrum of human agency than he. Throughout the centuries those arguing for obviously contradictory notions of "free will," "predestination," and "original sin" have cited Augustine as authoritative. These debates continue to this very day, as this symposium illustrates. As I worked my way through the conflicts of the late fourth and early fifth century, I began to wonder if the conflict between Augustine and Pelagius, Prosper and Cassian, and many others was really about human agency in the first place. Were

---

1. Wendell Berry, "Discipline and Hope," in *Recollected Essays 1965–1980* (San Francisco: North Point, 1981) 193.

these often fierce arguments displaced from a more serious set of questions plaguing a church in transition? I am, of course, not alone in wondering about this, but if this is true, what was this argument really about and what conclusions should we draw for the life of the church?

Gottschalk and Eriugena

In the middle of the ninth century a Saxon monk by the name of Gottschalk ignited a controversy in the realm of the Frankish King Charles the Bald. He preached that God's predestination was double. That is, some people were destined for good and salvation, others for ill and damnation. His critics, the king among them, were concerned that his teaching would undercut the moral motivation of Christians. After all, if their fate was already determined by God's sovereign decision, what difference did it make how they lived? Gottschalk's views were condemned at synods in Mainz in 848 and Quierzy in 849. Charles the Bald presided over the latter synod and approved the burning of Gottschalk's works.[2] But Gottschalk had many friends, and in spite of his condemnation and eventual imprisonment, the controversy continued to rage.

Eventually Hincmar, archbishop of Rheims, requested the aid of John Scottus Eriugena, a scholar in the court of Charles the Bald. Very little is known of Eriugena. His name identifies him as from Ireland. His work suggests he was strongly influenced by Neoplatonism.[3] He was evidently part of the Irish migration that during the sixth through the tenth centuries brought thousands of monks and scholars to the continent to found monasteries and establish schools. The brilliant court of Charles the Bald and the famous Cathedral school at Laon had attracted some of the great minds of the era, including Eriugena. According to Dermot Moran, "Laon had both a cathedral and a chapel, an important library and scriptorium, and connections with other monasteries. . . . It was also noted for its large 'Irish colony.'"[4] Small wonder Eriugena found it a congenial place to study and teach.

Eriugena was evidently not an ecclesiastic. Far from quieting the controversy, "His intervention," Mary Brennan writes, "left Hincmar further abashed."[5] Eriugena enthusiastically inveighed against the views of Gottschalk, but in the process he

---

2. On this see Dermot Moran, *The Philosophy of John Scottus Eriugena: A Study of Idealism in the Middle Ages* (Cambridge: Cambridge University Press, 1989) 27–34; and John Scottus Eriugena, *Treatise on Divine Predestination*, translated by Mary Brennan (Notre Dame, IN: Notre Dame University Press, 1998) ix–xiv.

3. Moran, *The Philosophy of John Scottus Eriugena*, 103–22.

4. Ibid., 20.

5. Eriugena, *Treatise on Divine Predestination*, x.

opened himself up to charges of heresy. His work against Gottschalk, *Treatise On Divine Predestination*, attacked the notion of double predestination and insisted on the freedom of the human will. Gottschalk, he argues, "tries to deny the most equitable rewards of justice and the most merciful gifts of grace."[6] Eriugena asserts, "Where there is inevitability there is no will."[7] In fact, he insists, "if the will of God is free—and to believe otherwise is wicked—and if the free will is devoid of all necessity, then no necessity has hold of the will. . . . All necessity is excluded from the divine will. Therefore it is excluded from his predestination."[8]

Eriugena, however, was not a Pelagian. "Free choice," he insists, "must not be defended in such a way that good works are attributed to it without the grace of God; nor must grace be so defended that, as it were from the safety afforded by it, evil deeds may be habitually performed."[9] Grace and predestination cannot become a cover for misbehavior, and good works are not to be seen as merely a human accomplishment. Eriugena goes on to insist that while human beings were damaged by the sin of Adam, "he [Adam] did not lose the substance which is to be, to will, to know. . . . For God did not create in man [sic] a captive will but a free one, and that freedom remained after the sin."[10]

This was all too much for Hincmar and his colleagues. Eriugena's work was condemned in 855 and "inelegantly described (echoing St. Jerome) as 'Irish porridge.'"[11] This conflict, typical in many ways, reflected the centuries-earlier conflicts between Augustine and Pelagius and, slightly later, between John Cassian and Prosper of Aquitaine. Pelagius, more likely a Briton than an Irishman, had incurred the wrath of Jerome and exercised the pen of Augustine. The latter's solution to the problem of Pelagius has cast a long shadow over the history of the church, as the topic of this symposium suggests. This ninth-century conflict illustrates the theological and pastoral challenges Augustine's views entailed—challenges he tried, with mixed success, to address in his own writing, as we will see.

Ironically both Eriugena and Gottschalk based their arguments on Augustine. Some of Eriugena's critics thought, quite rightly, that he was a bit cavalier in his use of the saint. In fairness to Eriugena though, Augustine was not entirely consistent and could be read on this and other topics in a variety of ways, and in fairness to Gottschalk, it seems that his views of human agency were closer to the mature views

---

6. Ibid., 1.4 (in what follows I will cite the sections of the treatise rather than the page numbers in Brennan's translation).

7. Ibid., 2.1.

8. Ibid.

9. Ibid., 4.3.

10. Ibid., 4.6.

11. Ibid., xi.

of Augustine than were those of Eriugena. Be that as it may, in spite of his condemnation Eriugena apparently stayed in the court of Charles and suffered no further consequences. Gottschalk, on the other hand, perhaps ironically, died in prison.

Eriugena in his appeal to reason was perhaps ahead of his time. According to Brennan it was this appeal that aroused the most resentment.[12]

> Reason is given a hearing on an equal footing with the time-honored authorities of Scripture and the Fathers; this balancing of reason and authority was to be greatly elaborated in [Eriugena's later work] the *Periphyseon*. The secular language of the liberal arts is applied in theological discussion, a procedure duly and formally anathematized by Prudentius of Troyes and Florus of Lyon in their rebuttal [of Eriugena's work on predestination].[13]

Reason, of course, would trouble tradition and authority in ever increasing ways over the following centuries.

This conflict reflected the concerns that had originally occupied Augustine, Pelagius, and their heirs. These concerns were both theological and pastoral. In the conflict between Gottschalk and Eriugena the bishops were concerned that Gottschalk's preaching of double predestination could result in moral indifference or despair in monks as well as ordinary Christians. The same charges had been made against Augustine's views. Eriugena, like Pelagius, seemed to give free rein to the human will and to limit the sovereignty of God. This for many was clearly unacceptable.

The terms of the conversation have not shifted a great deal over the centuries. Calvin and Pighius and Luther and Erasmus wrestled over the same ground a thousand years after Augustine and Pelagius and seven hundred years after Gottschalk and Eriugena.[14] The issues are as alive today as they were in fifth-century Hippo and sixteenth-century Geneva. Nevertheless, in spite of all the theological and philosophical wrangling of Augustine and Pelagius, Gottschalk and Eriugena, and Calvin and Pighius, I would suggest the real issue was pastoral. It addressed a question very much alive in the monasteries of Gaul and North Africa as well as the churches of Rome and Hippo: How is one to live as a Christian? This is still the real question.

The Church in the Late Fourth and Early Fifth Century

The Western church in the late fourth and early fifth century was experiencing a time of dramatic change and upheaval. The old Roman political and civic order was

12. Ibid.

13. Ibid.

14. See John Calvin, *The Bondage and Liberation of the Will* (Grand Rapids: Baker, 2002) and E. Gordon Rupp and Philip S. Watson, eds. *Luther and Erasmus: Free Will and Salvation* (Philadelphia: Westminster, 1969).

eroding. Barbarian invasions, violence, and war threatened the settled life of towns and the emerging power of the church. By the early sixth century, Robert Markus argues, the culture and society that had fostered Augustine and his peers had been replaced by a culture and society that could properly be called medieval.[15] It is difficult to say how the conflicts and chaos of those decades impacted the thinking of the main subjects of this study: Augustine, Pelagius, Prosper of Aquitaine, and John Cassian. But they were not writing in a vacuum, and the key question was not simply how one understands grace and nature, or God's sovereignty and human free will, but, as suggested above, *how one lives a Christian life.* What did it mean to be a Christian, a faithful follower of Jesus of Nazareth and Paul of Tarsus? Perhaps especially, what did it meant to be a Christian when Rome was sacked and the seemingly eternal order of Rome was being swept away.

Varieties of Monasticism

A young Augustine describes in his *Confessions* his early plan, even before he was baptized, for a kind of semi-monastic community. In reality it was, as Peter Brown puts it, modeled on a Greek "philosophical community."[16] It entailed a group of sophisticated, well-to-do young men living a kind of common life supported by a wealthy patron so as to engage in "a life of philosophical detachment." But "by the autumn of 386," Brown writes, "everything had changed in Augustine himself—everything, that is except for the social setting in which he intended to live his new life."[17] By now he was a baptized Catholic set on being celibate. The group gathered around him in Cassiciacum in the foothills of the Alps near Milan was not very different from that he had hoped to gather in his "philosophical community," but this time the focus was upon the leisured reflection on the Christian life and love of God. In fact, Brown writes, "they became Platonic lovers. They were united by the vision of a single Beloved, a Supreme Beauty who was both utterly distant from them and yet hauntingly present."[18]

This monastic/philosophical interlude did not last long. By the autumn of 387 Augustine was on his way to North Africa. In Thagaste he and his intellectual colleagues formed another monastic community. This one not only lacked a wealthy patron but was consciously modeled on the Jerusalem community described in the

15. See Robert A. Markus, *The End of Ancient Christianity* (Cambridge: Cambridge University Press, 1991).

16. Peter Brown, *Through the Eye of a Needle* (Princeton: Princeton University Press, 2012) 161.

17. Ibid., 162.

18. Ibid., 165.

books of Acts.[19] The pooling of their resources, they thought, would enable them to live in unity with God and with each other. Brown describes how Augustine eventually gave up his wealth as had the "rich young man" confronted by Jesus.

> Nor was the wealth realized from Augustine's property given directly to the poor. Gifts to the church tended to be spoken of, in a pious formula, as if they were gifts "to the poor of the church." More probably, Augustine's estates and those of his friends were quietly donated to the church of Thagaste. In return each may have received an annuity or the usufruct of a portion of the revenues of their estates. They would then contribute this income to the common fund of the new community.[20]

When he moved to Hippo as first priest and then bishop this community came with him. Brown comments:

> From the time of his ordination as a priest at Hippo in 391 to his death in 430 Augustine's life and thought were inextricably linked to the monastery that he had founded. . . . But unfortunately, the precise course of its development as an institution is shadowy. For most of the time, except when provoked by the occasional scandal, he took the existence of the monastic backdrop to his daily life for granted and seldom discussed it. As a result, it remains for us the dark side of the moon of the life of Augustine.[21]

In its origin and functions, Augustine's community, at least at the beginning, was very different from a form of monasticism coming to the West from the Eastern deserts. In earlier centuries of the church the martyrs had been the model of Christian perfection. Their suffering and death at the hands of callous Roman officials had fueled a cult of the martyrs that had focused the worship and motivated the courage of thousands. With the recognition and then privileging of the church by the Roman Emperors of the fourth century, the martyrdoms ceased. According to Robert Markus, "The emotional energies previously absorbed by the duty to rise to the demands made on a persecuted Church were largely redirected towards disciplined ascetic living."[22] Monasticism was, in fact, now seen as a form of martyrdom, and monks were Christian soldiers giving battle to the world, the flesh, and the devil. In this battle leisured philosophical reflection was not the norm. Rather such a battle required a fierce asceticism, a commitment to virginity, and increasingly to poverty. The Eastern monks were uncompromising in their commitment to ascetic discipline

19. Ibid., 168.
20. Ibid., 169.
21. Ibid., 173.
22. Markus, *The End of Christianity*, 70.

even though, as Markus puts it, "the severity of ascetic observance was subject to a good deal of variation."[23]

Eastern monasticism made its way west and had perhaps it greatest impact in Gaul. On an island near Marseilles, Lerins, a new community, was founded. According to Brown it was "the most successful of island monasteries that had been chosen for their sheer 'horror.' Spiritual Counts of Monte Cristo, the upper-class converts to the monastic life who lived at Lerins and on similar bare islands, claimed to have brought a touch of the awesome desert of Egypt to within sight of the Cote d'Azur."[24] Figures like Martin of Tours and, perhaps most importantly, John Cassian communicated the Eastern forms of monasticism to Gaul. Cassian's *Conferences* are dialogues regarding the monastic life with some of the great figures of the Eastern deserts.[25] This form of heroic monasticism made its way even to Ireland and its remote and inhospitable islands. Ascetic rigor fueled the forms of religious life that flourished in Ireland, Scotland, and the north of England and eventually spread across Europe through the monastic foundations of Columbanus and his heirs.[26]

In Gaul the result was a two-tiered notion of Christianity. There were the "saints" of the monasteries and the ordinary laypersons of the cities and countryside. With Brown, "the writings that came from Marseille, Lerins, and Arles concentrated to an unusual degree on defining the boundary between the new demands of the ascetic movement and the average Christianity of well-to-do secular persons."[27] The presence of these ascetic communities alongside cultivated lay persons and local bishops "provoked constant debate as to which Christianity was authentic and which was a half-hearted compromise. Equally vigorous was the debate among monks themselves as to who were true monks and who were tepid amateurs. This situation generated arguments on almost every aspect of Christian behavior and of Christian society— from the nature of grace and free will to the fate of the Roman empire."[28] However these monks understood and answered these questions they were convinced that there was an advantage to their lives of rigorous asceticism. They were convinced they were the "spiritual elites" of the world separated from the spiritual dilettantes by poverty, virginity, and obedience. All this was called into question by the conflict between Pelagius and Augustine.

23. Ibid., 75.

24. Brown, *Through the Eye of a Needle*, 412.

25. See Boniface Ramsey, ed. *John Cassian: The Conferences* (New York: Paulist: 1997). Subsequent quotations from Cassian are from this volume.

26. See Brendan Lehane, *The Quest of Three Abbots* (London: Murray, 1968); and John T. McNeill, *The Celtic Churches: A History AD 200 to 1200* (Chicago: University of Chicago Press, 1974).

27. Brown, *Through the Eye of a Needle*, 413.

28. Ibid.

The Rise of Pelagius

It is bitterly ironic that Pelagius, a man of scrupulous morality and, at least to his way of thinking, confident orthodoxy should become perhaps *the* arch-heretic of the Catholic, and for that matter, the Protestant Church. Subsequent to his condemnation, orchestrated by Augustine and his friends, his name has been used as an epithet and warning. B. R. Rees observes, "For centuries now the adjective 'Pelagian' has been a convenient term of abuse in the Christian Church and Pelagius himself a bogeyman for upright clerics to evoke when wanting to frighten wayward members of their flock."[29] The list of people accused of being "Pelagian," "Semi-Pelagian," or "Synergist" is long and distinguished. Fourteenth-century "Archbishop Thomas Bradwardine," Rees continues, "detected a Pelagian hiding beneath every academic gown, just as Reinhold Niebuhr in twentieth century America saw Pelagians in every pew."[30] Charges of semi-Pelagianism perhaps even cost John Cassian, whom Rees calls "one of the most attractive of the Western fathers," official status as a saint.[31] Why was Pelgius deemed such a threat?

Pelagius came to Rome from Briton as a moral reformer. To Pelagius the Catholic Church, at both center and periphery, was compromised and morally flaccid. In his magisterial biography of Augustine, Peter Brown observes that Pelagius

> . . . had no patience with the confusion that seemed to reign on the powers of human nature. He and his supporters wrote for men "who wanted to make a change for the better." He refused to regard this power of self-improvement as having been irreversibly prejudiced; the idea of an "original sin," that could make men incapable of not sinning even more struck him as quite absurd. He was annoyed by the way in which Augustine's masterpiece, the *Confessions*, seemed merely to popularize the tendency toward a languid piety.[32]

In spite of this, as Rees points out in his *The Letters of Pelagius and his Followers*, Pelagianism "was not a coherent theological statement."[33] Its adherents held wildly differing views, and Pelagius became embroiled in theological controversy as a result of the implications of his moral teachings rather than his explicitly developed theological reflection. As Brown puts it, "Pelagi*nism* as we know it, that consistent body of ideas of momentous consequences, had come into existence; but in the mind of

29. B. R. Rees, *Pelagius: A Reluctant Heretic* (Woodbridge, Suffolk: Boydell and Brewer, 1991) ix.

30. Ibid.

31. Ibid., 108.

32. Peter Brown, *Augustine of Hippo: A Biography*, (Berkeley: University of California Press, 2000) 343.

33. "Letter to Demetrias" 3.2 in B. R. Rees, *Pelagius: Life and Letters* (Rochester, NY: Boydell, 1998) 1. Subsequent quotes from the letter are from this edition.

Augustine, not of Pelagius."[34] Augustine saw serious theological problems lurking in the "icy Puritanism" and heroic individualism of Pelagius. He would not rest until he secured his condemnation.

Pelagius's views are well illustrated in his letter "To Demetrias." Demetrias was a wealthy young woman who had forgone marriage for a life of virginity and devotion to God. She was only one of a large circle of wealthy and prominent young Romans who were attracted to the rigor of Christian perfectionism in what they saw as a compromised Roman society and church. Pelagius offers Demetrias a bracing challenge to obedience and faithfulness. He insists that she has within her, as do all humans, the capacity to do good and not evil. He writes, "It was because God wished to bestow on the rational creature the gift of doing good of his own free will and the capacity to exercise free choice by implanting in man the possibility of choosing either alternative, that he made it his peculiar right to be what he wanted to be, so that with his capacity for good and evil he could do either quite naturally."[35] This ability to choose between good and evil was a gift of God's grace and was not destroyed by the fall of Adam. Such a pale notion of grace would not have satisfied Augustine.

It was, Pelagius told Demetrias, an insult to God to imagine that he would give commands that humans were incapable of obeying of their own free will:

> What blind madness! What unholy foolhardiness! We accuse God of a twofold lack of knowledge, so that he appears not to know what he has done, and not to know what he has commanded; as if, forgetful of the human frailty of which he is himself the author, he has imposed on man commands which he cannot bear. And at the same time, O horror!, we ascribe iniquity to the righteous and cruelty to the holy, while complaining, first, that he has commanded something impossible, secondly that man is to be damned by him for doing things which he was unable to avoid, so that God—and this is something which even to suspect is sacrilege—seems to have sought not so much our salvation as our punishment.[36]

In his message to Demetrias and other prominent, wealthy Romans, Pelagius in the words of Brown, "appealed to a universal theme: the need of the individual to define himself, and to feel free to create his own values in the midst of the conventional, second-rate life of society. . . . He would offer the individual absolute certainty through absolute obedience."[37] But this would mean that for Pelagius and his followers, the vast majority of "good Christians" in the Roman world would be damned.

34. Brown, *Augustine of Hippo*, 346.
35. "Letter to Demetrias," 3.2.
36. Ibid., 16.2.
37. Brown, *Augustine of Hippo*, 347.

Pelagius represented, Brown continues, "the most pungent protest in all Late Roman literature, against the subtle pressure, which Augustine had experienced in Hippo, to leave the Christian life to recognized saints and to continue to live as ordinary men, like pagans. Pelagius wanted every Christian to be a monk."[38]

Augustine saw all of this as nothing less than an attack on divine grace. He insisted that human beings were not just damaged by Adam's sin, but fatally wounded. The only hope of human beings, defiled as they were by original sin and then actual sins, was the grace of God moving them inexorably to obedience and faith. It could only be by the grace of God untainted by human will and unsupported by human merit. It was God's work from first to last. Furthermore, it was God's choice from first to last. God chose who would be saved by his grace. The human will had nothing to do with it. Augustine saw human beings after Adam as suffering from a fatal flaw that could only be healed by divine grace. Pelagius, for his part, saw human beings as certainly flawed, but fully capable of obedience to the will of God.

Brown sums up their differences with a fascinating analogy: "Augustine had long been fascinated by babies; the extent of their helplessness had grown upon him ever since he wrote the *Confessions*; and in the *Confessions*, he had had no hesitation in likening his relation to God to that of a baby to its mother's breast, utterly dependent, intimately involved in all good and evil that might come from this, the only source of life."[39] Pelagius, on the other hand, "was contemptuous of babies. 'There is no more pressing admonition than this, that we should be called *sons* of God' he had written to Demetrias. To be a 'son' was to be an entirely separate person, no longer dependent on one's father, but capable of following out of one's own power, the good deeds that had been commanded."[40]

To use another, perhaps inapt, analogy from the American political scene, Pelagius was a kind of theological "Libertarian" convinced that human beings should rise or fall on their own merits without the support and interference of the "government." Augustine, on the other hand was an advocate of a kind of theological "nanny state" where individuals are able to progress only with the complete support of the institution of government—in this case the grace of God and the church. Pelagius is not the only example in the earliest years of the church of a puritanical perfectionism, but he is the most prominent. Had his view of the Christian life prevailed, it is difficult to see how Christianity would have survived.

On the other hand, could Augustine be accused of infantilizing the ordinary Christians, and tacitly, if unintentionally, encouraging a life of moral indifference?

38. Ibid., 349.
39. Ibid., 352.
40. Ibid.

Many of his critics thought that this was exactly what he was doing. Robert Markus argues that Augustine's attack on Pelagius, Julian of Eclanum, and others was "a defense of Christian mediocrity."[41] But, to be fair, it could also be called a defense of ordinary Christians. For Pelagius and his followers, however, there was no such thing.

As I have stated, had the Catholic Church followed the way of Pelagius it is unlikely that it would have survived. Would not such heroic asceticism have limited the appeal of Christianity to a small circle of fanatic loyalists? The preference for celibacy alone would not only have acted as a deterrent to prospective members, but as the Shakers found, if required of its members, guaranteed the movement's eventual extinction. Yet did not Augustine's way of preserving both God's grace and the place of the ordinary Christian within the church also lead to both serious theological problems and spiritual lassitude?

N. P. Williams argues:

> There is no struggling against a force which represents all the might of omnipotence, directed by all the intellectual resources of omniscience. God is in the position of a chess-player, gifted with telepathic and hypnotic power of an infinitely high degree, who not only foresees all the other player's moves, but actually makes them, acting through the other's mind and brain, and consequently has won the game before it has even begun.[42]

Both Augustine and centuries of Augustinians (and Lutherans and Calvinists) have strenuously objected to such a depiction of divine predestination, but I frankly find it difficult to avoid Williams' conclusions. It was exactly this that troubled monks in both North Africa and Gaul. It is to this struggle that we now turn.

Hadrumetum and Lerin: Augustine's Challenge to Monasticism

Augustine's counter blasts to what he saw as Pelagius's heresy produced blowback from a perhaps surprising source. Not only did Augustine's uncompromising insistence on God's grace call Pelagius's perfectionism into question, it threatened to undermine the lives of ordinary monks. In 426, only a few years before his death, Augustine had to deal with a controversy that had arisen in a monastic community in Hadrumetum in North Africa. The implications of Augustine's teaching troubled some of the monks. As Rebecca Harden Weaver puts it,

> To the extent that the intervention of divine grace, apart from merit, determines a person's ultimate destiny, the character of a person's actions does not effect that determination. Furthermore, to the extent that grace shapes

---

41. Markus, *The End of Christianity*, 45–62.

42. N. P. Williams, *The Grace of God* (London: Longmans, Green, 1930) 28.

a person's actions, it is not human agency but the divine operation upon human agency that determines the person's destiny. The problem was a crucial
one for these monks. Their monastic ideal rested on the notion that, by one's
own agency, although not without grace, one can so shape one's life according
to the monastic discipline as ultimately to attain to God. The questioning,
therefore, of the relationship between actions and their outcome, between the
pattern of one's life and one's ultimate destiny, was a challenge to the entire
monastic undertaking.[43]

In other words, if my actions bear no relation to the outcome of my life, why am I a
monk in the first place? Why take up this rigorous and difficult life?

This launched what has been called, inaptly, the Semi-Pelagian controversy. It
was ostensibly laid to rest at the Council of Orange in 529, but as demonstrated
in the ninth-century controversy surrounding the writings of Gottschalk and Eriugena, let alone the Reformation and Post-Reformation controversies among both
Protestants and Catholics, the council hardly settled the matter. Augustine was himself a chief protagonist early in the conflict. His disciple Prosper of Aquitaine took
up his cause after his death. John Cassian, on the other hand, was an able proponent
of the monastic way of life, espousing a view of free will and grace that held both in
a creative tension.

Cassian's "Thirteenth Conference: On God's Protection" famously defended
both free will and God's grace: "The grace of God and free will certainly seem mutually opposed to one another, but both are in accord."[44] Human beings are *not* incapable of willing the good: "When he [God] notices good will making an appearance
in us, at once he enlightens and encourages it and spurs it to salvation."[45] Cassian,
located in Gaul, was a man of immense prestige and clearly not Pelagian, but his
views represented a threat to the purity of the Augustinian position. It seemed to
reintroduce the notion of human merit Augustine had so recently sought to stamp
out in his many works against Pelagius. Prosper of Aquitaine was eventually to take
up the cudgel against Cassian.

Before the growing crisis in Gaul could be addressed Augustine had to deal
with the conflict in his native North Africa. In a flurry of letters to and from Augustine and the monks of Hadrumetum the old bishop sought both to reassure
the monks of the validity of their lives and to insist on his understanding of grace,
free will, original sin, and predestination. Augustine appreciated the anxiety of the
monks. He insisted that his views, "rightly understood" as Weaver puts it, "in no

---

43. Rebecca Harden Weaver, *Divine Grace and Human Agency* (Macon, GA: Mercer University
Press, 1996) 1.

44. *John Cassian,* Conference 13, XI.4. (See n. 25.)

45. Ibid., VII.4.

way undercut the monastic life. The questionable nature of this assumption would become increasingly apparent as the controversy developed, both in Africa and later in Gaul."[46] In trying to sustain the monastic way of life and preserve uncompromised his view of the grace of God, Augustine was attempting to square the circle.

One monk, whether a critic or supporter of Augustine is not clear, when rebuked by his abbot suggested, since his actions were all determined by the foreknowledge and grace of God, the abbot should take it up with God.[47] This nicely illustrated the problem within Augustinianism that had originally troubled the North African monks and would trouble Cassian and much later Hincmar of Rheims and John Scottus Eriugena. What use is moral striving and efforts to obey the law of God if all were already determined? Augustine would labor mightily to establish that all Christians should strive to pursue the good, regardless of his doctrines of grace and predestination. In subsequent generations some convinced Augustinians would even suggest that, although it was certainly true that all was determined by the mysterious counsels of God, this was not something that should be preached! One should be careful about promoting a theology that "misunderstood" could lead to despair and moral lassitude. "Ordinary Christians" could not be expected to grasp the niceties of Augustine's thought.

Be that as it may, it seems that Augustine's intervention eventually quieted things at Hadrumetum, or at least, Weaver tells us, we hear nothing more from them. But a more serious challenge was ahead. She writes: "The monks of southern Gaul . . . regarded Augustine with less awe than did their North African counterparts." They too "found his teachings a challenge to their striving for Christian perfection. It was in South Gaul," Weaver concludes, "what had begun as an amicable misunderstanding came to assume the character of a heated debate."[48]

Prosper and Cassian and the Future of Augustinianism

Prosper, a younger contemporary of Augustine, Pelagius, and Cassian, was born in the Roman province of Aquitaine around 390. He was an obviously well-educated and pious layman, an enthusiastic supporter of Augustine, a friend to prominent bishops, and a servant of popes. When the monks of Gaul demonstrated the same difficulties with Augustine as had the monks of North Africa, Prosper took up his cause.[49] The Gallic monks were not as disposed as those of North Africa to show

---

46. Weaver, *Divine Grace and Human Agency*, 16

47. Ibid., 23–24.

48. Ibid., 35.

49. Ibid., 38–41. Much of what follows is drawn from her account of the conflict.

deference to Augustine. Nor were they particularly enamored of the institutional church in general or bishops in particular. They were as concerned as their African brothers about the ways Augustine's doctrines of predestination and grace undermined their way of life, but they were also suspicious that Augustine was infected by Greek fatalism and Manichean dualism.[50]

The works that had quieted things in Hadrumetum only stirred things up further in Gaul. Letters expressing concern went from Prosper and Hilary, Bishop of Arles, to Augustine. The result was Augustine's two final works, "On the Predestination of the Saints" and "The Gift of Perseverance."[51] In spite of the learning and erudition of these works, they hardly settled the matter. Shortly after they were written, Augustine was dead. It was left to Prosper, among others, to take up his cause. He did so very ably for the next twenty-five years.

At about the same time, during the mid-twenties of the fifth century, John Cassian, Abbot of St. Victor in Marseille, was producing the work he is most known for, *The Conferences.* The work is presented as a collection of dialogues between Cassian, his travelling companion Germanus, and some of the most renowned of the Eastern desert fathers. I have already briefly discussed Cassian's views on free will and the grace of God. In Conference Thirteen, as we saw above, Cassian insisted that both God's grace and human will were critical, and he refused to set them at odds. "The God of the universe must be believed to work all things in all, so that he stirs up, protects, and strengthens, but not so that he removes freedom of will that he himself once granted."[52] In sections twelve through sixteen of the Conferences, Cassian, starting with Paul, cites passages across the biblical narrative that underscore both human responsibility and divine grace. Here we find no tortured logic but a rather serene assertion that the Bible makes it clear that humans do indeed have free will but that it is truly God who works in them, as Paul puts it in Phil 2:11, "to will and to act in order to fulfill his good purpose." Cassian left both divine grace and human initiative intact and refused to push to either the logical extreme of Augustine or Pelagius.

This approach would not have pleased Augustine and did not please Prosper. Evidently Cassian's work was not available to Prosper until after the death of Augustine, but in response he composed a treatise, *Liber contra Callatorem*, against Cassian's Conference Thirteen.[53] Weaver is not sure that Prosper either fully understood

---

50. Ibid., 42.

51. See *The Fathers of the Church: St. Augustine—Four Anti-Pelagian Writings* (Catholic University of America Press, 1992).

52. Cassian, "Conference 13," XVIII, 5.

53. Weaver, *Divine Grace and Human Agency*, 121–31.

Cassian or was completely fair with him, but this was only the beginning of his long and spirited defense of his hero. Prosper continued to interpret and defend Augustine long after Cassian's death in 435. Prosper himself died in 456. His work was important not merely for his defense of Augustine (which included seeking the support of the pope for his position) but editing selections of Augustine's work.[54] This work, *Liber senteniarum* "would provide crucial elements of the language by which the controversy was to be resolved in 529 at the Council of Orange."[55] It was resolved more or less in Augustine's terms.

The Enduring Significance and Challenge of Augustine

Augustine *has* cast a long shadow—for good and for ill. Perhaps nowhere has his shadow lingered as it has with regard to his complex of teachings on original sin, predestination, grace, and free will. More than one scholar has argued that Augustine's particular formulation of the relationship between God's initiative and the human response was, in spite of his attempts to argue otherwise, an innovation. It was an innovation intended to slam the door on Pelagius's overly optimistic view of human capacities, his insistence that humans could remain sinless, and his apparent denigration of the grace of God. Pelagius represented a genuine threat to the health and future of the church. His rigid perfectionism needed to be challenged, but Augustine's answer to the problem created problems that he in the end could not solve. Although on paper at least the church assented to Augustine's severity, in the pulpit, confessional booth, and pastor's office the more generous views of Cassian frequently prevailed. Generations of priests and pastors taught that human beings could exercise their will for the good, aided by the grace of God. For all that, God was not willing that any should perish, regardless of the church's official doctrine.

Nevertheless, the monks, Pelagius, and Augustine offered the church of the early fifth century three distinct and enduring models of Christian living. First was the *elitism* of the monasteries. The monks argued their form of Christianity was clearly superior to that of the run-of-the-mill Christian in Rome, Hippo, or Alexandria. They were closer to God, closer to salvation, and closer to truth. For many centuries, for better and for worse, monks and nuns represented a critique, an alternative, and a challenge to ordinary believers. Augustine was rightly troubled by this dualism. How was he as a pastor to challenge those ordinary believers to a form of faithfulness appropriate to their places in life, a faithfulness no less acceptable than that

54. Ibid., 154.
55. Ibid.

of the monks with whom he himself lived? A two-tiered Christianity did not seem appropriate to the expectations and experience of the apostles.

The second form was the *perfectionism* of Pelagius. For him there were *not* two classes of Christians but one. His followers were committed to a ruthless obedience and flawless existence. They were bound to scorn both the ordinary Christians and the monks who lived by what they considered half measures. Perfectionism has always plagued the church. Throughout its history perfectionists have preached their impossible ideal and looked with disdain on those apparently incapable of making the spiritual cut. The entirety of Protestantism could be viewed as a series of perfectionist movements that eventually moderated and settled into Augustinian mediocrity. But such movements, like the poor, are always with us, and the perfectionist bifurcations continue unabated. With perfection being difficult to accomplish— whether perfection of life, theology, or practice, the calving of denominations will continue. Perhaps this Protestant tendency is the true outcome of Pelagianism.

Finally, following elitism and perfectionism is "indifferentism." Augustine was painfully aware of the awful muddle that was the church in Hippo. He saw regular folks, neither monastic elites nor Pelagian perfectionists, stumbling along, trying to be faithful, but liable to failing and falling. He recognized that wheat and tares were sown together and that it was perilous to try to disentangle them. God knew who were his and would make that plain in due time. After all, it was not their good deeds and faithfulness that made the difference, but the sovereign choice of God before time began. This did not excuse him from preaching faithfully and offering the sacraments, especially that of baptism. It did not excuse them from the call to obedience, however obscure its origin and outcome. But in the end it was all God.

Each of these options has proponents to this very day, and each has something to commend it. They were developed as the church struggled, first, to accommodate itself to its new status of a permitted and then preferred religion in the Roman world. Second, they matured as the church faced the dissolution of the old Roman order and was called to take a more central role in the political and social life of the emerging medieval order. Although both Pelagius and Augustine and their heirs strove to base their systems on the early apostles and especially on the Apostle Paul, their world was not his world and their opponents were not his opponents. Paul's world was and remained a Jewish world. The questions and concerns that motivated him to write his letters largely grew out of how this new thing that had occurred in Jesus of Nazareth was continuous with the covenant God had made with Israel. To this world we briefly turn.

Jewish Contributions to Divine Initiative and Human Response

First century and early rabbinic Judaism certainly believed in the sovereignty of God, but it equally affirmed the responsibility of individuals to be obedient to God's commands. In *m. Aboth* 3:16 R. Akiba is famously reported as saying, "All is foreseen, but freedom of choice is given; and the world is judged by grace, yet all is according to the excess of works [that be good or evil]."[56] Some have taken this to mean that the rabbis were able to live with an unresolved tension. Others have interpreted this passage to mean that, while the outcome of the world is sure and judgment is coming, each individual must live a life of obedience to Torah of their own free will. Friedrich Avemaria concludes his survey of the tension between God's command and Israel's obedience by arguing: "This interaction is clearly dialogical. God and his human counterpart remain two neatly distinguishable personal subjects. The idea of an absorption of human agency into the agency of God, as it was to be developed in nineteenth-century Hasidism, is virtually absent from rabbinic literature."[57]

Gabriele Boccaccini in an examination of the tension between divine and human agency in second temple Judaism suggests that it was Paul who came "closer to individual predeterminism" when he claimed that all Jews and Gentiles were under the power of sin and dependent on the grace of God. "Yet," Boccaccini concludes, "Paul's metaphor of slavery, while confirming the impossibility of doing good deeds, also implies the freedom of the will, through which the slave accepts (or refuses) the offer of redemption."[58] Paul was also clear that his converts to Messiah Jesus were called to a form of obedience that was rooted in Torah. I will have more to say about this.

As time went on the Augustinian idea of human beings as powerless and incapable of doing good without the intervention of the grace of God perplexed and outraged Jewish thinkers. Maimonides, another great North African, insisted: "Free will is granted to all men. If one desires to turn himself to the path of God and be righteous, the choice is his. Should he desire to turn to the part of evil and be wicked, the choice is his."[59] It is clear that Maimonides was making this argument against a form of Augustinian thinking for he goes on to say: "A person should not entertain the thesis held by the fools among the gentiles and the majority of the undeveloped

56. See Herbert Danby, trans., *The Mishnah* (Oxford: Oxford University Press, 1933).

57. Friedrich Avermaria, "The Tension Between God's Commands and Israel's Obedience as Reflected in the Early Rabbinic Literature," in *Divine and Human Agency in Paul and His Cultural Environment*, ed. John M. Barclay and Simon Gathercole (London: T. & T. Clark, 2006) 70.

58. Gabriele Boccaccini, "Inner-Jewish Debate on the Tension Between Divine and Human Agency in Second Temple Judaism," in *Divine and Human Agency in Paul and His Cultural Environment*, ed. John M. Barclay and Simon Gathercole (London: T. & T. Clark, 2006) 21.

59. Maimonides, *Teshuvah 5*, Halacha 1, 2.

among Israel that at the time of a man's creation, The Holy One, blessed be He, decrees whether he will be righteous or wicked. This is untrue. Each person is fit to be righteous like Moses, our teacher, or wicked, like Jeroboam."[60] A bit later he makes an argument common among critics of deterministic schemes: "Were God to decree that an individual would be righteous or wicked . . . how could He command us through the prophets: 'Do this.' 'Do not do this.' 'Improve your behavior.' Or 'Do not follow after your wickedness.'"[61]

This does not mean that Maimonides rejected divine sovereignty or believed in a form of dualism. "One must know," he insists, "that everything is done in accord with his will and, nevertheless, we are responsible for our deeds." Even this, he argues, is part of God's will and good creation: "[God] desired that man have free choice and be responsible for his deeds, without being pulled or forced. Rather, he, on his own initiative, with the knowledge which God has granted him, will do everything that man is able to do."[62] None of this is to suggest that Maimonides was a perfectionist in the mold of Pelagius. He knew that humans would sin and need to repent. Nevertheless, like Pelagius he thought the ability to do good or evil was a gift of God at creation and not something destroyed by Adam's fall.

The Augustinian notion of the predetermined fate of powerless individuals struck Leo Baeck in the early twentieth century as a form of romanticism. He wrote, "Christianity accepted the inheritance of ancient—Greek and oriental—romanticism. At an early date, the traditional national religion of the Hellenistic lands had been joined by a victorious intruder, probably from the north: another religion, phantastic and sentimental—the Dionysian or Orphic cult. . . . It had all the traits of Romanticism: the exuberance of emotion, the enthusiastic flight from reality, the longing for experience."[63] In Paul, Beack argued, "Judaism and paganism were now reconciled and brought together in romanticism, in the world of mystery, of myth, and of sacrament."[64] As I have written elsewhere, "In the end, according to Baeck, faith for Paul was everything. Human beings could effect nothing; all was by God's intention, God's grace."[65] For German Lutheranism, the form of Christianity best

60. Ibid.

61. Ibid., Halacha 4.

62. Ibid.

63. Leo Baeck, "Romantic Religion" in *Jewish Perspectives on Christianity*, ed. Fritz A. Rothschild (New York: Crossroad, 1990) 60–62.

64. Ibid.

65. John E. Phelan, Jr. "(Re)reading Paul: Jewish Reappraisals of the Apostle to the Gentiles" in *Doing Theology for the Church: Essays in Honor of Klyne Snodgrass*, ed. Rebekah A. Eklund and John E. Phelan, Jr. (Eugene, OR: Wipf and Stock, 2014) 82.

known to Baeck, this was the pinnacle of religious understanding. For Baeck, it was the nadir.

Ultimately it was Augustine's form of Christian faith that so troubled Maimonides and Baeck. Augustine's rejection of Pelagius's perfectionism involved a rejection of effective human agency, in spite of his arguments to the contrary. His insistence on predestination, original sin, and the determinative power of God's grace was seized on by Luther, Calvin, and other reformers to oppose what they saw as the Pelagian character of late-Medieval Catholicism. Though there were reactions to Luther's strictures among the Mennonites, Pietists, Methodists, and others, Protestantism has struggled ever since with the relation of "works" and "obedience to God's will" to salvation. More than once this struggle has morphed into a form of antinomianism.

Concluding with Paul

Are elitism, perfectionism, or indifferentism our only options? Does Paul himself offer us another way to approach the question of how we should live? I would argue that my colleague Klyne Snodgrass offered us a way forward some twenty years ago in his article "Justification by Grace—To the Doers: An Analysis of the Place of Romans 2 in the Theology of Paul."[66] Klyne points to the obvious difficulty that NT scholars have had with Rom 2. Paul's insistence that "it is those who obey the law who will be declared righteous" (2:13b) is shocking to ears schooled on Augustine, Luther and Calvin. "One will find," Klyne writes, "statements ranging from a denial that Paul believes judgment is according to works without respect of persons to the assertion that words like 2:7 are only a foil for the argument against Jews, to the softening of such words by viewing them merely as missionary speech to awaken the conscience, or attempts to encourage ethical behavior. J. C. O'Neill omitted all of chapter 2 as irrelevant to Paul's purpose."[67]

I will not repeat here the argument of Klyne's groundbreaking and still important article. I will rather offer his conclusion, with which I wholeheartedly agree: "The final question, 'Can Paul have believed that salvation is to the doers?' must be answered with a resounding 'Yes!' One of the main problems that has led to such confusion in the study of Paul (and indeed in the church) is the inadequate and cognitive definitions that have been given of faith. Any definition that does not do justice to the concept of obedience is unacceptable."[68] A bit later he writes, "Salvation

---

66. *New Testament Studies* 32 (1986) 72–93.

67. Ibid., 73.

68. Ibid., 85.

is by grace and people do not have to be godly or obedient before they come to God in Christ, but every part of Paul's writings would reject that they could remain ungodly in Christ. The righteousness of God includes that activity and power showing how previous sins could be passed over, how sin is defeated and how a life pleasing to God is now possible by the increased activity of the Spirit."[69] I would add that this interpretation of Rom 2 fits well with another maligned and ignored text: "You see," James wrote of Abraham, "that his faith and actions were working together, and his faith was made complete by what he did" (James 2:22).

In his other work Klyne has argued that another key for understanding Paul is his notion of "participation."[70] Paul's use of "in Christ" and "body of Christ" language speak to the intimacy the believer has with Christ through the Spirit. This intimacy with Christ leads to intimacy with other believers who share the same intimacy in the same body. This intimacy is not the intimacy of the mystic in singular union with God. It is the intimacy of the community, the intimacy of a *people*. It is this intimacy, this peoplehood that I fear we have lost. This is especially evident in the evangelical world with its individualistic notion of salvation, its suspicion of spiritual practices, and its fear of communal accountability, let along individual accountability.

We hear a great deal today about "communities of practice." Ancient Israel and rabbinic Judaism clearly represented communities of practice. Certainly there are monastic communities within the Roman Catholic Church that are communities of practice. Of course, to a significant extent all local churches are communities of good and, yes, bad practices. The NT demonstrates that the early church was also a community of practice. These practices were both communal and individual, and all were rooted in the *Torah* (excluding what Paul called "the works of the law"—that is those elements of Torah that separated Jews and Gentiles), and all anticipated God's coming in judgment to set the world right. For Christians these practices are shaped by the moral teachings of Torah, the commands of Jesus, and the instructions of Paul and the rest of the apostles. This complex set of instructions requires rereading, reinterpretation, and reapplication in every generation. The rabbis over the centuries have modeled a process of communal conversations over the meaning and implications of the text. They record their controversies, the preferred interpretation, and yet leave the alternative interpretations in place. Be that as it may, for the Paul and his community, to live for God did not mean to live without sin (contra Pelagius); it did not mean to be part of a small elite company (contra the monks); and it certainly

---

69. Ibid., 86.

70. See Klyne Snodgrass, "Jesus and a Hermeneutics of Identity" in *BibSac* 168 (2011) 133–45; and "Paul's Focus on Identity" *BibSac* 168 (2011) 259–73.

did not mean to live as if the fate of every person was already determined (contra Augustine). It meant to live lives of obedience sustained by a community

It is time to step out of the long shadow of Augustine. Our problem today is not the severe and icy puritanism of Pelagius's perfectionism. It is rather a placid "languidly pious" individualism that rests upon past experiences. It is rather a lack of rigor, a failure of obedience. It is rather *presumption* on the grace of God instead of *living* by the grace of God. What would it mean to accept both the grace of God in Jesus Christ and the responsibility, the *communal* responsibility, to be formed by the commands of God and the law of Christ?

RESPONSE TO PHELAN

Rebekah A. Eklund

First, I want to thank Jay Phelan for his fine paper and for the honor of responding to it, although I have already complained to him that, having expected a paper on (say) Paul, I received a paper on semi-Pelagianism. Like Phelan, I am a NT scholar, which leads me to believe that NT scholars rush in where angels fear to tread—that is, into the debate between Augustine and Pelagius. Also like Phelan, I am interested in the life that NT texts have taken on in the church and in theology over time. I have also been thinking a great deal about divine grace and human freedom lately, because I am currently teaching a book by Hans Urs von Balthasar called *Dare We Hope "That All Men Be Saved"?* to a class of undergrads who are, for the most part, deeply uncomfortable with the idea of punishment in general and eternal damnation in particular. Von Balthasar, of course, issues his own direct challenge to the Augustinian tradition, which I will not rehearse here.

Instead, I want to consider the question at the center of Phelan's paper: how is one to live as a Christian? Phelan's paper raises a wealth of interesting issues. In this brief space I will pass over many of those issues to focus on two: the first concerning sanctification and the problem of a two-tiered Christianity; and the second concerning the problem of indifferentism and whether we are under an Augustinian shadow or a Pelagian one.

Justification, Sanctification, and Two-Tiered Christianity

As one of my Jesuit friends recently reminded me, the concept of a two-tiered system of Christianity was not necessarily inherent to earliest monasticism. In fact, the first monks often narrated themselves not as spiritual elites but as the worst of sinners, those most in need of salvation. But the specter of a two-tiered Christianity looms over the Pelagian debate.

This first reflection arises in part from the claim in Phelan's paper that Pelagius's views on obedience necessarily mean that the vast majority of Christians in the Roman world were damned, presumably because Pelagius thought that one must be morally perfect—or if not perfect, then very, very good—to achieve salvation. I wonder if a certain distinction between justification and sanctification might be helpful here. To be sure, too sharp a split between the two has caused its own problems and is difficult to support in the NT, particularly if justification is seen as essential and growth in holiness as optional, if justifying is God's work and maturity ours. But if the main question is how one is to live as a Christian, perhaps we might consider the role that sanctification, or growth in holiness, might play in relation to the problems created by both Augustine and Pelagius, rather than focusing solely on the question of securing salvation.

For example, if Pelagius in effect collapses the two tiers of Christianity by moving everyone onto the first tier—we are *all* called to be the spiritual elites—I wonder if he has, in part, confused the issue of salvation or justification with the issue of sanctification, or the maturing and growth in godliness expected of all Christians with the assistance of the Holy Spirit and the *ekklesia*.

Which brings me to babies. I was struck by Peter Brown's contrast between Augustine's view of himself as a baby on his mother's breast, utterly dependent, and Pelagius's view of the Christian as a "son," no *longer* dependent on the parent. Both, of course, find their places in Scripture. In Ps 131 the psalmist sings, "I have calmed and quieted my soul, like a weaned child with its mother," and the author of Hebrews presents us with the image of maturing Christians who can move someday from milk to solid food. I see no reason why we cannot accept both as faithful images of the Christian journey with God, although I would reject the Pelagian note that maturity requires independence. Maturity, in fact, strikes me as not only an increase in our own capacities and responsibility but an ever-deepening awareness of and dependence on God's grace.

Spiritual Lassitude/Indifferentism

Phelan's paper admits that Augustine "would labor mightily to establish that all Christians should strive to pursue the good." The paper seems to take this as a contradiction, that if Augustine were true to his own teaching, it would lead to "despair and moral lassitude." I wonder if concerns about predestination as the path to moral laxity or indifference is a genuine problem or a perceived one that has never materialized in practice. I have been worshipping in a Presbyterian church for the last year, and the people there are certainly prone neither to despair nor moral lassitude.

In addition, Augustine's own life seems to bear witness to precisely the opposite. In Joseph Bernardin's essay on "St. Augustine as Pastor," Bernardin writes that Augustine taught the necessity of repentance and prayer, exhorted the rich to give to the poor as if to Christ, emphasized the danger of hearing the word but not doing it, taught that the Christian life was a life of discipline and that spiritual growth required perseverance—and that all of these, of course, were gifts of grace, grace all the way down, but this let nobody off the hook in terms of their daily practices.[1]

Here is Phelan's description of Augustine's own churches: "regular folks, neither monastic elites nor Pelagian perfectionists, stumbling along, trying to be faithful . . . [Augustine] recognizes that wheat and tares were sown together and that it was perilous to try to disentangle them. . . . [The sovereign choice of God] did not excuse him from preaching faithfully and offering the sacraments. . . . It did not excuse them from the call to obedience." This sounds to me like a description of "a long obedience in the same direction," not a description of indifferentism. It sounds a little bit like all of us—regular folks, neither monastic elites nor Pelagian perfectionists, stumbling along, trying to be faithful.

Therefore, I confess that I fear Pelagius may have cast an even longer shadow over at least parts of the church than Augustine, and I say that as someone who is not Augustinian on the question of double predestination. But tell me which is more worrisome: Christians who think their salvation requires nothing more than a single prayer or a mental assent but who fail to practice justice, show mercy, and participate in the faithful practices of the worshiping community? (Augustine and Pelagius might agree on this particular concern!) Or, Christians who tear themselves to pieces worried that their prayer was not sincere enough, that there is some unforgivable sin that they are sure to commit, that God's grace will eventually wear thin in the face of their continual, small, everyday sins?

I wonder if we are living in Pelagius's shadow just as much as Augustine's, not because we have inherited his icy perfectionism (for the most part) but in the widespread and almost unconscious belief in unfettered human capacity freely to choose or reject God, in the elevation of free will and human decision, or in the thousand tiny ways we try to earn God's favor or assure ourselves of our salvation. I think the hardest lesson I have ever learned is I am a beloved child of God, and that that is the end of that sentence.

Beverly Gaventa's marvelous Lund lectures before the symposium and her reflections on Romans made me wonder if Pelagius underestimated or misdiagnosed the extent of the problem, whereas Augustine may have misdiagnosed the extent of God's solution. That is to say, Pelagius fails to see that only God can rescue us from this body of death, whereas Augustine's view that God saves only some seems to fall short of the scriptural vision of God's redemption of all creation.

Since I am a NT scholar, I like the idea (also noted in Phelan's paper) that St. Paul himself is the best and most reliable guide we have, as complex as he is, into

---

1. Joseph B. Bernardin, "St. Augustine as Pastor," in *A Companion to the Study of St. Augustine*, ed. Roy W. Battenhouse (New York: Oxford University Press, 1955) 57–87.

the thorny question of the tension between divine grace and human responsibility. So if the primary question is how one is to live as a Christian, here are a few words of exhortation from Paul that could well take a lifetime to fulfill: "Present yourselves to God as those who have been brought from life to death" (Rom 6:13); "Present your bodies as a sacrifice, living, holy, and pleasing to God" (Rom 12:1); and finally, in a delightful apparent contradiction, "Work out your own salvation with fear and trembling, for it is God who is working in you both to will and to work for his good pleasure" (Phil 2:12–13).

WISDOM'S RESPONSE TO THE DIVINE INITIATIVE

Tremper Longman III

While wisdom is a pervasive theme in many different books of varied literary types in the OT, our primary focus will be on the three books about which there is general consensus that their primary focus is on wisdom, namely Proverbs, Job, and Ecclesiastes. I will include an afterward about the Song of Songs, which may be connected to wisdom but in a different manner from the other three.

As we explore Proverbs, Job, and Ecclesiastes in reference to the theme of human response to divine initiative, we first note that, while wisdom is well known for its human response, precious little is obvious in terms of divine initiative. Wisdom does not speak of revelation, covenant, or divine law. Wisdom does not interact with the history in which God reveals himself to his people in the burning bush and the exodus. God does not speak to the sages in the book of Proverbs or to Qohelet in Ecclesiastes as he speaks to the prophets.[1] God speaks, and dramatically so, in the book of Job, but note that he speaks at the end of the book after considerable human speech that we will see are abortive attempts to respond to the divine initiative.

While it might be expected, then, to speak of divine initiative first and then human response, for wisdom literature we will take the opposite order and speak of human response first and then address the question of divine initiative. We will first look at Proverbs, then Job, and finally Ecclesiastes. While each book provides its own unique contribution, it is important to see that all three affirm the "fear of the Lord" as the heart of a proper human response to the divine initiative.

---

1. According to W. Brueggemann (*In Man We Trust: The Neglected Side of Biblical Faith* [Atlanta: John Knox, 1972] 17) the initiative comes not from the divine but from the human in wisdom literature: "Wisdom affirms that the authority for life is to be discerned in our common experience. What is right and good is not identified by answers in the back of the book, but only by patient, careful discernment of what we ought to be doing to be us." Though as is not atypical of Brueggemann, we can find assertions which are in tension with this human-centered view of wisdom when he speaks, for instance of "the theological foundation in the Lordship of Christ" (p. 41) in wisdom as well.

The Human Response

Proverbs: "The fear of the Lord is the beginning of wisdom/knowledge" (1:7)

The book of Proverbs opens with a prologue (1:1–7), typical of ancient Near Eastern instructional literature.[2] This prologue introduces the book by talking about its origins in Solomon, its content as wisdom, and its audience as the immature as well as the wise. In the first six verses wisdom could be understood simply as practical advice and ethics ("to receive the teaching of insight, righteousness, justice, and virtue," v. 3[3]). The concluding verse of the prologue moves our understanding of the nature of wisdom to its most profound depths: "The fear of the Lord is the beginning of knowledge, but fools despise wisdom and discipline" (1:7). The importance of the "fear of the Lord" to the wisdom task may be noted not only in its strategic appearance at the climax of the prologue, but also throughout the book. Not only does it form an inclusio at the beginning and end (9:10) of the discourses that constitute the first part of the book of Proverbs (chs. 1–9), it occurs throughout (1:29; 2:5; 3:7; 8:13; 10:27; 14:2, 26, 27; 15:16, 33; 16:6; 19:23; 22:4; 23:7; 24:21; 28:14; 29:25; 31:30).

In short, wisdom is not only a practical or even an ethical category but a theological one. Wisdom is also not an abstract quality but the result of a relationship. Wisdom is only possible if a person has a relationship with the true God characterized by fear. There is no wisdom apart from fear of Yahweh.

Why fear? Why not the love of God or joy in the Lord? Fear sounds so negative to us. According to John, does not "perfect love cast out fear" (1 John 4:18)? We will come back to the New Testament's attitude toward the fear of God, but for now we stay in the context of the OT. Our first comment is that the fear spoken of here is not the kind of fear that would make a person run away and hide. That kind of pure dread would be counterproductive to the interests of wisdom. Fear here is the emotional response to someone much greater than ourselves. It is more than respect; "awe" may be too passive a term, but it gets close. The fear of the Lord is an acknowledgement that God is the Creator and we are his creatures. One who fears will learn from the Lord and will follow the Lord's instructions. In other words, and this is important, the fear of the Lord entails obedience. Fear breeds humility and eschews pride, a virtue and a vice respectively often addressed in the book of Proverbs (3:5, 7; 6:17; 11:2; 15:25, etc.). Those who fear the Lord are not wise "in their own

---

2. K. Kitchen, "Proverbs and the Wisdom Books of the Ancient Near East," *Tyndale Bulletin* 28 (1977) 69–114.

3. All translations of Proverbs are from T. Longman III, *Proverbs*, BCOTWP (Grand Rapids: Baker, 2006).

eyes," but listen to God and his agents (the sages/father) and will be open to learning from their mistakes, which only a fool will repeat (10:17; 12:1).

Ecclesiastes: "Fear God and keep his commandments, for this is the whole duty of humanity"[4]

Ecclesiastes is a book of wisdom quite different from the book of Proverbs. Proverbs celebrates wisdom and values the benefits that will accrue to the wise and warns concerning the pain that awaits fools. Proverbs is a compilation of speeches (particularly in chs. 1–9) and proverbs (in chs. 10–31) that promote the fear of the Lord and the proper attitudes, emotions, and actions that follow from that fear. The book of Proverbs may be a compilation of the wisdom of a number of sages, but they all speak with one voice.

Ecclesiastes, on the other hand, is a book that presents two voices.[5] Qohelet (often translated "the Teacher" or "the Preacher") speaks in the body of the book (1:12—12:7), but a second unnamed wisdom teacher's words frame Qohelet's words and thus constitute the perspective of the implied author. His introductory speech (1:1–11) simply introduces Qohelet and his rather depressing ideas, while the epilogue (12:8–14) evaluates Qohelet for the second wise man's son (see 12:12).

Thus, to understand the book of Ecclesiastes and its contribution to our study, we must ask two questions. What is the perspective of Qohelet, and what is the perspective of the frame narrator? It will be the latter's perspective that we will see most closely aligns with the canonical contribution of the book. In this respect the book of Ecclesiastes is similar to the multi-voiced book of Job. In that book we hear from Job, the three friends, and Elihu, but they do not represent the message of the book. For the message of the book, we must attend to the voice of Yahweh who speaks out of the whirlwind at the end of the book. It is not as if the other voices in Job or Qohelet's voice in Ecclesiastes do not contribute to the message of the book, but we cannot simply quote them and say "thus says the Lord." With Ecclesiastes we will see that Qohelet means something quite different from the second wise man when he talks about the "fear of the Lord."[6]

---

4. Eccl 12:13. All translations from Ecclesiastes are from T. Longman III, *Ecclesiastes*, NICOT (Grand Rapids: Eerdmans, 1998).

5. This is a commonly held view. See M. Fox, "Frame-Narrative and Composition in Biblical Literature," *HUCA* 48 (1977) 83–106; C. L. Seow, *Ecclesiastes*, AB 18C (New York: Doubleday, 1997); C. G. Bartholomew, *Ecclesiastes*, BCOTWP (Grand Rapids: Baker, 2009); M. Shields, *The End of Wisdom: A Reappraisal of the Historical and Canonical Function of Ecclesiastes* (Winona Lake, IN: Eisenbrauns, 2006).

6. For more on this, see T. Longman III, "The Fear of the Lord in the Book of Ecclesiastes," *BBR* 25 (forthcoming).

We begin with Qohelet, who introduces himself in 1:12 and speaks in the first person ("I, Qohelet"), ending his speech with a reflection on death in 12:1–7. He reflects on his search for the meaning of life but concludes that life is meaningless. He tries to find meaning in pleasure, wisdom, wealth, work, and more but always comes up empty. For Qohelet three facts of life render it meaningless. First, death takes away the purpose of life (see 2:12–17; 12:1–7). Second, since there is nothing beyond death where the righteous might get the reward they deserve, the injustice of life on earth renders life meaningless (7:15–18; 8:10–15). Third, the inability of humans, even sages like Qohelet, to discern the proper time renders life meaningless (3:1–15). After all, according to the wisdom project, to say and do the right thing requires a person to know the proper time. Since there is no greater purpose to life, Qohelet in the final analysis urges his listeners to grab whatever enjoyment they can out of life (*carpe diem*, 2:24–26; 3:12–14, 22; 5:18–20; 8:15; 9:7–10).

It is within this broader perspective that we should evaluate Qohelet's occasional admonitions to fear God. The phrase "fear God" (or some variant) occurs seven times in the book of Ecclesiastes (3:14; 5:7 [Heb 5:6]; 7:18; 8:12 [twice], 13). The verb "fear" is always from *yr* and God is *ʾĕlohîm* (never Yahweh; sometimes the pronoun is used). Qohelet has a distant relationship with God at best. Indeed, he urges a cool detachment in a relationship with God (5:1–7). Thus, within the context of Qohelet's broader teaching and also in the particular context of its use, Qohelet is not urging the kind of awe-struck fear that leads to obedience advocated by the sages in the book of Proverbs. Instead, he urges the kind of fear that would make one duck and run for cover. There is no benefit in a relationship with God because there is no purpose to life.

To make our point more concrete, we will examine one of the passages in which Qohelet urges the fear of God (5:1–7; Hebrew 4:17—5:6). Earlier Qohelet famously announces that he will conduct his search for meaning "under the sun" (1:13–14). The phrase is best understood as limiting his investigation to what he can "see" rather than what he can "know" through revelation. However, Qohelet is no atheist or agnostic. He speaks about God throughout the book, though in what has been widely recognized as a distant manner signaled in part by his exclusive reference to God as *ʾĕlohîm*.

Qohelet's most sustained reflection on God (5:1–7; Hebrew: 4:17—5:6) confirms the impression that his relationship with God is distant at best. Indeed, what guides his advice about how to relate to this God is his assertion that "God is in heaven and you are on earth" (5:2b). Due to this distance between God and humanity, few benefits can accrue from relating to this God, and thus it is best to keep interaction with God to a minimum.

Indeed, right after he announces that God is in heaven and humans ("you") are on earth, he advises his hearers to let their words be few. In 5:1–2a he tells people to be slow to offer sacrifices and also to speak to God. It is not clear from the Hebrew text that Qohelet believes that all sacrifice is foolish and evil, but in any case he is far from advocating a vibrant and active relationship with God. When it comes to praying to God, he comes close to saying that the one who prays is basically hallucinating, evident in his analogy between the dreams of someone who works too hard and someone addressing many words to God (5:3; see also 5:7a).

Besides sacrifice and prayer, Qohelet also offers advice when it comes to vows (5:4–6). In brief, he tells his hearers that it is dangerous to offer a vow, but if one has offered a vow to God, then one had better fulfill it. It is a foolhearty mistake to tell the messenger who has come from the temple to collect the vow that it was a mistake. God might not pay a lot of attention to a worshipper, but according to Qohelet the person who does not pay the vow will draw the angry attention of the otherwise distant deity.

At the end of this reflection on God, Qohelet urges those who hear him to "fear God." The context indicates that Qohelet's fear of God has more to do with being afraid than reverence. The one who fears God will acknowledge that he is distant and uninvolved unless, of course, a person crosses him. Whereas the book of Proverbs urges those who fear God to enter into a relationship with him that is likened to an intimate relationship between a young man and a woman (Woman Wisdom),[7] Qohelet rather suggests maintaining a healthy distance.

In summary, Qohelet feels distant from God. For him there is no substantial divine initiative. He feels that life has no meaning. So his response is *carpe diem* and the cultivation of a very careful relationship with God who provides no real benefits to life. Indeed, in 7:15–18 he urges those who listen to him to "fly under the radar" by being neither too wise nor too righteous, on the one hand, or too wicked or too much a fool on the other. Otherwise, one might attract the attention of this God who provides no benefits since he has observed both "a righteous man perishing in his righteousness" as well as a "wicked person living long in his evil" (7:15). Thus, in this sad context as well Qohelet urges the fear of God, which we understand to be the type of fear that makes one run away and avoid God. Indeed, the person who fears God will follow both wisdom/righteousness and folly/wickedness (7:18).

The second voice is that of an unnamed wise man whose voice may be distinguished from Qohelet's by speaking of Qohelet in the third person ("he, Qohelet"; see 1:1–11; 7:27; 12:8–14). He is speaking to his son about Qohelet. This second

---

7. I have argued that "Woman Wisdom" ultimately stands for Yahweh himself in *Proverbs*, 58–61, 221–23.

wise man also urges the fear of God, but in a different context that suggests that his admonition is similar to the sages' in the book of Proverbs.

In 12:8–12 he evaluates Qohelet's speech for his son. As I have argued elsewhere but will here only summarize,[8] Qohelet begins by approving of Qohelet's message that life is difficult and then one dies—but with a caveat. In v. 10 by saying "Qohelet sought to find words of delight and he wrote honest words of truth," he affirms what Qohelet says. In other words, he is saying to his son, "Qohelet is correct in his understanding that life *under the sun* is meaningless." Indeed, life is meaningless apart from a vibrant relationship with God, but the frame narrator does not want the son to stay "under the sun." Therefore, he ends on a positive note by urging his son to "Fear God and keep his commandments, for this is the whole duty of humanity. For God will bring every deed into judgment, including every hidden thing, whether good or evil" (12:13–14). The context which includes the connection with Torah obedience and expectation of a judgment is the signal that here the second wise man uses "fear God" in a similar way to that which we saw in the book of Proverbs. Our case will be strengthened a bit later in the paper when we consider the divine initiative to which this is the called-for human response.

The Book of Job: Does Job Fear God for No Good Reason?

What is the human response in the book of Job? Again it is the "fear of God." The "fear of God" comes up in the very first verse describing the main protagonist: "There was a man in the land of Uz whose name was Job, and that man was innocent and virtuous, fearing God and turning away from evil" (Job 1:1).[9] That Job fears God is the assessment not only of the narrator but also of God himself (1:8; 2:7), and this is not challenged by the accuser (a "son of God" or angel who plays the role of God's agent in the world). There is no doubt that Job fears God in the sense expressed by Prov 1:7, though there is a question about his motivation. "Is it for no good reason that Job fears God?" (1:9). Does Job fear God because of who God is or because of the rewards that result from such fear?

Even when the rewards are taken away from Job, he maintains his fear of God (1:20–23 and 2:9–10). However, over time, while not turning his back on God, he comes to question God's justice and desires to challenge God face to face. He

8. Longman, *Ecclesiastes*, 274–81. See more recently T. Longman III, "Qohelet as Solomon: 'For What Can Anyone Who Comes after the King Do?' (Ecclesiastes 2:12)," in *Reading Ecclesiastes Intertextually*, LHB/OTS, ed. Katharine Dell and Will Kynes (New York: T. and T. Clark, 2014) 42–56. The latter represents a significant advance in my understanding of the function of v. 10, a reading that is reflected in this article.

9. All translations from the book of Job some from T. Longman III, *Job*, BCOTWP (Grand Rapids: Baker, 2012).

expresses his intentions to his "three friends" with whom he enters into a lengthy debate. They represent the view of retribution theology, which mechanically links the fear of the Lord with rewards and sin with punishment. Thus, if someone is suffering, they must be sinners. The friends press their case against Job and urge him to repent to set things right again. Job, for his part, knows he is not a sinner who deserves to suffer. However, he too accepts retribution theology and believes that only a sinner would suffer like he suffers. Thus, he believes that God is unjust and the solution to his problem is to confront God and set him straight.

The fear of the Lord comes up several times in the context of the debate. In Eliphaz's first speech he is relatively respectful of Job's previous piety but shocked at this complaining outburst. He thus prods him by saying, "Is not your 'fear' your comfort? Is not the innocence of your ways your hope?" (4:6). Here, the comforting fear is the fear of Yahweh, which if he has it, so Eliphaz implies, it will lead to his ultimate restoration. In his response Job counters by charging his friend with treason of their friendship by saying, "One who withholds loyalty from his friend forsakes the fear of Shaddai" (6:14). Job does not admit to so forsaking the fear of Yahweh, but he is saying that even in such a situation friends should stay devoted. They think he has betrayed Yahweh and use that to justify their attack. Job says that even if this were the case they should remain loyal.

The next time Job refers to fear of God it is in the negative sense of terror (not unprecedented elsewhere, see Ecclesiastes). He wants to talk to God, to set him straight. Job, after all, also holds to the belief that only sinners should suffer. He knows he is innocent, so God must be unjust (9:21–24). He wishes he had an arbitrator or mediator to lessen his "fear of God," so he can stand up to him.

Eliphaz next comes back to the theme of the "fear of God" in his second speech (15:4). Here he castigates Job's wisdom. He suggests that his arguments undermine "fear of God." Next, it is again Eliphaz, this time in his third speech, who raises the issue of the fear of God, he ridicules Job's claim of piety by mockingly asking him "Does he reprove you for his fear?" (22:4).

In the disputations, when "fear of Yahweh" is used positively as a virtue, it is used by one of the three friends, usually Eliphaz to question Job's proper attitude for God. Of course, readers of the book know what the characters of the book do not. Job does not suffer because of a lack of fear of God. Ironically, Elihu, the young brash man who comes in after the debate with the three friends, tries to prod Job to a proper fear of God, which he thinks he lacks, by emphasizing God's greatness and power (37:24).

Though the expression "fear of God" does not appear in Yahweh's speeches or in Job's response to them, we certainly can understand the effect of these speeches as inducing such fear. In chs. 38–42 God confronts Job with his wisdom and power, reducing him to his knees, not because of a sin that led to his suffering, but because of his growing impatience with God. Here we see Job regain a sense of the fear of God.

In this survey of the theme of the fear of God in the book of Job we have intentionally passed over its most famous use in ch. 28. We have done this because the question of this chapter's place in the book is a serious question. In terms of its content it is a magnificent assertion of God's wisdom. Human beings can do marvelous things like mine the earth for precious gems and metals, but wisdom is beyond them. The last lines of the poem answer the question of the location of wisdom: "Behold, the fear of the Lord is wisdom, and turning aside from evil is understanding" (28:28).

The issue has to do with the location of Job's speech. It occurs at the end of the disputation but is followed by Job's further protestation of innocence and complaint (chs. 29–31). Chapter 28 anticipates the conclusion of the book in its assertion of God's wisdom, but more turmoil follows before the resolution in Job's repentance. Perhaps the best explanation for this is that the book well represents the psychology of a sufferer.[10] In the midst of pain people can have moments of clarity but then fall back into despair.

The Divine Initiative

According to Proverbs, Ecclesiastes, and Job, the "fear of the Lord" is the heart of the human response to the divine initiative. But what is distinctive in the Wisdom literature about the divine initiative? Again, we will proceed by looking at these three books individually.

Woman Wisdom in the Book of Proverbs

Typically, wisdom literature, and in particular the book of Proverbs, has been characterized as more human-centric than theocentric. We find no "thus says the Lord's" in Proverbs. Wisdom is often seen as universal, rather than Israelite, in its perspective, more humanistic than particularistic. Proverbs has even been called secular literature.[11]

---

10. A view advocated by A. Lo, *Job 28 as Rhetoric: An Analysis of Job 28 in the Context of Job 22–31*, VTSup 97, (Leiden: Brill, 2003), which I have affirmed. See Longman, *Job*. Alternatively, as argued by J. Walton, *Job*, NIVAC (Grand Rapids: Zondervan, 2012) the chapter might be attributed to the narrator.

11. O. Eissfeldt (*The Old Testament: An Introduction* [New York: Harper and Row, 1965] 47) says, "The basis for the commendation of wisdom and piety is on the one hand purely secular and rational." This view has been properly disputed by L. Bostrom, *The God of the Sages: The Portrayal of God in the*

It is true that the wisdom of Proverbs often appeals to observation, experience, and tradition (built on observation and experience) as its source. Consider 6:6–8: "Go to the ant, you lazy people! See its paths and grow wise. That one has no military commander, officer or ruler; it gets its food in summer, gathers its provisions at harvest."

Here we have no divine oracle, but rather the sage urges his pupils to learn from observing the ants. In another proverb dealing with laziness the sage appeals to experience: "How long, you lazy person, will you lie down; when will you rise up from your sleep? 'A little sleep, a little slumber, a little folding of the arms to lie down'—and your deprivation like a person with a shield" (6:9–11).

As a subset of learning from observation and experience, we see the wisdom teachers learning from their mistakes. That is why they praise those who learn from their errors and treat those who do not as utter fools: "Those who guard discipline love knowledge; and those who hate correction wander aimlessly" (10:17). Similarly in 12:1 we find "Those who love discipline love knowledge; and those who hate correction are dullards."

However, the sage does not have to experience or observe something personally in order to learn and pass on that information. They can learn from those who gained wisdom in the past. In other words, the instructions of wisdom can come from the tradition of those who precede them:

> Hear, sons, fatherly discipline,
> and pay attention to the knowledge of understanding.
> For I will give you good teaching;
> don't forsake my instruction.
> For I was a son to my father,
> tender and the only one of my mother.
> He taught me and said to me:
> "Let your heart hold on to my words;
> guard my commands and live." (4:1–4)

Thus, we see in Proverbs and in wisdom literature generally many admonitions and prohibitions that appeal to observation, experience (including learning from one's mistakes), and tradition. But how is this divine initiative? How does this relate to the fear of the Lord as the proper human response?

In this regard, we should begin with a consideration of Prov 20:12: "An ear to hear and an eye to see—Yahweh made both of them." According to Proverbs observation, experience, tradition, and learning from one's mistakes are indeed all

---

Book of Proverbs (Stockholm: Almqvist and Wiksell International, 1990) 36–39.

important sources of human wisdom. However, at the heart of wisdom is God himself. Apart from God there is no true insight into the world. God is the only source of true wisdom. According to Prov 20:12 even the ability to observe and experience comes from the Lord.

We come to the role of the figure of Woman Wisdom in the book of Proverbs. Woman Wisdom speaks for the first time in the second discourse of the book (1:20–33). She is in the midst of the people in a public place urging the immature to come and listen to her. She is upset that they reject her invitation and threatens them that she will ignore them if they turn to her later in the midst of a crisis. In later discourses the father tells his son to find Woman Wisdom and enjoy her benefits (3:13–20). He wants his son to develop an intimate relationship with her (4:5–9).

Woman Wisdom speaks again in Prov 8, but first she is introduced by a third party, probably the father who is the implied author of the book. He describes her again as speaking in very public places ("the crossroads" and the "gate/entrances" of the city, vv. 2b, 3) and emphasizes the elevation of her location ("the high places on the path," v. 2a).

Woman Wisdom begins to speak about herself beginning in 8:4. She describes herself, and the attentive listener will note that her virtues are those of wisdom itself. She is the very embodiment of wisdom. She also associates herself with "wealth and honor" (v. 18a). The most interesting and for centuries frequently discussed parts of her self-description are in vv. 22–31 where she claims to be the first-born of creation. She observed God putting the world together, and if we are correct to translate the difficult *ʾāmôn* in v. 30 as "craftsman,"[12] then she also participated in creation. She ends her speech with an appeal that the "sons" listen to her and enter into a relationship with her (vv. 32–36).

The sages' presentation of Woman Wisdom comes to a climax in Prov 9:1–6. Here the narrator describes her magnificent seven-pillared house which is located on the "pinnacle of the heights of the city" (9:3) where she has prepared a magnificent feast. She then sends her servants out to invite "the simpleminded" to a wonderful banquet. Those who accept the invitation will live.

At the end of Prov 9 we are introduced to a second woman for the first time, namely Woman Folly. She too is located "at the heights of the city" (9:14b). She too has prepared a meal that looks delicious, but it is stolen and to be eaten in secret. The narrator tells us that those who accept her invitation "are in the depths of Sheol" (9:18b).

Proverbs 9 is a pivotal chapter in the book. It culminates the first part of the book composed of discourses or lectures of Woman Wisdom, or more often the

---

12. See Longman, *Proverbs*, 196.

father. In this chapter both Woman Wisdom and Woman Folly invited the simple-minded to a meal. They are competing for the same audience.

With which Woman will the reader decide to dine, Woman Wisdom or Woman Folly? But who are these women? Certainly, at minimum, Woman Wisdom represents the wisdom of Yahweh. But I believe we can go further. Woman Wisdom stands for Yahweh himself. After all, her house is at the highest point of the city, and in ancient Israel, as throughout the entire ancient Near East, the house at the highest point of the city would be the sanctuary.

Who then is Woman Folly? Her house is also at the highest point of the city; therefore, she represents all the false gods and goddesses that vie for Israel's attention. Proverbs 9, thus, presents a fundamental choice between following Yahweh or following a false god.

What then is the divine initiative? It is the appeal of Woman Wisdom to whom we are to respond with fear.

Before moving on to the book of Ecclesiastes, let me consider what we have covered from the perspective of the NT. How are Christians to read the divine initiative in Proverbs? According to Jesus in Luke 24, the whole of Scriptures anticipate his coming (cf. vv. 25–27, 44–45). When we read Proverbs from a NT perspective and in particular consider Woman Wisdom, we are drawn to Jesus, who is the epitome of wisdom. As he grew up, he grew in wisdom (Luke 2:40, 52). When he began to teach, he amazed those who heard him as having wisdom like none other (Mark 1:27–28). Paul called him the one "in whom are hidden all the treasures of wisdom and knowledge" (Col 2:3). These passages, of course, are just examples of many such expressions. Most interesting in terms of our present subject, Woman Wisdom, are those passages which associate Jesus with Woman Wisdom. We will only cite one, Col 1:15–16: "The Son is the image of the invisible God, the firstborn over all creation. For in him all things were created: things in heaven and on earth, visible and invisible, whether thrones or powers or rulers or authorities; all things have been created through him and for him." Like Woman Wisdom Jesus is the first born of creation and the one through whom all things are created (see also John 1:1–3). Further, just like Woman Wisdom in Prov 8:22–31, Jesus as Woman Wisdom is the force behind the "thrones or powers or rulers or authorities."

For the Christian reader of Proverbs Woman Wisdom is none other than Jesus. Our response is to develop a relationship with Jesus and to listen to and obey his words.

Law, Prophets, and Writings in the Book of Ecclesiastes

Where is the divine initiative in the book of Ecclesiastes? We above noted a crucial distinction between Qohelet and a second unnamed wise man who addresses his son in the epilogue of the book, and again we must be mindful of the two voices of the book as we answer this question. What stimulates the human response to the divine in the book of Ecclesiastes?

We begin with Qohelet, and our treatment here can be brief since there is no significant human response because there is no, at least according to Qohelet, significant divine initiative. We can be brief also because we have already examined the most significant text in this regard (5:1–7), the most telling statement of which is "For God is in heaven, and you are on earth" (5:2). Qohelet, of course, is not an atheist or even an agnostic. Indeed, it would be a misnomer to call him a deist. It is not that God is so Other that he is uninvolved with humanity. Rather, God is no help, so it is better to keep a low profile with him. Thus, the proper attitude toward God is indeed "fear," but a fear that avoids rather than heeds. As Qohelet looks at life "under the sun," God has little impact on his thinking. He tries to find the meaning of life in a variety of areas, but does not even consider God as the source of meaning, and thus his search is a futile one.

It is a different story with the second wise man as he speaks to his son and encourages him to "Fear God and keep his commandments, for this is the whole duty of humanity. For God will bring every deed into judgment, including every hidden thing, whether good or evil" (12:12–14). We discussed this above in terms of human response. The frame narrator's fear is different from that of Qohelet because it leads to obedience and is done in awareness of a future judgment. If we were to impose anachronistic theological terminology somewhat loosely, we could talk about this as justification (establish a right relationship with God by fear), sanctification (living a life of obedience), and eschatology (knowing that God's judgment is coming in the future). But here too, in my estimation, we also have a subtle, but clear allusion to the divine initiative.

Before asserting this claim further, it is imperative to speak briefly about the date of Ecclesiastes. In another publication I have set forward all the evidence (comparative language, socioeconomic context, and philosophical ideas) that are relevant to topic.[13] All these lines of evidence make it clear, as the vast majority of scholars today of all theological persuasions agree, that the book is a product of the postexilic period. The language is closer to late Hebrew. The socioeconomic background to the

---

13. T. Longman III, "Determining the Historical Context of Ecclesiastes," in *The Words of the Wise are Like Goads: Engaging Qohelet in the 21st Century*, ed. M. J. Boda, T. Longman III, C. G. Rata (Winona Lake, IN: Eisenbrauns, 2013) 89–102.

book—note for instance the mention of coinage which only began in the Persian period—reflects the same period, as does the thought world. While we can say with some measure of confidence that the book is postexilic, attempts more specifically to define the time period as either Persian[14] or Greek[15] are less successful, though in my estimation the latter is more likely. This position is relatively uncontroversial these days. Since the time of Luther (or at least Grotius), the view that the figure of Qohelet is modeled on Solomon rather than actually being Solomon has been forwarded by many Bible-affirming scholars (Moses Stuart, Franz Delitzsch, E. J. Young to name just a few).

With this late date in mind, let us take another look at the frame narrator's final words (12:13–14) to his son, the implied reader, and thus to us, the actual readers. In the postexilic period the Hebrew canon took form in three major parts, which we know as the Law (Torah), the Prophets (Nebiim), and the Writings (Ketubim), the Tanak for short. The weakness of my argument is that we cannot be exactly certain when in the postexilic period the book was written or how early the three part canon division began to take shape. This division is at least as early as the preface to the book of Ecclesiasticus, no later than 130 BC.[16]

That admitted, it is suggestive to align the three part admonition with the three parts of the Hebrew canon. After all, "fear God" makes one think of the wisdom tradition, which is found in the Ketubim; "obey the commandments" clearly alludes to the Torah, and the reference to the judgment alludes to the Nebiim.

In short, at the end the father urges his son on to what I would call an "above the sun" perspective. He (and we) should heed the divine initiative as presented in the Tanak. He acknowledges the truth of Qohelet's thinking (12:10) to be sure. If one stays under the sun, there is no other conclusion then that life is meaningless, but one should not stay under the sun and try to figure out life by what one "sees/ observes." Rather humans should avail themselves of God's revelation as presented in the Tanak.

---

14. So C. L. Seow, "Linguistic Evidence and the Dating of Qoheleth," *JBL* 115 (1996) 38 and C. L. Seow, "The Social World of Ecclesiastes," in *Scribes, Sages and Seers: The Sage in the Eastern Mediter-ranean World*, ed. L. G. Perdue (Göttingen: Vanderhoeck and Ruprecht, 2008) 189–217.

15. For instance, L. G. Perdue, "The Book of Qohelet 'Has the Smell of the Tomb about It': Mortality in Qohelet and Hellenistic Skepticism," in *The Words of the Wise are Like Goads*, 103–16.

16. R. Beckwith, *The Old Testament Canon of the New Testament Church and Its Background in Early Judaism* (London: SPCK, 1985) 110–80.

The Voice of God in Job

God does not speak directly to humanity in Proverbs or Ecclesiastes. In Proverbs God speaks through the father as he instructs his son and through the figure of Woman Wisdom. Job is famously different from the other two wisdom books as God speaks to Job out of the whirlwind.

At first God seems wrongly absent and uncaring to Job. Interestingly, as we observed earlier, Job feared God right from the beginning of the story. The narrator, God, and even the accuser agree on this assessment. Though there is no question about his fear of God, there is a question about whether Job fears God only because of the benefits.

Thus, God allows the accuser in two stages to remove the rewards that accompany his relationship with God. Even so, Job stays faithful (1:23; 2:10). However, after his three friends come and mourn with him for seven days, Job finally expresses his frustration with his predicament. Often characterized as a lament, Job's complaint in ch. 3 does not follow the pattern of a lament. Unlike a lament Job addresses his comment to the air rather than directly to God. He does not sever his relationship with God by any means, but his complaint motivates his three friends to verbal action against him. They articulate the view that sin leads to suffering and that suffering can only be explained by sin. Job too holds this retribution principle, but he knows that he is not wrong. Thus, while the three friends diagnose Job's problem as a sin problem, Job believes the problem is caused by God's injustice. Accordingly, the three friends argue that Job needs to repent in order to relieve his distress. Job believes that the solution can only be found if he confronts God and sets him straight. Both Job and the three friends set themselves up as sages who are able to diagnose a problem and suggest a remedy. However, their debate does not lead to resolution.

After their disputation reaches an end Elihu steps in (chs 32–37). He too believes he knows what the problem and the solution are, but when he speaks, he ends up saying the same thing as the three friends. Job is a sinner whom God has caused to suffer. He needs to repent. Because Elihu offers nothing new, no one—human or divine—bothers to interact with his ideas.

When Elihu ends his speech, God appears in the whirlwind to confront Job. Here we have the divine initiative that evokes human response. God's appearance in the whirlwind indicates that he is none too pleased with Job. Thus, we are not surprised that the bulk of the divine speeches are challenging questions designed to remind Job that it is God, not him, who is wise and powerful. God's address to Job reminds one of an aggrieved professor with a know-it-all student. At the end of his patience the professor turns to the student and says, "Do you really know so much?

Okay, it is pop quiz time." God peppers Job with question after question, not waiting for Job to answer because he, Job, and the reader know that only God knows the answers.

How does Job respond to the divine initiative? As we have already indicated, he responds with the fear of the Lord. Job feared God at the beginning of the story, but here his fear moves to a new depth of maturity. By pursuing God in spite of his suffering, Job showed he was not in it only for the rewards, but he still thought he deserved them. When Job finally repents "in dust and ashes," he demonstrates the fear of God that leads to silence in the face of the mystery of suffering. He no longer accuses God of injustice but submits to God's greater wisdom and power.

Excursus: Physical Intimacy in the Song of Songs

It is not unusual to identify the Song of Songs as wisdom literature. One can make the case that wisdom literature concerns the nitty-gritty of everyday life,[17] and certainly a book like Proverbs is concerned with proper behavior in the realm of sexuality (see particularly chs. 5–7). However, if the Song is wisdom, it is a different type of wisdom from Proverbs, Ecclesiastes, and Job. A better genre analysis would call it an anthology of love poems. With that caveat, it is still interesting to reflect on the Song in terms of the theme of the human response to the divine initiative.

In the first place, even more than the previous wisdom books, the idea of divine initiative seems a strange one for the Song of Songs, which seems to have an intentional avoidance of even the mention of God. The book celebrates the physical intimacy between an unnamed man and an unnamed woman (see 4:1—5:1), though there is also the awareness of the difficulty of such union (see 5:2—6:3).

However, with Trible,[18] we believe that the Song of Songs must be read within the canon as a whole, and that is where the theological dimension of the Song reveals itself. The Song celebrates the man and the woman in the garden feeling no shame as they enjoy each other's bodies. This, says, Trible, brings us back to the Garden of Eden, where Adam and Eve are "both naked . . . and felt no shame" (Gen 2:25). Between the Garden of Eden and the garden of the Song of Songs stands the fall. The introduction of sin leads to alienation between the man and the woman, so they have to cover themselves due to their new-found shame. Thus, the Song is about the redemption of sexuality.

17. B. S. Childs, *Introduction to the Old Testament as Scripture* (Philadelphia: Fortress, 1979) 573–75.

18. P. Trible, *God and the Rhetoric of Sexuality* (Philadelphia: Fortress, 1978).

What is the divine initiative then? It is God creating male and female and giving them the gift of sexuality, whose primary purpose is to bring them closer together, to make them "one flesh." What is the human response? It is to enjoy God's good gift of sex as God intended it in the Garden of Eden.[19]

Conclusion

In our examination of wisdom's response to the divine initiative we focused on the books of Proverbs, Job, and Ecclesiastes with a glance at the Song of Songs. The influence of wisdom theology extends much further in the biblical corpus, but we wanted to focus our attention on these four books.

The divine initiative manifested itself in surprising ways when compared to other parts of the OT. Indeed, with the possible exception of Job, the divine initiative was not always obvious. God does speak directly to Job out of the whirlwind, but in Proverbs God's voice is connected most directly to Woman Wisdom and secondarily to the father who speaks to his son. In Ecclesiastes, we have two speakers. Qohelet does not recognize the divine initiative and so his response is troubled. The second wise man, though, urges his son to hear God in the Tanak. In all three books, the fundamental human response is the same. We are to "fear God" with a type of fear that does not make us run away, but rather one that leads to obedience.

19. See D. Allender and T. Longman III, *God Loves Sex: An Honest Conversation about Sexual Desire and Holiness* (Grand Rapids: Baker, 2014).

RESPONSE TO LONGMAN

James K. Bruckner

Thank you to Dr. Longman for his engaging paper on Proverbs, Ecclesiastes, and Job and the human response to the divine initiative in them. The central issue in understanding biblical wisdom as a response to God lies in his distinction of the "fear of the Lord" as an active commitment and relational practice in contrast to a passive experience of "being afraid" of God. The best juxtaposition of these concepts that I know is Exod 20:20 where the Lord appears in thunderous light on Mt. Sinai: "*Do not be afraid*; for God has come . . . in order that *the fear of* [*the Lord*] may remain with you." Longman's fuller description is apt: "The fear of the Lord is an acknowledgement that God is the Creator and we are his creatures. One who fears will learn from the Lord, follow the Lord's instructions [*qere* Torah]; . . . it entails obedience . . . breeds humility and eschews pride . . . listening to God and his agents and being open to learning from . . . mistakes."

He observes that this kind of relational and active fear is the unifying theme in these three wisdom books. There are differences: in Proverbs "Wisdom has built her house," i.e., in the seven pillars of the earth; in Ecclesiastes "everything under the sun" is open for review; in Job the whirlwind and the cosmological zoo tour are the apex of Job's experience. Each of these images of understanding and enjoying the good creation requires an admission ticket, inscribed with the words "The fear of the Lord."

Yet, the fear of the Lord is not the only response to God described in wisdom literature. Longman's focus on both positive and negative responses ("abortive attempts") to God in these three varied books of wisdom is quite helpful and representative of the wider OT canon: the fool in Proverbs, the Preacher's failed attempts to find satisfaction (e.g., in knowledge, pleasure, or hard work), and the failure of Job's friends in the course "applied theology." We might further consider other examples of human response in the biblical literature. There are many *negative* responses to judgment, even negative response to forgiveness (since it presupposes an acknowledgment of sin). There are *positive* responses to God's law and even to the wrath of God as an agency against injustice and the wicked, as well as the happier positive responses to forgiveness and restoration. We may want to talk about these as well, but now let us turn to some questions, book by book.

Proverbs

Longman's main description of the divine initiative in Proverbs is "the appeal of Woman Wisdom, to whom we are to respond with fear." Specifically this appeal is that a good life begins with seeking wisdom through the fear of the Lord. The primary argument here is that Woman Wisdom "stands for Yahweh himself." It is extended through NT examples to claim that "Woman Wisdom is none other than Jesus."

My question is whether Longman is collapsing categories here. Yes, Jesus is the incarnation of the Word and of *Yahweh's* wisdom in the NT, but to say that Jesus is the Sophia of Proverbs begs the question of the creation of wisdom and its simple personification as the Lord's primary attribute (wisdom) in Proverbs. In Jewish interpretation of the OT, Woman Wisdom is never a god/goddess or hypostatization.[1] The evidence that the house at the highest point of the city would have been the sanctuary begs the question of identity. Where else would a personified characteristic of Yahweh dwell but in God's house? Perhaps it would dwell in the highest point of the creation, in the heavens, but again, with Yahweh; alternately, following William Brown, it would dwell in the Sabbath, the seventh day.[2]

The statements that Woman Wisdom *represents* the wisdom of Yahweh and that "God does not speak directly to humanity in Proverbs [but] . . . speaks . . . *through the figure of* Woman Wisdom" seem more prudent. The Lord's attribute of wisdom remains for us as a postincarnation calling to the faithful: "Seek wisdom," i.e., Prov 1–9 does not need Jesus to remain a true and living Word.

The evidence of Col 1 as applied to Woman Wisdom also raises a host of questions, perhaps too many to engage here. Certainly Jesus is: 1) an embodied person; 2) *begotten* of the father, not made (Nicene Creed); 3) of the Godhead (Trinity). Certainly Sophia is: 1) not a person, but a personification; 2) not begotten, but created; and 3) not a goddess of the Godhead, but the primary characteristic of a creating Yahweh. The verbs in Prov 8 concerning Woman Wisdom are all passive.[3] In Colossians, however, Jesus the Son is the subject of active verbs, accomplishing the

---

1. See the extensive discussion on the history of interpretation of Sophia in M. Pierce Matheney, Jr., "An Introduction to the History of Interpretation" in *An Introduction to Wisdom Literature and the Psalms*, ed. H. W. Ballard Jr. and W. D. Tucker Jr. (Macon, GA: Mercer University Press, 2000) 129–54.

2. William Brown, *The Seven Pillars of Creation* (Oxford: Oxford University Press, 2010).

3. Woman Wisdom was possessed (*qānāh*) by the Lord; formed, poured (*nāsak*); and "writhed" or "danced" (*ḥûl*; not *yālad*). These are all creative acts.

redeeming and creating. Wisdom simply "was there" when the Word was creating. Consequently, the cited Col 1 text ought not to be interpreted to say that *Woman Wisdom* is "first-born" of creation, for she is neither embodied nor an actual person in Proverbs. That move collapses the timeline of biblical revelation and oversimplifies each text.

Rather than saying, "For the Christian reader of Proverbs Woman Wisdom is *none* other than Jesus," would it not be better to say that Jesus is the culmination and perfection of the Woman Wisdom tradition? Even then Longman's conclusion would stand: "Our response is to develop a relationship with Jesus and to listen to and obey his words."

Ecclesiastes: Is Life Meaningless?

In Ecclesiastes, Longman astutely observes that the divine initiative is stated in the future tense by the father-narrator: "God *will* bring every deed into judgment, including every hidden thing, whether good or evil (12:14). This reference to the prophets' warning of an ultimate judgment is matched by the "subtle but clear allusion" in 12:13 to the other two parts of the Tanak, wisdom (fear God) and the Torah (keep his commandments). This Tanak thesis is rightly corroborated by a late date for Ecclesiastes during the final formation of the Hebrew canon.

Longman describes this Tanak reference as a father's plea for his son to live with an "above the sun" perspective, rather than in the meaningless "under the sun" perspective represented by Qoheleth's experimentation with life. The failed human response is represented in the negative voice of Qoheleth himself, who urges that one keep a healthy distance from a fearsome God. This interpretation is similar to Martin's Luther's suspicion that Qoheleth represented Egyptian wisdom *only* and to Scofield, who maintained that Ecclesiastes was not written by Solomon but *for* Solomon, and is an example of a person thinking "apart from God." This is not a divine initiative at all.

While I am generally convinced of the Tanak reference and the late date for the final form, is the dichotomy between the final narrator as God's initiative and Qoheleth as a man afraid of God actually so sharp in the book? Are we to discard the paradoxical wisdom of the Preacher as he writes his own concluding comments, especially the advice not to forget to delight in the Creator's world, while keeping God's judgment in mind? For example, here are some texts that are not included in the paper:[4]

---

4. See also Eccl 12:6–7.

> Young people, it's wonderful to be young! Enjoy every minute of it. Do everything you want to do; take it all in. But remember that you must give an account to God for everything you do. (Eccl 11:9 NLT)

> Don't let the excitement of youth cause you to forget your Creator. Honor him in your youth before you grow old and say, "Life is not pleasant anymore." (Eccl 12:1 NLT)

This balance is also in view when Qoheleth urges the reader to "Enjoy life!" God is in view in every case. Longman quotes 5:1–7 as evidence of a distant, dangerous God, but shortly following in 5:18–19 (which is not quoted) is a deep appreciation for God as a giver of good gifts.[5]

> Here is what I have seen to be good and fitting: to eat, to drink and enjoy oneself in all one's labor in which he toils under the sun during the few years of his life *which God has given him*; for this is his reward. Furthermore, as for every man to whom *God has given* riches and wealth, He has also *empowered* him to eat from them and *to receive* his reward and *rejoice* in his labor; this is the *gift of God*. (Eccl 5:18–19 NASB)

The point of my question is whether the narrator is not simply reinforcing Qoheleth's concluding comments and directing the remembrance of the Creator to the Tanak. The "above the sun" and "under the sun" dichotomy seems too sharp and too neat. We continue to live "under the sun" with its issues of *hebel*, vapor, fleeting meaning, and frustration, even now, and even when God and God's Word are held at the center of life.

Does *hebel* mean "Meaningless" or "Frustrating"?

Longman also notes that the narrator agrees with Qoheleth's conclusion that life "under the sun" is "meaningless." Here I want to raise a basic translation issue. Does *hebel* really mean "meaningless" as the NIV and NLT translate it?[6] Is not the real problem for Qoheleth that, as far as he knows, everyone *dies* in the end ("fleeting life" and "few years of his life")? His exclamation, *habel habālīm* is almost always in response to the awareness that *death* has the last word.[7] But does he mean to communicate that it is "utterly meaningless"?

5. See also Eccl 2:24–25; 3:13; 8:15; 9:7, 9.

6. Only the NIV and NLT translate/paraphrase *hebel* as "meaningless." Most others have "vanity," which also falls short of the meaning of *hebel*.

7. Ecclesiastes uses the term *hebel* nineteen times. In eleven of the cases, including the beginning and the end of the book, death and mortality are the issue (Eccl 1:2–4; 2:14–16; 2:18–19; 2:21; 3:19–20; 4:7–8; 12:8). In the others, life is "vain" when it is "painful and grievous" in some way (see Eccl 1:14; 2:23; Cf. Ps 89:47).

In the OT *hebel* is best known as Abel's name, with the primary meaning "breath" or "vapor" which is there and gone again, thus, abstractly, "fleeting" or "frustrating," but does that justify "meaningless"? Though I cannot hold on to my breath, my breathing is not meaningless. The text itself helps us to define *hebel* by the repeated synonymous parallel use with "striving after the wind" (Eccl 1:14; 2:11, 17, 26; 4:4, 16; 6:9).[8] Like a "frustrating vapor," yes; like a breath, or steam, it is gone; like Abel, who is neither meaningless nor irrelevant in the canon; weightless, but not worthless. *Hebel* tells the truth about the impermanence of human activity in contrast to the permanence of God.[9] Longman actually comes close to expressing this when he summarizes, "Life is difficult, and then one dies."[10] The Greek term used here is *mataiotēs*, used in Rom 8:20 and translated by the NIV, "For the creation was subjected to *frustration*, not by its own choice but by the will of the one who subjected it in hope." I would like to hear Longman's reflection on the NIV and NLT translation/paraphrase decisions to go with "meaninglessness" in Ecclesiastes. This is a key, since the word *hebel* actually defines Qoheleth's human response to the divine initiative in creation and his call to enjoy it, with God in mind.

Holding Ecclesiastes Together

Chapter 3 is the hermeneutical key that may hold the message of Qoheleth and the narrator together. Chapter 3 is a description of a pre-Tanak "fear of God." In 3:1–10 there is a season for everything under heaven. The frustration of seeking and not finding satisfaction in knowledge, pleasure, or hard work (presented in chs. one and two) culminates in chapter 3. Each attempt is fraught with frustration, and ultimate satisfaction is ultimately deferred. In 3:11 everything is simply seasonal, "appropriate in its time," not ultimate or eternal; there is "a time for every season under heaven."[11] In 3:19–22, like the animals, we will breathe our last breath and return to the dust, without much certainty beyond that. This is certainly *vanity* or *frustrating* but not *meaningless*, since Qoheleth also knows the divine initiative that God will certainly judge wickedness and righteousness (3:16–17; see also the future reference in 12:14). To this end God has set eternity in our hearts but kept back any details about it to see if we will fear and trust God (3:11–15, 18). What more does

8. Other synonyms that are used with *hebel* are "shadow," "ephemeral," and "fleeting."

9. Compare Kathleen Farmer, "Book of Ecclesiastes," *Eerdmans Dictionary of the Bible*, ed. David Noel Freedman (Grand Rapids: Eerdmans, 2000) 367.

10. This is in line with Michael Fox: "There is no single unspoiled value in this life." See *A Time to Tear Down and a Time to Build up: A Rereading of Ecclesiastes* (Grand Rapids: Eerdmans, 1999; repr. Wipf & Stock, 2010) 280.

11. From "Turn, Turn, Turn" by the Byrds, 1965, which sets Eccl 3 to music.

the narrator know about that eternity? For that matter, what more do we know, for we too have very few details, even in Christ.

Qoheleth's words in these passages are not much different from the narrator's postscript in ch. 12, who offers an *imprimatur* for Qoheleth to his son (v. 12, "these words are given by one shepherd"). The narrator then reiterates the *wisdom* of fearing God, the expectation of prophetic *judgment* to come, and adds simply, "Keep his commandments." The phrase about the commandments is what makes Longman's distinction between being *afraid* of God and *fearing the Lord* crucial to understanding the book, for that is the precise issue in Exod 20:20, the setting for the Ten Commandments, "*Do not be afraid*; for God has come . . . in order that *the fear of* [*the Lord*] may remain with you." The narrator's reference to the commandment punchline does not negate what has gone before but completes it.

Job

God in Job

Longman highlights the powerful whirlwind tour of chs. 38–41 as God's primary initiative in Job. In this encounter God overwhelms Job with questions and silences him: "Like an aggrieved professor . . . God peppers Job with question after question." My first question is about the fact that God shows up at all, and indeed, as the Lord Yahweh, personal and in close to the suffering Job. Is this not a significant divine initiative for one who is suffering?

My second question is whether the point of the extended whirlwind tour of God's cosmological zoo really is simply a peppering of unanswerable questions? Is not the content of this divine initiative to turn Job's attention to the creative power of God and the creation itself as a means of healing in the midst of his illness? Is it not to administer hope to the hopeless and provide a new perspective on the created world as a complex and wondrous place? Further, if we take Job as a paradigmatic text for a historically exiled Israel, does not the whirlwind cosmic tour open the eyes of exiled Jews to the power of God to create, redeem, and recreate a people who have lost everything in Babylon and abroad? That is certainly how Isaiah uses the wonder of creation in the preaching hymns of Isa 40–48.

My third question concerns the Lord's direct speech and initiative at the end of the book (42:1–8). While the whirlwind is the necessary beginning, is not God's intervention announcing Job's vindication to his erstwhile friends the necessary ending? There the Lord reveals himself to be a redeeming judge who vindicates Job's protest and condemns the friends' application of retribution theology to Job's case. God does *not* commend Job's "fear of God that leads to silence." Rather, the Lord commends Job's *words*; he commends Job's struggle to come to a more mature understanding of suffering that is beyond the rough sledgehammer of a strict reward/ retribution theology. Are not these concluding words of God the most significant initiative of God in the book? The text says (with God's repetitive emphases),

> The Lord said to Eliphaz the Temanite, "My wrath is kindled against you . . . because you have not spoken of me *what is right as my servant Job has.* Now therefore . . . go to *my servant Job* . . . and *my servant Job will pray* for you. For I will accept him so that I may not do with you according to your folly, because you have not spoken of me *what is right, as my servant Job has.*" (Job 42:7–8 NASB)

Does not God here vindicate Job's persistent vocalization of his desire for the personal presence of God in the midst of his suffering? Is not Yahweh echoing his pride in "my servant Job," a phrase stated twice in ch. 1 to the *ha-śātān* (Job 1:8; 2:3)? Does not the Lord sustain the value of Job's struggle toward a theological maturity concerning innocent suffering?

Job in Job

Longman keenly identifies the presenting issue of the book: "There is a question about whether or not Job fears God only because of the benefits." At the beginning the adversary claims that Job will not maintain his fear of the Lord because it is based in an ironclad righteousness-reward/unrighteousness-retribution theology. Job's response to God is confused at first because of this rigid theology, since he knows he is not unrighteous. He concludes that God must be wrong and calls for a face to face meeting (9:21–24). After the encounter Job concludes that his *theology* must be the problem, retracts, and repents of it. I would argue that it is this persistence in theological revision that God commends.

In the end, as Longman notes, Job fears God *without* benefits. Job shows that he was "not in it only for the rewards (though he thought he still deserved them)." Job repents because he is overwhelmed by God: "He demonstrates the fear of God that leads to silence in the face of the mystery of suffering . . . Job submits to God's greater wisdom."

My final question is whether we cannot say a bit more than this. Is Job's submission and silence his only response? He actually says quite a lot in his last words to God, when he retracts his theological position, expressing his amazement that he is actually talking directly with the Lord:

> Then Job replied to the Lord: "I know that you can do all things; no purpose of yours can be thwarted. [You asked,] 'Who is this that obscures my plans

without knowledge?' Surely I spoke of things I did not understand, *things too wonderful for me to know.* [You said,] 'Listen now and I will speak; I will question you, and you shall answer me.' My ears had heard of you but *now my eyes have seen [rāʾāh] you.*" (Job 42:1–5 NIV)[12]

Could it be that Job retracts and expresses sorrow over his theological blundering ("repent" is not *šûb* here, but *nāḥam*, he is sorry) because he is overwhelmed by seeing his Redeemer face to face rather than by God's sovereignty? There is at least some excitement in this submission. The words, "now my eyes have seen you" echo a key passage from ch. 19:

> Oh that my words were written! Oh that they were inscribed in a book! . . . And as for me, I know that my Redeemer lives, And at the last He will take His stand on the earth . . . Even after my skin is destroyed, yet from my flesh *I shall see [ḥāzāh]* God; Whom I myself shall behold [*ḥāzāh*], and whom *my eyes shall see [rāʾāh]* and not another. (Job 19:23, 25–27a, NASB)

Who is the Redeemer in the OT but Yahweh? Job retracts his objections about his innocent suffering because he has personally met his Redeemer! Job is fully invested in this new-found relationship with the Lord, even in the midst of his continuing dust and ashes.[13] Is the Lord rough with him? Surely he is, but what is that compared to what he has lost in his lifetime? Is this not *a rough friendship* rather than a sovereignty beat down? Is not the purpose of Job to challenge a rigid retribution theology and offer the possibility of the presence and friendship of an unexpected Redeemer within the wondrous and sometimes terrifying creation?

---

12. The brackets indicate that the NIV has added these voicing cues, based on God's similar, but ironic, words in Job 38:2–3. These could indeed be Job's heartfelt words, indicating his willingness to be instructed further by the Lord.

13. This would also solve the problem of the placement of ch. 28, "a magnificent assertion of God's wisdom." Why does Job's disputation persist after this speech? Lo's solution that the sufferer relapses would make sense if the book had nothing new to offer past ch. 28. Walton's solution of a narrator's voice is possible, but is it not something else? Job persists exactly because a "magnificent assertion" is not what the question of innocent suffering requires or what an innocent sufferer needs. The Lord appears in person and engages the conversation. That is something new, beyond the magnificent assertion, and ultimately a satisfying response for Job.

WHICH HUMANS? WHAT RESPONSE? A REFLECTION ON PAULINE THEOLOGY

Beverly Roberts Gaventa

Confronted with the question of how human beings respond (or might respond, or could respond, or should respond) to the divine initiative, I suspect many American Christians would call to mind an occasion of the gospel's proclamation. We may imagine a congregation and a preacher.[1] If we are thinking of the earliest Christian communities, perhaps we see Peter at Pentecost or Paul in Athens. In whichever setting, whether ancient or modern, we think of the gospel being preached or taught in some way to a group of people who respond by deciding about the gospel and then acting on that decision. The people on the receiving end may demand to know what they should do (as they do at Pentecost; see Acts 2:37), or they may slip away shaking their heads at such nonsense (as many seem to do in Athens; see Acts 17:32–34). In all of these scenarios, the people we imagine are in a position to hear and decide, to listen and learn or refuse to learn.

What happens to these scenarios from the life of the early church when we reflect on a single ugly fact, namely, that slavery was ubiquitous in the Roman world?[2] The names of slaves are scattered across the pages of our Bibles, as are references to slaves and slavery, and there is little to suggest that Christians critiqued the practice. Although masters (presumably Christian masters) are admonished to deal justly with slaves (Eph 6:9; Col 4:1), the practice of slavery is not questioned. To the contrary, slaves (presumably Christian slaves) are admonished to obey their masters (Eph 6:5–8; Col 3:22–25; 1 Tim 6:1–2a; Titus 2:9–10; 1 Pet 2:18–21), even when those masters are "harsh" (1 Pet 2:18). The fact that Christianity emerges

---

1. The use of "we" is complicated in an increasingly fractured religious landscape. In this paper I employ it as a shorthand reference to North American Christians, based on my own experience in Protestant churches and seminary classrooms.

2. Accurate figures are impossible, given the nature of the sources available. Some have conjectured that, in the first century CE, roughly 30 percent of the population of Italy was enslaved; empire-wide, the figure may have been closer to 20 percent. See John Madden, "Slavery in the Roman Empire: Numbers and Origins," *Classics Ireland* 3 (1996) 109–28. Walter Scheidel represents a recent and minimalist view when he suggests a slave population of approximately 10 percent when the entire imperial population (Italy, Egypt, and others) is taken into account. See his "Slavery" in *The Cambridge Companion to the Roman Economy,* ed. Walter Scheidel, (Cambridge: Cambridge University Press, 2012) 92.

unquestionably in a slave society impinges on a number of issues in the study of early Christianity,[3] but for the moment I want to focus on this question of how we "respond" to the divine initiative.

One of the things we know about slaves is that they were subject to sexual "use" by their owners.[4] We also know that among the "responses" early Christian texts seek from believers is that they avoid sexual immorality. Concern about sexual misconduct appears as early as 1 Thess 4:3–8 (widely regarded as Paul's earliest letter), frequently in 1 Corinthians (5:1–3, 9; 7:2–9), as well as in the "apostolic decree" of Acts 15.[5]

A terrible realization surfaces: early Christian texts admonish sexual propriety, but slaves had no choices about their sexual conduct. As Seneca observed, "Unchastity is a crime in the freeborn, a necessity for the slave, a duty for the freedman."[6] What does this fact mean within the Christian community? Were these slaves to be judged, tolerated, or accepted? Scholars differ on these questions, and the evidence does not all point in the same direction. Jennifer Glancy states the dilemma with piercing clarity: "Either the [Pauline] community excluded slaves whose sexual behavior could not conform to the norms mandated within the Christian body, or the community tolerated the membership of some who did not confine their sexual activities to marriage."[7] This realization is disturbing, as it should be, especially to those who have inherited a view of the early church as an idyllic period to be emulated.

Many questions are tangled up in this discussion, both questions having to do with the limits of our historical knowledge and questions about the implications of early Christian writings, but my concern at present is quite specific: How are we to talk about "the human response to the divine initiative" in circumstances in which major elements of what we consider "human response" are not possible? I introduce

---

3. See especially the discussions in Jennifer Glancy, *Slavery in Early Christianity* (Oxford: Oxford University Press, 2002), and J. Albert Harrill, *Slaves in the New Testament: Literary, Social, and Moral Dimensions* (Minneapolis: Fortress, 2006).

4. For primary evidence in support of this assertion, see Keith R. Bradley, *Slaves and Masters in the Roman Empire: A Study in Social Control* (New York: Oxford University Press, 1987) 116–19; Glancy, *Slavery in Early Christianity*, 21–29.

5. I hope it is clear that I take up this issue as one element within a larger response, which Paul might term "the obedience of faith" (as in Rom 1:5). I do not at all wish to limit the human response to God to appropriate sexual conduct, especially in our environment where much Christian ethical discussion has focused on sexuality almost to the exclusion of other areas of human life, prompting some to identify Christianity with prudishness. The point, as should come clear below, is simply to problematize the default assumption of ability or capacity in discussions of our response to God.

6. *Controversies* 4. Praef.10; cited by Carolyn Osiek and Margaret Y. MacDonald in *A Woman's Place: House Churches in Earliest Christianity* (Minneapolis: Fortress, 2006) 103.

7. Glancy, *Slavery in Early Christianity*, 49. See also the excellent and accessible discussion of female slaves by Osiek and MacDonald in *A Woman's Place*, 95–117.

the complex issue of slavery and early Christian instructions about sexual conduct as a way of problematizing any account of the human response to the divine initiative that prioritizes human *capacity* (whether moral, intellectual, or physical).[8] In this paper I argue that an account of the human "response" that depends on human capacity is deeply flawed from the point of view of Pauline theology and that Paul's understanding of the body of Christ offers a starting point for more adequate reflection on the human response to God.

Romans 6:12–14; 12:1–2

Paul's letters contain many places for thinking about the human response to the divine initiative, but I want to begin with two pivotal passages in Romans, both of which appear to presuppose a capacity-based understanding of human response.[9] In Rom 6:12–14 Paul writes:

> Therefore do not let sin rule as a king in your mortal body so that you obey its desires. And do not present your limbs to sin as weapons for wrong, but present yourselves to God as people once dead but now alive, and your limbs to God as weapons of righteousness. For sin will not be able to rule over you like a king, since you are not under law but under grace.[10]

The notion of "presenting" the person recurs in Rom 12:1–2:

> For this reason, I exhort you, brothers and sisters, by God's mercies, to present your bodies as a sacrifice to God—living, holy, pleasing to God—which is your fitting worship. And do not be conformed to this age, but be transformed by the renewal of your thinking so that you discern God's will—the good and pleasing and fully mature.

Romans 6 follows closely on Paul's argument in 5:12–21 that the universal reign of sin and death has been defeated by God in Jesus Christ, making it possible for human beings to present themselves to God as weapons in the on-going conflict between God and anti-God powers.[11] How we describe that possibility is revealing.

---

8. Both here and below I use "capacity" or "ability" to refer to limits imposed on persons by others (as in slavery) as well as those that are biological in origin (as in dementia). I believe that usage is appropriate for this project, given that both sorts of incapacity challenge widely held notions of human response to God. Further, I use "response" both of initial "responses" to the gospel (usually referred to as "conversion") and of the further "responses" manifest in Christian life.

9. Much of what follows focuses on Romans in particular, since my work for the last several years has been with that letter.

10. Translations are the author's unless otherwise noted.

11. That sentence reflects an argument I am developing in a commentary on Romans. For some introduction, see Gaventa, *Our Mother Saint Paul* (Louisville: Westminster John Knox, 2007), especially pp. 115–60.

It is typical for commentators to emphasize the role of human choice here. For example, J. D. G. Dunn writes that "the believer . . . must continually choose" between the dual lordships, both of which persist in their influence.[12] He adds that believers "can put themselves at God's disposal," that "each act involving moral choice is an act of moral commitment, where the decisive commitment of conversion-initiation has to be renewed and realized ever afresh."[13]

In view of the ubiquity of slavery in Paul's world and a host of conditions in our own world, however, the question returns: How does one present one's "members" (one's own body) to righteousness if that physical body belongs to a human master who is in control of all action, even the most intimate relationships? How does one present one's person as a living sacrifice if that person belongs to another human being? How would the slaves and freed persons (former slaves who still were under obligation to their masters) in the Roman congregations hear these admonitions?[14]

It is tempting to get Paul off the hook by arguing that he does not "really" mean what he says. Human beings are not actually weapons, and these are not "real" sacrifices. This is metaphorical language, and therefore no one would take it too seriously. Many discussions of Gal 3:28, for example, limit its applicability by arguing that Paul means that there is no slave nor free in the church, or there is no male nor female in church.

Admittedly, support for such a reading strategy lies close to hand. First Corinthians 7:22 offers as an antidote: "The slave who is called in the Lord is the Lord's freedman; similarly, the free person who is called is Christ's slave." Here Paul undertakes to trouble the categories of "free" and "slave" by implicitly declaring that the only status that matters is status in relationship to Jesus Christ. Even the one who is enslaved to a human master is, in Christ, simultaneously free.

Paul's contemporary Epictetus would approve of this argument, stripped of its christological location. Epictetus, himself a freed slave, contends that the person who is concerned about "externals" (such as health or wealth or reputation) is already a slave.[15] Notice, however, that Epictetus' comments have to do largely with the free person who is no better than a slave because he is enslaved within his own fears.

There is genuine wisdom in Epictetus' declarations about the distortions produced by concern with "externals," as there is theological wisdom in Paul's argument that God is able to produce freedom even in the context of enslavement. Nonetheless,

---

12. James D. G. Dunn, *Romans 1–8*, WBC 38 (Dallas: Word, 1988) 305.

13. Ibid., 350–51.

14. For one suggestive attempt at addressing that question, see Peter Oakes, *Reading Romans in Pompeii: Paul's Letter at Ground Level* (Minneapolis: Fortress, 2009) 143–49.

15. E.g., *Diatribai* 2.2.12–13.

the reality remains that there were in the first century many people who, apart from the cooperation of others, simply could not observe at least some of the practices they were being taught. They were not free to do whatever they decided was right or whatever they believed God required of them.

Which Humans?

Introducing the complexity of early Christian slavery into a discussion of Paul's understanding of the gospel and response to it may seem irrelevant for the present. To the contrary, however, it is only the tip of the iceberg, as it places before us a difficult question. How do we arrive at an understanding of the human response to God that does justice to those situations in which much of what we conventionally regard as "response" is either difficult or impossible to achieve? There are many such situations. Any number of human beings, living with and among us, simply cannot respond with faith (if by that we mean with cognitive assent) or respond with the full person; they cannot "choose" for the Lordship of Christ. Because of the discussion of Roman slavery above, we might think first of all of those who live in virtual slavery, whether they are child soldiers or sex workers. However, it is not only slavery in modern guise that constitutes a problem for "response." What "response" to God is expected from those who live with severe intellectual disability, severe mental illness, or addictions of various sorts?[16]

This is an odd starting point. We customarily begin with an individual who is fully capable of making decisions and acting on those decisions. If incapacity of any sort is introduced into the discussion, that happens as an afterthought or an exception. There are, however, at least two reasons for beginning with persons who are in some way incapacitated or disabled. The first is practical. Incapacity is a fact of human life. We either experience it or are exposed to it at some point in our lives. All of us exist only one diagnosis or one accident—literally, one misstep in the shower—away from having a disability. The second reason is theological. Beginning with incapacity reveals the limited and indeed deeply flawed ways in which we think about humanity in relationship to God. It reveals the way we privilege certain kinds of human gifts over others, and it presses us to think more deeply about what constitutes a genuinely human "response" to God's initiative and how that response is generated.[17]

16. There are, to be sure, significant differences within this range of human experiences. My point is simply that all of them, whatever the cause, are marked by some degree and type of diminished capacity.

17. There is a danger here of instrumentalizing persons with disability, treating them as nothing more than persons through whom we learn things, but that danger seems to me preferable to silence.

At several points in what follows, I focus on the particular incapacity known as dementia, and I do so with the help of the seminal work of John Swinton on that subject.[18] Swinton takes up the deep fears attached to dementia, fears of loss of memory, even loss of the "self." He patiently uncovers the reductionistic understandings of the human being at work in many of our ways of thinking about and interacting with persons with dementia. Routinely persons suffering from dementia are characterized as "no longer themselves," "no longer there," even as "abandoned" by God.[19] I will at least touch on elements of Swinton's constructive proposals below, but for now the relevant issue is that at a certain stage in the life of someone with dementia the possibility of "response" to God is limited, at least "response" as we customarily think of it as an individual's cognitive assent and subsequent actions. I cannot begin to do justice to this rich book, but I will draw on it both to problematize some of our answers about human response and to suggest some better ways in which to conceptualize our response to the divine initiative.

What Response? Pauline Problems for Our Answers

Considering Swinton's insightful work on dementia and then returning to the letters of Paul, especially to his admonitions about presenting the self to God, we might be forced to conclude that Paul is—at best—not helpful. His emphasis on faith, on presenting the self, seems as blinkered by assumptions about human intellectual and physical capability as are our own starting points. We might even conclude that he is a problem rather than a resource.

That would be a premature and unfortunate conclusion. The problem instead is that we have a distorted reading of Paul, based on our own distorted understanding of the human being in relationship to God. Admittedly, Paul does not address dementia or any other incapacity directly,[20] but thinking about dementia together

18. *Dementia: Living in the Memories of God* (Grand Rapids: Eerdmans, 2012). I cannot recommend this gently argued, deeply disturbing book too highly, both for its practical wisdom and for its profound engagement with questions of theological anthropology. Swinton is professor of practical theology and pastoral care at the University of Aberdeen, having entered the study of theology after many years working as a psychiatric nurse.

19. Swinton addresses at some length the discourse (both lay and professional) around persons with dementia that assumes they are already "dead" or would be "better off dead" (*Dementia*, 110–34). They are thought no longer to be "real" persons. There is a distinctly uncomfortable resemblance to some ancient discourse about slaves as not really human. Aristotle famously refers to a slave as "an animate piece of property," "a tool to live with" (*Politics* 1253b). On slavery as death, see the classic work of Orlando Patterson, *Slavery and Social Death* (Cambridge, MA: Harvard University Press, 1982).

20. He does refer to his own "thorn in the flesh" in 2 Cor 12:7 and his illness (an eye problem?) in Gal 4:12–16, but those do not serve as his starting points for theological reflection.

with reading Paul's letters may reveal some problems with the way we typically think about human responses to God.

The first problem, which I hinted at in my opening comments, is that we have an inadequate understanding of God's action in the world in Jesus Christ. Much of popular American Christianity proceeds as if the gospel is a kind of *offer* God makes to humanity, one that is conditional on human response. The logic, to put it crassly, resembles that of the marketplace: In the death and resurrection of Jesus, God offers humanity eternal salvation *if only* humanity will repent, believe, and then live following God's instructions.[21]

The notion that the gospel is a kind of *offer* made by God can draw heavily on such Pauline texts as these:

> For I am not ashamed of the gospel, because it is God's own power bringing about salvation for everyone who believes [who trusts God?], the Jew first and also the Greek. For in the gospel God's righteousness is being revealed apocalyptically, from faith and for faith, as it is written: "The righteous one will live out of faith." (Rom 1:16–17)

> But now, apart from the Law, God's righteousness has been made plain, although it is witnessed by the Law and the Prophets, the righteousness of God through the faithfulness of Jesus Christ[22] for everyone who believes. (Rom 3:21–22)

> If you confess with your mouth that Jesus is Lord and you believe in your heart that God raised him from the dead, you will be saved. . . . "For everyone who calls on the name of the Lord will be saved." (Rom 10:9, 13)

These passages all attend to human faith, but they stand alongside other passages in Romans and elsewhere that reflect the notion that, in Jesus Christ, God is acting unilaterally to reclaim the world from the powers that have held it captive, most notably sin and death. For example, in 5:12–21, Paul writes in universal terms about the extent of the gospel, when he contends that both Adam's disobedience and Christ's obedience implicate the whole of humanity (and see 11:26, 32). Romans 8:18–25 likewise, with its language of the groaning of creation, suggests that redemption includes the whole of the created order.

---

21. It is worth noting that the terminology of "repentance" and "forgiveness" is almost totally absent from Paul's letters.

22. Translating this phrase, "the faith of Jesus Christ," has become a notorious *crux interpretum* and the secondary literature is vast. Here I opt for "faithfulness of Jesus Christ" both to reflect the possible parallel with God's own faithfulness in 3:3 and to suggest a parallel with human faith(fulness) in the end of the verse.

When we read the conditional claims of 1:16–17, 3:21–22, and 10:9, 13 in this larger setting, the possibility emerges that, for Paul, God's saving action extends to the whole of humankind. Not all will see and understand that action at present, to be sure, but the human response does not become a kind of entry pass. This is admittedly a deeply complex and controversial topic, and it is possible that at least one role of Paul's doxological conclusion to his discussion of God's dealings with Israel (11:33–36) is to undermine any simple conclusions. At the very least, however, these cosmic elements in Paul should be allowed to temper any easy reliance on an exchange theory, in which God makes in Jesus Christ an offer which human beings then are free to accept or decline.

In addition to this exchange theory of the gospel, we have a distorted understanding of *pistis*, which we regularly reduce to "belief" in a narrow, intellectual, even propositional sense, without taking into account the range of meaning of the Greek noun *pistis* and the related verb *pisteuein*. For example, in Rom 3:3 Paul refers to "God's *pistis*," which surely does not mean God's "belief" but God's "faithfulness." In 3:2 he uses the verb *pisteuein* of Jews, not because they "believed" but because they were "entrusted" with God's "oracles." Operating with a constricted understanding of *pistis* as "belief" in turn makes it quite difficult to articulate an understanding of the human response to God that reflects the experiences of those who are cognitively impaired (to take but a single example).[23]

For the last several decades, as Pauline specialists have emphasized his interest in building up communities, especially communities that cross ethnic lines, the point has often been made that Paul's letters are not simply about "ideas."[24] Frequently the observation is made that it is anachronistic to describe Paul as a "theologian."[25] These assertions can be exaggerated in ways that imply that reference to God (or Christ, or the Spirit) is incidental to Paul's "real" project which is social or political, but in a limited sense they are important correctives. Faith is not for Paul simply *belief* in a fixed set of claims or propositions. It is not merely a cognitive act of consenting to a set of propositions.

However we translate the *pistis/pisteuein* word group, it is crucial to reflect on the range of ways in which Paul speaks about human faith and how it comes

---

23. As Swinton observes, becoming "deeply forgetful and intellectually vulnerable within liberal Western cultures that prioritize intellect and reason over other aspects of being human has quite specific meaning, and that meaning is deeply negative" (*Dementia*, 80).

24. An early and influential argument that Paul's letters are not "composed exclusively of theological ideas or compact mythic complexes" appears in Wayne A. Meeks' justly influential work, *The First Urban Christians* (New Haven, CT: Yale University Press, 1983) 2.

25. For an example, see Philip F. Esler, *Conflict and Identity in Romans: The Social Setting of Paul's Letter* (Minneapolis: Fortress, 2003) 5.

into being. When referencing his own recognition of Jesus as God's Messiah, he writes about "revelation," or perhaps better, "apocalypse" (Gal 1:12). Elsewhere he describes himself as having been "overtaken" by Jesus Christ (Phil 3:12). Often, he refers both to himself and to others as having been "called" to faith (e.g., Rom 1:7; 8:28; 1 Cor 1:24).

In Romans faith is connected with the activity of the Spirit. Paul describes the love of God as "having been poured into our hearts through the Holy Spirit, which was given to us" (5:5). Scholars dispute whether "love of God" here is subjective (God's love for "us") or objective ("our" love for God), but in either case that love comes about through the work of the Spirit. By adding the phrase "which was given to us," Paul makes it clear that the Spirit does not come because it is invoked, but because it is given. When in Rom 8 Paul unpacks this brief word about the Spirit, he reinforces this point. It is the "spirit of adoption" by which "we" are able to cry to God as father (8:15). It is because "we" have the first fruit of the Spirit that we groan, etc. This suggests that the language of "believing" and "confessing" needs to be read in the larger context of the Spirit's actions that brings about God's redemption in human lives.[26]

There is another step involved here, as the problem extends beyond the mistranslation or misinterpretation of a few Greek words. The misunderstanding of faith is a symptom of our corrupted understanding of the human being. Our understanding of the human response unreflectively depends on the notion of abilities, whether those are cognitive or moral or physical abilities, rather than on the notion of giftedness. When we speak of human beings presenting themselves to God in Rom 6 or 12, we think of those human beings as capable of rational thought, as having free will, as being capacitated for action. We begin with what we think of as "normal," and then—if pressed—we make allowances for those who are outside the "norm."[27]

That does not seem to be Paul's norm; instead, for Paul all humans are fully disabled apart from God's intervention in Jesus Christ. That is the arc of his argument in Rom 1–7. He begins by arguing that humanity rebelled against God's own godliness (1:18–25), but the consequence of that rebellion and of God's "handing them over" (1:24, 26, 28) is that humanity is incapable of doing what is right (3:10–18), is held under sin's power (3:9), and lives under the toxic reign of sin and death (5:12–21).

---

26. For an elegant exposition of this understanding in the theology of Karl Barth, see Benjamin Myers, "From Faithfulness to Faith in the Theology of Karl Barth," in *The Faith of Jesus Christ: Exegetical, Biblical, and Theological Studies*, ed. by Michael F. Bird and Preston M. Sprinkle (Peabody, MA: Hendrickson, 2007) 291–308.

27. Notice that I wrote "we": "we make allowances," once again treating the "capacitated person" as the norm.

Even the "I" who knows and loves God's holy law is incapable of doing the good (7:14–25). However diverse the human community may be (Jew and Gentile, able bodied and disabled), it is universally disabled because of sin and death. For Paul it is only with the advent of Jesus Christ that humanity is freed for—capacitated for—response to God (8:1–4).[28] That universal experience of redemption should prompt a universal outcry of praise and thanksgiving (as in Rom 15:1–13).

The problem with that line of argument is that it appears to place people with disabilities on the "in Adam" side of the line and those without disabilities on the "in Christ" side of the line. Precisely because of this notion of the incapacitated and re-deemed human community, however, Paul helps us to understand—or he should—that such abilities or capabilities as we have, however large or limited, are not our possessions. More important, they are not what make us human. They are purely and only gifts. Our capacities vary, but we are not defined by them. We are defined as creatures belonging to God who have been gifted in a variety of ways.

The texts are familiar territory. Perhaps the most pointed appears in 1 Cor 4:7: "Why do you make discrimination [among yourselves]? What do you have that you did not receive? And since you received it, why do you boast as if you didn't receive it?" Paul's counter-argument to those Corinthians who boasted in their own spiri-tual gifts is to remind them that everything they have they received as a gift. That same argument undergirds the discussion of spiritual gifts in 1 Cor 12, which is reprised in Rom 12:3–8. This orientation of Paul's anthropology toward the divine initiative is not limited to the notion of spiritual gifts. Faith itself is measured out by God (Rom 12:3); that is to say, faith is not a human act or decision but a result of God's own gift.

Swinton finds in his reflection on the experiences of people with dementia a radical reminder of this dependence on God. Recalling Gen 1:1 and (apparently) unwittingly paraphrasing 1 Cor 4:7, he writes: "Human beings are creatures who are wholly dependent on God. *There is nothing that anyone has that has not been given to them.*"[29] The implication of that biblical wisdom, so deeply antithetical to much of Western thinking, is that the human response to the divine initiative is itself also an outworking of the divine initiative.

---

28. Explication for this paragraph may be found in *Our Mother Saint Paul,* 113–36; and in Gaven-ta, "The Shape of the 'I': The Psalter, the Gospel, and the Speaker in Romans 7," in *Apocalyptic Paul,* ed. Beverly Roberts Gaventa (Waco, TX: Baylor University Press, 2013) 77–91.

29. *Dementia,* 161 (italics in the original).

The Body of Christ and the Human Response to the Divine Initiative

There is yet more to say, however. The divine initiative in the death and resurrection of Jesus Christ creates a human agent capable of response,[30] but crucially that agent exists within the body of Christ. Typically, we invoke the language of the body of Christ when discussing church unity or the variety of gifts. It is thereby sometimes handled—implicitly if not explicitly—as an image of human community or corporate humanity on its own, divorced from the language of Christ (an emaciated body). We are not, however, part of just *some* body, but of *Christ's* own body.[31] The "body of Christ" also provides a rich theological location for grasping not only our connections with one another, but also our shared weakness and our shared strength. Invoking the body of Christ also seems appropriate, since Paul introduces it in Romans almost immediately after 12:1–2; that is, presenting the self is not only an individual matter but also a matter of the whole body of Christ.

Lingering over the fact that this unifying body is Christ's own suggests, first, that the body of Christ is the place of our shared weakness, not simply by virtue of our own human limitations but because we were baptized into Christ's own broken, weak, shamed body. Admittedly I transgress exegetically with this point, at least a bit. Paul does not explicitly speak about Christ's broken body (not even in the "words of institution" in 1 Cor 11:23–26), yet his comments about the self-emptying of the powerful Christ in the Philippians hymn and elsewhere seem consistent with that notion. In Rom 15 Christ is said to have suffered rather than to have pleased himself, and in Gal 2:20 we find he "loved me and gave himself up on my behalf." Such texts suggest that it is entirely appropriate to import into Paul's understanding of Christ's body the wounds of the crucified, which are also the wounds of the resurrected.

If the body of Christ is itself broken, then our individual brokenness has its rightful place within that body, not outside it, not relegated to the margins. No weakness or disability of ours makes the body less, for it has already been rendered incapable and handed over to the powers of this age (1 Cor 2:8). At the heart of the divinely generated response to God, then, is a way of assessing both ourselves and others that is radically at odds with a capacity-based evaluation system.[32] We

---

30. On the creation of the human agent, see J. Louis Martyn, "Epilogue: An Essay in Pauline Meta-Ethics," in *Divine and Human Agency in Paul and His Cultural Environment*, ed. John M.G. Barclay and Simon J. Gathercole (London: T. & T. Clark, 2008) 173–83.

31. The body of Christ is not simply corporate humanity, as if human community in and of itself were an improvement over individuals. See the important cautions of Susan Eastman in "Double Participation and the Responsible Self in Romans 5–8," in *Apocalyptic Paul*, 93–110.

32. The classic exegetical argument behind this sentence remains that of J. Louis Martyn in "Epistemology at the Turn of the Ages," in *Theological Issues in the Letters of Paul* (Nashville: Abingdon, 1997) 89–110.

assess, not based on "defectology,"[33] but on God's new creation. This point extends well beyond the question of how those with diminished circumstances or capacities respond to God's initiative; it encompasses every facet of our lives, from the way we think about ourselves individually to the way we assess our congregations to the way we assess our national and international actions.[34]

Embracing what is usually regarded as weakness is not the only or the last word to be used for the body of Christ, however. At the same time that Christ's body is weak, broken, and offensive from one point of view, it is already powerful beyond our capacity to imagine. To think only of Romans and only briefly, Paul writes at the outset that Christ is "publicly displayed as Son of God in power" (1:4). Christ's obedience is powerful over sin and death themselves (5:12–21). Of course, the closing of Rom 8 is emphatic on this point: Nothing in creation can separate "us" from the love of God in Christ Jesus. The impressive list of those agents who try to bring about separation does not explicitly name disability or the fear of disability, yet the list encompasses all of human experience, which necessarily does include disability.

This point is echoed in one of the major threads of Swinton's work. He straightforwardly identifies the deep fear generated by dementia—fear of being lost, of being disconnected from our memories, of being disconnected from family, and even from a sense of self. Swinton contends, however, that this fear overlooks the fact that we all exist in relationship to one another and to God from whom we are not lost. Indeed, we cannot be lost to God; our memories are held by God. We are held by God from whose embrace we cannot be lost. Here Swinton calls on a range of biblical texts (including Ps 139:2–12; Isa 49:15–16, Jer 17:7–10; and Heb 13:5) and on pastoral experience.[35]

In Pauline terms this also means that we cannot be lost to the body of Christ, which is capable of holding us all, whatever our strengths and weaknesses. Paul introduces the notion in 1 Cor 12 as a way of countering competition and condescension over the evaluation of varying spiritual gifts. In Rom 12 it stands within the opening of a long section of the letter that repeatedly touches on the temptation to be

33. Swinton, *Dementia*, 41–45.

34. I have attempted to spell out the implications of this radical epistemology for the lives of women in *Our Mother Saint Paul,* 63–75. In his thoughtful response to my paper Nicholas Perrin introduces the notion of human beings as "image-bearers who are to respond as ones being conformed to *the* image," that is, the *imago Dei.* It may be that he finds a more prominent role in Paul than I do for the notion of creation in the image of God. Setting aside that disagreement, however, I would recall that Paul's references to Jesus as God's son often emphasize his power precisely as power in the weakness of human flesh (as in Rom 8:3; Phil 2:5–11).

35. *Dementia*, 186–226. Among the compelling witnesses is Christine Bryden, herself experiencing the early stages of dementia, who wrote, "I will trust in God, who will hold me safe in his memory, until that glorious day of Resurrection, when each facet of my personality can be expressed to the full" (ibid., 194).

condescending to others. Paul admonishes in 12:3, "Do not think bloated thoughts about yourself but think sober thoughts. . ." and in 12:16 he adds, "Don't think arrogant thoughts but be governed by humble thoughts. Don't start being smart from your own resources." The reasons for this concern come into view in ch. 14, where Paul addresses the conflict between those Christians who adhere to kosher law and those who do not, both of whom appear to be convinced that their own practices should dominate. It is not for Christians to decide or judge one another, since it is God alone who judges: "Who are you to judge the household slave of another? She stands or falls before her own lord. And in fact she will stand, because the Lord is powerful to cause her to stand" (14:4).

What implications does this understanding of the "body of Christ" have? First, it means that the body belongs to Christ, which means we humans cannot expel or be expelled from it. The boundaries of this body are not ours to set or patrol.[36] When reading Romans, anytime we find ourselves inclined to limit those boundaries we need to hear the repeated word "all," which runs through Romans as a warning against a human imposition of limits (e.g., 1:5, 7, 8, 16; 2:9, 10; 3:19, 20; 11:26, 32). Further, however different our capacities for response may be, we are all in the same place. There can be no separation between "us" and "them."

How does this weak and powerful body that belongs to Christ respond to the divine initiative? To begin with, the body of Christ is first characterized as *receiving*. In 1 Corinthians Paul introduces the body in the context of his explication of *charismata*, spiritual *gifts* (12:4–11). He does not leave it to the audience to connect the dots, since he explicitly invokes God's action in vv. 24–31. Similarly, Rom 12 says that it is God who "measures" faith (v. 3) and again speaks in terms of the various spiritual gifts that are at work within the body. Perhaps the most important thing to say about the body of Christ in response to God is that the body of Christ knows it is in the receiving mode. It knows that its capacities are the result of divine gift rather than human will or action.

That does not at all mean quiescence or passivity. As Paul depicts Christ's body, its role is receiving, but it is also *upbuilding*. In both Rome and Corinth it appears that Christians were engaged in tearing down one another. In Corinth conflicts focused on spiritual gifts, and in Rome they centered on food laws. In both cases Paul insists that the role of the body is to build up rather than to tear down. If the role of the body of Christ is not to patrol the boundaries, it is to upbuild.

---

36. A possible exception to this statement appears in 1 Cor 5:1–5, where Paul demands that the Corinthians expel the man who is living with his father's wife, presumably his stepmother. However, Paul's statement in v. 5 is sufficiently ambiguous that it is not clear exactly what Paul anticipates. It may well be that the expulsion from the local congregation (if that is in view) is prelude to his eschatological salvation.

That upbuilding can sometimes be twisted into a concern about the internal life of the community that demonizes the outside. In our time, when anxiety about the church's future pervades many conversations, not to mention the way anxiety about outsiders pervades our culture, we are awash in evidence of this tendency. Paul insists that we have been welcomed by Christ (Rom 15:7), we strangers, and thus he admonishes welcoming one another.

Finally, and perhaps most important, the body of Christ is a body that comes together for the praise of God. Doxology is not often prominent in discussions of Pauline theology, but it should be. After all Romans, Paul's most influential letter, contends that at the core of the human problem is the refusal to worship God (1:18–25; 3:10–18). As Rom 8 depicts the work of the Spirit, among the first acts of the Spirit is enabling us to cry out to God (v. 15) and to give voice to prayer, however inarticulate (v. 26). The letter culminates with the claim that Jew and Gentile alike come together in praise of God (15:7–13; see Phil 2:9–11).[37] The response of the body of Christ to its welcome is to join in the acknowledgment and praise of God.

Toward the end of his study of dementia, John Swinton narrates the story of Mary, a young woman with multiple disabilities.[38] In addition to intellectual disability, Mary is unable to speak, although she makes sounds. She experiences constant muscle spasms, has limited vision, and is dependent on others for all her physical needs. Since infancy Mary has been included in a Quaker community and is taken to services regularly. According to Swinton's account, sometimes during the Quaker meeting she will shout out, sometimes producing "long, rather winsome wails." When the service moves into periods of silence, she also becomes silent. Some years ago Mary was diagnosed with leukemia. As her mother, deeply upset, was explaining the diagnosis, Mary in turn became upset and began to weep.

Several different explanations of Mary's behavior can be offered.[39] Reading this account with the apostle Paul inclines me to think that Mary's responses have been shaped by her experiences of Christ's body within the Quaker community. People like Mary, who are not able to make faith statements as we usually think of them,

37. For the exegetical argumentation behind this paragraph, see Gaventa, "From Toxic Speech to the Redemption of Doxology in Paul's Letter to the Romans," in *The Word Leaps the Gap: Essays on Scripture and Theology in Honor of Richard B. Hays*, ed. J. Ross Wagner, C. Kavin Rowe, and A. Katherine Grieb (Grand Rapids: Eerdmans, 2008) 392–408; and "'For the Glory of God': Theology and Experience in Paul's Letter to the Romans," in *Between Experience and Interpretation: Engaging the Writings of the New Testament*, ed. Mary F. Foskett and O. Wesley Allen Jr. (Nashville: Abingdon, 2008) 53–65.

38. *Dementia*, 238–39. This account comes out of a study conducted at the Centre for Spirituality, Health, and Disability at the University of Aberdeen: www.abdn.ac.uk/chad.

39. One of the starting points of Swinton's book is his insistence that Christian theology not cede discussion of dementia to neuroscience or regard theology and science as competitive enterprises. That is to say, multiple explanations are possible (*Dementia*, 5–8).

who do not "believe" in our restricted sense of the term, are held by the response of others, and they are shaped by that response. Notice that Mary is not exhorted to respond in a particular way (at least according to the account). Her community shapes her for cries unutterable, for silence, and also for weeping with those who weep. In turn, those of us who are so impoverished that we think (sic!) the human response to God is about what we individuals think and do, perhaps we are held in that same body by those whose wisdom is of a different sort. All of us together produce nothing more than the cry for God's deliverance (Rom 8:18–25).

This paper has been a kind of thought experiment intended both to problematize some of the conventional ways in which we speak of "responding" to God and to consider an alternative. I recognize that introducing the issue of human incapacity is complex and enormously difficult, and I do not pretend to have solved the problem. My hope is that this way of putting the question can serve as a control on our reductionism and a stimulus to broader reflection on Pauline (and other biblical and theological) resources.

RESPONSE TO GAVENTA

Nicholas Perrin

In her article "Which Humans? What Response? A Reflection on Pauline Theology," Beverly Gaventa brings to bear her expertise as a Pauline scholar in describing human response to the divine initiative. Here she challenges current American Christian understanding of human responsiveness by problematizing "any account of the human response to the divine initiative that prioritizes human *capacity* (whether moral, intellectual, or physical)" (italics original). Toward rectifying this (mis)understanding Gaventa turns to Paul's notion of the body of Christ, a notion which, as she sees it, allows us to reflect more accurately and faithfully on human responsiveness to the divine.

Gaventa begins by raising the interesting, if not disturbing, question as to how first-century Christian slaves could be expected to adhere to norms of sexual purity, when they themselves (at least in some cases) would have been subject to recurring sexual exploitation. Her goal here is not so much to resolve this particular first-century ethical problem (which as she points out has plenty of modern-day analogues) but to offer it as a case study in which our typical expectations of human responsiveness must be chastened by the grim reality that human autonomy is not always a given. For Gaventa, this seemingly exceptional case (which is perhaps not so exceptional after all) opens the door to a much broader question, namely: "What 'response' to God is expected from those who live with severe intellectual disability, or severe mental illness, or addictions of various sorts?" Accordingly, rather than offer an account of human response constructed on the basis of "normal" experience, which principally excludes those who have been spared such challenges, Gaventa proposes a baseline which includes those who typically constitute the so-called exceptional case.

For Gaventa the broad failure to adopt this more inclusive approach is not unrelated to three (characteristically American) misunderstandings of the Apostle Paul. First, by construing the gospel as a kind of offer, the Western church has fallen prey to an exchange theory "in which God makes in Jesus Christ an offer which human beings then are free to accept or decline." Second, rather than recognizing faith as an aspect of the Spirit's work, we have also mistakenly reduced faith to cognitive assent. Finally, and most decisively, "this misunderstanding of faith is a symptom of our corrupted understanding of the human being," an understanding which "unreflectively depends on the notion of abilities—whether those are cognitive or moral or physical abilities—rather than on the notion of giftedness." For Gaventa all such missteps could be avoided if we attend more closely to Paul's doctrine of the body which recognizes its weakness and brokenness—and by extension the limitations of individuals within it. With this backdrop in place, Gaventa then goes on to characterize human responsiveness to the divine by two marks: (1) the awareness that we receive all things as divine gifts and (2) the activity of upbuilding the body of Christ.

In response to Gaventa's thought experiment, I would register my own agreement and disagreement. As for my principal agreement, I am grateful for the way in which Gaventa encourages us to be—to hijack a phrase from economics—"thinking at the margins." Because our theological and philosophical tradition has largely derived notions of human consciousness and freedom from majority experience, it has also failed to account for human disability and as a result has unreflectively excluded an important segment of humanity. This is demonstrable, for example, not only in the Reformers' construal of the *imago Dei*, but also in Enlightenment ethical reasoning. (We cannot help but wonder with a wry smile whether *Critique of Pure Reason* could have possibly been written had Kant adopted mentally retarded children!) Contemporary theological reflection on human responsiveness must continue to take more serious account of those with limited faculties.[1]

At the same time, I suggest that Gaventa's proposal may be improved. I find myself wanting greater clarity, especially when she says, "Perhaps the most important thing to say about the body of Christ in response to God . . . is that the body of Christ knows it is in the receiving mode." First, if Gaventa defines human responsiveness as an awareness of being "in the receiving mode," how exactly does this square with her rejection of the popular-level construal of the gospel as an offer? While I think all would object to a crass decisionalism that validates only explicit, crisis-point conversions, I wonder if Gaventa's proposal (so far as I understand it) would have us swing the pendulum to the other extreme whereby explicit confessions of faith are invalidated simply because they are explicit. If someone offers me a gift and I gratefully accept it at the moment of transaction, how is this principally inferior to a scenario in which I receive a gift that has been granted to me perhaps without my formal acceptance? Alternatively, if Gaventa means to assert that God's gifts, including the gift of faith, are granted without reference to the human receptivity or, in some cases, in contravention of it, where does this leave human freedom? (I raise this point as

---

1. See, most recently, Olli-Pekka Vainio, "*Imago Dei* and Human Rationality," *Zygon* 49 (2014) 121–34.

a five-point Calvinist!) I understand the space constraints of an essay, but the point demands further clarification.

Second, I found it somewhat curious that our author should name "upbuilding" as the only other element of divine response alongside personal awareness of receiving. While of course no disciple of Paul would be opposed to the body of Christ building itself up, this is only one element among a number of Pauline exhortations. It is unclear why Gaventa prioritizes this Pauline prescription over against all the others, including for example his injunction to "admonish one another" (Rom 15:14; cf. Col 3:16). In this connection it appears that for Gaventa the antithesis of upbuilding is exclusionary behavior: "If the role of the body of Christ is not to patrol the boundaries, it is to upbuild." Yet it is simply impossible to read Galatians or 1 Corinthians without coming away with the impression that Paul is actually very concerned about the church's patrolling its boundaries—and aghast that they have not done a better job with that very function.

Finally, I wonder if Gaventa's proposal, for all its excellent intentions, is ultimately reductionistic. She writes: "Our capacities vary, but we are not defined by them; we are defined as creatures belonging to God who have been gifted in a variety of ways." In my view this summation is theologically insufficient. Who are we? According to the scriptural witness, we are image-bearers who are to respond as ones being conformed to *the* image (Rom 8:28–30; 1 Cor 15:42–58; 2 Cor 3:18; Col 1:15–20, 3:10). As I read Paul, it is neither our creatureliness nor our consciousness-as-receivers that frames our uniquely human response to the divine but rather our status within the eschatological *imago Dei*.

The quest for a theological account of human response that does justice to the full range of our broken humanity is a commendable quest indeed. Gaventa serves us well by calling us to avoid positing a one-size-fits-all phenomenology on the classic basis of the human rational faculty. At the same time, I am not certain that her counter-proposal (involving a description of human responsiveness in the lowest-common-denominator terms of our creatureliness) finally succeeds, either as an accurate description of Paul's handling of the issue or as a constructive path forward. In my view the Scriptures would suggest that all human response is contextual and constrained, and all individuals are morally obliged to respond fully to God, fully within the confines of their individual faculties. This, I suspect, is the point of Jesus' parable of the Talents. This too seems to be the same principle lingering behind Paul's paraenetic phrase "in proportion to [each one's] faith" (Rom 12:6). Or, as Paul puts it elsewhere, "For if the eagerness is there, the gift is acceptable according to what one has—not according to what one does not have" (2 Cor 8:12). While Gaventa is right to deny that human responsiveness is identical with the exercise of human capacity, and equally right to insist that the church has all too often smuggled in Western assumptions of human autonomy, we still somehow must do justice to the notion (discernible in Paul among other biblical writers) that our capacities, however limited, are nonetheless the platform on which human responsiveness finds expression.

ON LAW AND THE NOACHIC COVENANT: "CAN THE JUDGE OF THE WHOLE WORLD NOT HIMSELF DO JUSTICE?" (GENESIS 18:25)

Jodie Boyer Hatlem

In what follows I will insist that the necessary but not wholly sufficient ground for human encounter with God is a cry for justice. This logical construction "necessary, but not sufficient" bears much weight in my proposal. I also suggest that life is the necessary but not sufficient condition for hearing the command of God, and this life always includes a social element. In making these assertions I am following one of my teachers, David Novak, who has insisted that Scripture indicates that certain basic forms of sociality are necessary but not sufficient conditions for hearing revelation.[1]

What do I mean by this? Necessary and sufficient conditions for my involvement with this symposium include divine initiative—both through creation, whereby my life is entirely contingent and dependent (I cannot guarantee the drawing of my next breath), and in no small part because of God's entirely surprising act of calling me to himself. Neither of my parents were Christians; that I started attending church at the age of three is just the kind of utterly surprising impossible possibility that God's grace and initiative is always enacting.

There are also necessary human and social conditions for these things. A necessary condition for my drawing breath was the very human space of my mother's womb. The sufficient condition for my encounter with God was the rickety old bus of the Buckley Gospel Tabernacle, where God's strange invocation of grace came to

---

1. Necessary-sufficient language runs throughout Novak's theological work. A particularly apt example for this paper is in his essay "Is Natural Law a Border Concept Between Judaism and Christianity," in *Tradition in the Public Square: A David Novak Reader*, ed. Randi Rashkover and Martin Kavka (Grand Rapids: Eerdmans, 2008) 223: "The theologically legitimate hope for redemption is quite different from the utopian schemes that presume the world can redeem itself. But when this elementary justice functions as a presupposition rather than an ideal, it is only taken to be necessary for a communal life worthy of the image of God, not as a sufficient ground for a communal life that promises to be divine is its self-satisfaction. In other words, natural law taken as a presupposition rather than as an ideal is minimal, not maximal, in its demands and in its promises. As a presupposition only, it is certainly not salvific. It only offers *rights*, not *the good*. As such, it is but a regulatory principle, preventing revealed and traditional law from falling below the bar of elementary justice, which the very presence of that law in the world requires as its precondition."

me through the flawed and yet holy lives of the saints in Buckley, Michigan. They did the entirely unreasonable thing of taking a three-year-old each week on a church bus just so that kid (with hardly any rational capacity yet) could sit in Sunday School and the nursery.

The sufficient condition of my giving a paper today is ultimately also this God who called me to serve and who allows me to draw breath, but a necessary condition was also the invitation to attend this conference and present a paper.

Abraham and the Justice of God

In Gen 18:25 Abraham asks: "Can the Judge (hašōpēṭ) of the whole world not himself do justice (mišpāṭ)?" The context of the question is Abraham's pleading for the cities of Sodom and Gomorrah. Some have read this text as an affirmation that "justice" is a standard external to the God who judges. This finds expression in the natural law theory of Hugo Grotius and some forms of Jewish and Christian logos philosophy.[2] Karl Barth rightly rejects this form of natural law thinking. How then should we read this passage? Is Abraham calling God to his own nature as Rowan Williams suggests?[3] Is Abraham applying the principle of noncontradiction to God?[4] Is justice a standard extrinsic to God, or is justice, as Abraham understands it, related intrinsically to God as judge? Or, is the human cry for justice a necessary but not sufficient condition of doing the work of a theologian? This particular text is central to nineteenth-century Italian rabbi Elijah Benamozegh's Kabbalistic reflections on the possibility of human imitation of divine immanence (šĕkînāh). He says if humans are to imitate the pathos and suffering love of God, it is absolutely essential that the Judge of the earth does justice.[5]

In his 2000–2001 Gifford Lectures Stanley Hauerwas's titular claim is that "those who bear crosses work with the grain of the universe."[6] He has nevertheless recently become fond of saying that "justice is a bad idea for Christians."[7] In what follows I will argue that Hauerwas's affirmation of the suffering *logos* is structurally very similar to Elijah Benamozegh's claims about the imitation of God's pathos and

2. Grotius, *On the Law of War and Peace*, trans. F .W. Kelsey et al. (Oxford: Clarendon, 1925) 40.

3. Rowan Williams, *Tokens of Trust: An Introduction to Christian Belief* (Louisville:Westminster John Knox, 2007) . Williams returns to this question multiple times after first raising it on pp. 15–17.

4. David Novak, *Natural Law in Judaism* (New York: Cambridge University Press, 1998) 44–46.

5. Elijah Benamozegh, *Israel and Humanity*, trans. Maxwell Luria (New York: Paulist, 1995).

6. Stanley Hauerwas, *With the Grain of the Universe: The Church's Witness and Natural Theology* (Grand Rapids: Baker, 2001) 6.

7. See for instance, Stanley Hauerwas, "Jesus, The Justice of God' in *War and the American Difference: Theological Reflection on Violence and National Identity* (Grand Rapids: Baker, 2011).

Benamozegh's "Noachism." For Benamozegh, Noachism universalizes Judaism and Mosaic law without denying Jewish particularity or diversity for other nations. I argue that the necessary but not wholly sufficient ground for human encounter with God is a cry for justice. In making this claim I place Hauerwas, and by extension his chief "natural theologian" Karl Barth, in conversation with Jewish theologian, ethicist, and the Gifford lecturer for 2017, David Novak. Novak's natural law thinking, grounded in the seven commandments of the children of Noah, is an incredibly important account that might aid Christians striving to engage reason and baseline moral relations with non-Christians in a way that is fundamentally governed by Scripture and the person of Jesus Christ. Moreover, Noachism might prove to be the proper starting point to make up for contemporary Christian theology's tremendous lack with respect to legal thinking in general.

Abraham has been invited to reason with God in the passage on Sodom and Gomorrah, and by extension so have we. Genesis 18:25 invites us to consider the possibility that God's standard of justice is radically other than our standard of justice, but this text, which is central to Hasidic reflection on the "imitation of God," also insists "Yes, the Judge of the earth does justice." If there were no correlation between our standard of justice and God's standard of justice, then imitation of God (or for Christians, Jesus) would be impossible. This dialogue with God, where Abraham seemingly calls God back to his true nature, presents important challenges to theologians, like myself, who have been shaped by Karl Barth's understanding of revelation.

Barth insists that divine commands are always ad hoc.[8] He presents Genesis as an unfolding of revelation wherein God's speech is always a one-time event, not predicated upon, and not easily translated into rules, principles, or merely human formulations. Indeed, it can be argued that Barth reads all of the human-divine encounters in Genesis through the lens of Abraham and Isaac on Mt. Moriah. Barth's reading of the context of this passage could not be more structurally dissimilar to Benamozegh's reading of Abraham's conversation with God regarding Sodom and Gomorrah.[9] Barth suggests that God stands wholly outside of human conceptions of justice and believes that divine commands should not be rendered in legal formulations:

8. Karl Barth, *Church Dogmatics 2/2: The Doctrine of God*, trans. G. W. Bromiley and T. F. Torrance (Edinburgh: T. & T. Clark, 1957) 674. Hereafter references to *Church Dogmatics* will be with the abbreviation *CD* along with the volume and part number.

9. Benomozegh, *Israel and Humanity*, 231; Barth, *CD* 2/2:215, 673; Karl Barth, "The Strange New World Within the Bible" in *The Word of God and the Word of Man,* (Gloucester: Peter Smith, 1978) 38.

> The reality of the form of the divine command, in which it demands as per-
> mission and is the Law as Gospel, is something which is in principle incom-
> prehensible. Definition and construction in principle lead inevitably either to
> *legalism* on the one hand or *lawlessness* on the other.[10]

For Barth the commandment of God, like manna in the wilderness, is new every morning, continually sustaining but with the proviso that any attempt to horde
up commands for the future, "to define" or "to construct principles," results in rot.[11]
It is hard to square this insistence of Barth with his affirmation that "law is the form
of the gospel."[12]

While Barth's disavowal of natural law and theology is well known, he seems to
have a large difficulty distinguishing between command and law. As such, he has a
hard time describing how Scripture is binding and showing how divine command
addresses itself as command to a communal recipient. There is an important debate
in Jewish thought over the relationship between the command of God (*miṣwāh*) and
the law (*hǎlākāh*). Orthodox Judaism tends to make law and command close to synonymous. On the other hand, Reformed Judaism abstracts general principles from
particular laws, and this creates considerable space between "command" and "law."
This difference can also be seen in the works of Martin Buber and Franz Rosenzweig. Buber much more sharply distinguishes command and law which leads him to
the position that divine commands are directed to "individual selves."[13] Rosenzweig
pushes for a much stronger connection between law and command. For this reason
he insists that the recipient of the command is not a "self" but the "Jewish community" extended in time.[14]

Novak argues that Barth takes a position more similar to Rosenzweig's than to
Buber's. Quoting Barth, he writes: "The question must actually be 'What ought we
to do?' And not 'What ought I to do?'"[15] Novak insists that any sharp distinction
between command and law risks making the command of God directed only to
every individual believer. In order for a command to have a communal recipient it
must come to us in some sense in the form of "law."[16]

---

10. Barth, *CD* 2/1:602.

11. Ibid.

12. Ibid., 757.

13. David Novak, "Karl Barth on Divine Command: A Jewish Response" in *Talking with Christians: Musings of a Jewish Theologian*, Radical Traditions (Grand Rapids: Eerdmans, 2005) 135.

14. Ibid .

15. Barth, *CD* 2/2:655, quoted in Novak, "Talking with Christians," 136.

16. Ibid.

This brings us to Barth's most important statement on the matter: "The law is the form of the gospel."[17] Novak argues for a lovely translation of this passage that "the law is the way that the Gospel shows itself, namely, how the Gospel manifests itself in the world."[18] The law is the gospel's *gestalt*.[19] While as a Jewish theologian he cannot affirm this, Novak insists that a parallel affirmation could be made where law is the form of God's command. Christians and Jews can then explore a similar phenomenology between law and command. As Novak writes, the phenomenology of the Gospel, which for Christians is the new covenant, "is not an object to be observed but a commandment to be obeyed."[20] This is neither legalism nor antinomianism but a dynamic relationship with the covenantal God who graciously commands. Moreover, both Christians and Jews could affirm that in these commandments one finds freedom precisely because we are asked to obey a God who wills, in love, that we be free.

For now I will simply comment that I am not as confident as Novak that Barth treats the commands of God as if they have a communal recipient.

Divine command, for Barth, cannot be a norm which is casuistically applied. As soon as it becomes so, it loses its freedom to speak a loud "no" to human pretensions. It is simply easier to understand the commands of God, which he describes as "individual, concrete, and specific orders," as addressed to an individual rather than to a community.[21]

This tension also shows up in Barth's discussion of Scripture. Here it is hard to see how the divine command is not addressed to an individual. He writes that the divine command "does not need any interpretation, for even to the smallest details it is self-interpreting."[22] Barth is pressed into this position because of the insistence that "definition and construction in principle leads inevitably either to legalism or lawlessness."[23] His fear is a natural theology that seeks to find general principles to apply to specific situations. In these instances "we will pour the dictates and pronouncements of our own self-will into the empty container of a formal moral concept."[24] It is only the self-interpreting command that we can receive wholly without condition. Barth seems to be committed to a sacramental quality to Bible reading where, as if in the Eucharist one participates in the once and for all sacrifice of

17. Barth, *CD*, 2/1:757.

18. Ibid., 130.

19. Ibid.

20. Ibid.

21. Ibid., 2/2:675.

22. Ibid., 665.

23. Ibid., 602.

24. Ibid., 2/1:664–65.

Jesus Christ, in Bible reading one participates in a relational receiving of a command given by God.[25] To the extent that Deborah and Mary and I hear the same command, we are a community of receivers.

Barth does insist that the law is the form, the shape, the garment of grace.[26] However, he also employs Luther's evocative image in saying that Jesus is "clothed in the law, hidden in the manger and the swaddling clothes of the commandments."[27] This is a much more vexed way to render the relationship between law and gospel. Is the law the garment of grace? Or is it mere "swaddling clothes" and something to be cast off with maturity? Does the law obscure the mystery of grace, or robe it resplendently in its necessary form?

Simply put, Barth's reading of Scripture as ad hoc command is in tension with his claim that law is the form of the gospel. Barth seems unable to account for the scriptural narrative itself wherein, as Novak succinctly puts it, the "creation of a community prepared to hear revelation is not simultaneous with the giving of revelation."[28]

The Barthian focus on the binding of Isaac as the defining divine-human encounter in Hebrew Scripture, coupled with a resistance to drawing principles from Scripture, naturally involves a suspicion of human conceptions of justice and humanistic reason. It also leads to a suspicion of the possibility that divine commands can actually have a communal recipient. Barth wanted to stress the contingent nature of revelation with his claim that it is "ad hoc."[29] Trouble arises, however, because Barth, in his early work on revelation, did not attend sufficiently to the specificity of the narrative in which revelation is particular and historical, where revelation of God's work occurs within human history already in progress, a "history that language not only describes but also comprises."[30]

Attention to David Novak's engagement with Barth is helpful. This is not a claim that the ground of revelation is a human capacity for language or that there is some sort of "natural access" to God or God's justice that can place someone before the fall or provide ontological conditions for God's commands. Instead, to quote Barth in another place, "the guarantee that humans can reason finds its ground in the [historical] fact that God addresses him as a rational creature."[31]

25. Ibid., 2/2:701.
26. Ibid., 563.
27. Ibid.
28. Novak, "Karl Barth on Divine Command," 137.
29. Barth, *CD* 2/2:674.
30. Novak, "Karl Barth on Divine Command," 139.
31. Barth, *CD* 3/4:327.

Sermon on the Mount, Imitation, and Justice as a Bad Idea

Barth not only suspected natural law, but he also struggled to admit that we humans can be bound to a law given in Christ. Barth praises the "so-called fanatics" who take the Sermon on the Mount literally, remarking that "it has been said too loudly and confidently that in the examples formulated in Matthew 5:21–48, the radical deepening of the OT law is not meant to be understood in terms of law, as so many precepts which we must literally practice."[32] He goes on to say that the righteousness that the Sermon demands cannot be separated from the one who enacts it. Further, he comes very close to delimiting law and gospel, law and command as synonymous—even when the command or gospel or obedience is understood as imitation of or obedience to Jesus Christ. He writes "the demand cannot be separated from the one who enacts it."[33] This is, of course, true for all commands received by a believer; Jesus is not a lawgiver like Solon or Hammurabi. The sermon reveals the kingdom, Jesus, and the new humanity. Moreover, it presents the church with a living and dynamic question "Will the church live or not live in the fullness of life already granted to it."[34]

Barth argues that the Sermon on the Mount "defines and describes the freedom which is given to the people of God."[35] Here command and law are closely aligned. Moreover, Barth insists that the new creature of the Sermon on the Mount is a present reality, not a dream or a promise. He writes that the Sermon represents "the fulfilling of all command and therefore is the command."[36] Yet, it is impossible to "construct a picture of the Christian life from these decrees."[37] Barth continues that "it would be utter folly to interpret the imperatives of the Sermon on the Mount as if we should bestir ourselves to actualize these pictures."[38]

There is a then a stark anomism, bordering on the lawlessness he denounces, operating in Barth's work. How can the Sermon on the Mount be an event in revelation addressed to a communal recipient without the possibility of communal obedience? In what way can law ever be thought to be the form of the gospel if there is no way to construct even an image of these pictures? How can gospel, the command

---

32. Barth *CD* 2/2:692.

33. Ibid.

34. A. Katherine Grieb, "Living Righteousness: Karl Barth on the Sermon on the Mount," in *The Word is Truth: Barth on Scripture*, ed. George Hunsinger (Grand Rapids: Eerdmans, 2012) 102. See Barth, *CD* 2/2:688.

35. Barth *CD* 2/2:696.

36. Ibid., 690.

37. Ibid., 688.

38. Ibid., 689.

of God, be an event, an event encountered in community, without obedience? Or, as Rosenzweig insists "law must seek to become commands which seek to be transformed into deed the very moment they are heard."[39]

Without these deeds there can be no connection between law and the living reality of command, between these particular laws and participation with Christ. The command "Love thy enemy" can be seen as structured by the gospel and the living Christ in multiple directions, but this command can only be experienced by specific deed in the context of obedience. You must actively experience this particular class of neighbor, the enemy, which you actively love.

Barth has the same kind of problem with the human capacity to imitate the justice of God as he does with the human capacity to obey God at all. This problem extends to Barth's view on the imitation of Christ. It is simply not clear how one is able to structure one's life communally after the witness of Jesus Christ without some capacity to correlate law and command. Barth answers such a challenge with an insistence that "one cannot learn or imitate this life of the divine seed in the new world. One can only let it live, grow, and ripen within him."[40] This proclivity finds expression in many Barthians' preference for ethics based not on propositions but on the living social reality of church, narrative, and sacraments.[41] Jesus, the justice of God, is to be known in the Eucharist, but almost not at all in human acts and crying out for justice. In this rendering, "life" and "justice" can only be seen as extrinsic principles wrongly abstracted from living participation with the God who commands. Problematically, such ethical projects are stridently focused on the importance of human obedience to divine commands, yet they tend to share Barth's aversion to concrete deontological formulation.

Community, Command, and the Noachide

In recent years Hauerwas has cited often and appreciatively Daniel Bell's lecture and article from this symposium that proclaimed "Jesus is the Justice God."[42] In that lecture and essay Bell worries that social justice advocacy in churches is often "presented as if it were an external standard to which Christianity is accountable."[43] This leads to an anxiety on the part of churches wanting to make the gospel credible by showing how it supports a Christian capacity "to do secular justice," and where, if

39. Franz Rosenzweig as cited in Novak, "Karl Barth on Divine Command," 135.

40. Karl Barth, "The Strange New World Within the Bible," 41.

41. For examples of this method see the overall structure of Samuel Wells and Stanley Hauerwas, eds., *The Blackwell Companion to Christian Ethics* (Oxford: Blackwell, 2006).

42. Daniel M. Bell, Jr., "*Jesus*, the Jews, and the Politics of God's *Justice*," *Ex Auditu* 22 (2006) 89.

43. Ibid.

the church fails to measure up to the "external/secular standard of justice," it may be judged socially irrelevant.[44] Bell argues instead that Jesus is the justice of God and that there is no standard of justice extrinsic to or more basic than what is revealed in the life, death, and resurrection of Jesus. Hauerwas agrees and argues that social justice advocacy models often wrongly assume "that justice can be understood apart from Christian convictions and practices."[45] They usurp the rightful place of Judaism because justice is presumed to be universal "in a manner that has no particular or intrinsic relations to the Jewish people."[46]

This is something of a recalibration for Hauerwas, and we must ask whether it squares with some of Hauerwas's most persistent Jewish conversation partners. In *With the Grain of the Universe* Hauerwas draws on Yoder and argues that the cross of Jesus, the definitive revelation of God, is "an extreme demonstration that agape seeks neither effectiveness nor justice."[47] With the help of Bell, Hauerwas can now say that justice is a good idea for Christians as long as we recognize that justice is a standard that can only be known fully in Jesus Christ.

Hauerwas's insistence that Jesus is the justice of God is not as divorced from any possible human imitation or social construction as it is for Barth. Hauerwas can still insist that the Sermon on the Mount is a social programmatic and that imitation of the life of Jesus reveals something about the inner intentions of creation. For Hauerwas, Jesus Christ, the paradigm after which all things are being made new, is supremely imitable. Indeed, the purest human correlate to divine ordering is the martyr. Christian belief is made more plausible by the vulnerable winsomeness and absurd invocation of the martyr. Witnesses are not evidence, but the totality of their lives and practice is the best place to look if one is curious about "how the world is arranged."[48]

Moreover, these witnesses have a vocation in the context of the larger vocation of the world. "For Barth, to be a Christian, to anticipate here now the future, universal praise of God, is to be a member of a limited and prophetic minority."[49] At the same time, Hauerwas's vison has tended to obscure what commonalities we might have with non-Christians, even with Jews, whose lives seem to be marked by and shaped by concerns of the Sermon on the Mount or the lived practice of Jesus.

44. Ibid.

45. Hauerwas, "Jesus, the Justice of God," 101.

46. Ibid., 102.

47. John Howard Yoder, *The Original Revolution* (Scottsdale, PA: Herald, 1971) 59 quoted in Hauerwas, *With the Grain of the Universe*, 219.

48. Ibid., 212.

49. Ibid., 197–98.

Novak's theology of the Noachide seeks to develop a vision of justice like Bell's that is intrinsic, rather than extrinsic, to the very nature of God. But, Novak's vision of justice, unlike Bell's, does not require an absolute, MacIntyrean agreement about shared goods, *telos* and the like. In the space remaining, I will argue that Novak's formulation of natural law as Noachide law opens up a different logic for explaining the moral correlation between God's law and the law of human reason. This formulation differs substantially from that found in secular, classically liberal, distributive renderings of justice. By its nature Noachide law seeks to outline basic requirements from a Hebrew perspective for evaluating the moral standards of non-Jews. Fidelity to the Noachide, it should also be emphasized, was also a precondition for reception of the Mosaic covenant, according to Novak and rabbinic thinking. The people of Israel were prepared for the covenant because they kept the Noachide.

Novak explicitly draws his thinking on the Noachide from Elijah Benamozegh. Benamozegh's *Israel and Humanity* takes up several related tasks, but one of the most important is to establish "that those who observe the Law are thus participating in the universal order."[50] Similar to Hauerwas' claim about those who bear crosses, Benamozegh takes what may appear to be an idiosyncratic idea and demonstrate that, in fact, natural law and Jewish law are synonymous. It is well-established "Hebraic belief," according to Benamozegh, that keeping "the precepts of the Torah" is "in some sense cosmic and ontological" in import.[51] Part 3 of *Israel and Humanity* begins with a chapter on the "Unity and Universality of the Law." Benamozegh insists that, according to both the rabbis and the Bible, humans collaborate with God by way of keeping the Torah. Already from his nineteenth-century perch, Benamozegh anticipates certain recent developments in Christian-Jewish theological dialogue. Abraham and Noah are apostles to the Gentiles even before Paul.[52] Hebrew law is two-fold, a particular law specifically to be kept by Jews (Mosaism) set within a wider, universal law applicable to sojourners and aliens in the land of Israel and to humanity in general (Noachism).[53]

Israelite religion is thus "of truly universal character . . . even while preserving Jewish individuality."[54] Early Christianity misunderstood the "*dual* religion" of Judaism, Benamozegh suggests, and "at first hesitated for some time between the two extreme courses: imposing Mosaism upon everyone, or abolishing it even for

50. Benamozegh, *Israel and Humanity*, 219.

51. Ibid.

52. See Michael Wyschogrod, *Abraham's Promise: Judaism and Jewish-Christian Relations*, Radical Traditions, ed. Kendall Soulen (Grand Rapids: Eerdmans, 2004) 232.

53. Ibid., 232–40. See for contemporary relevance David Rudolph, *A Jew to the Jews: Jewish Contours of Pauline Flexibility in 1 Corinthians 9:19–23* (Tübingen: Mohr Siebeck, 2011).

54. Benamozegh, *Israel and Humanity*, 238.

Israel."[55] Under this dual schemata, Benamozegh is able to treat a wide variety of vexing issues including tension between Paul and James and the solution of the Jerusalem Council in Acts, proselytizing in Judaism and Christianity, the relationship between Enlightenment and religion, what happens when Christians voluntarily observe particular Mosaic *miṣwôt*, and the relationship between Jewish monotheism and Christian Trinitarianism.

Benamozegh, drawing primarily from Maimonides as well as dozens of other Jewish rabbinical sources, lays out the meaning of "the seven commandments" for the Noachide, which, as he insists, each "represent[s] not a single commandment but rather an entire group of related obligations."[56] The Noachide can "augment" this cluster of seven obligations by taking "such Mosaic laws as [s]he wishes to practice" alongside those "obligations which cannot be set aside for any reason."[57] Quoting from the Babylonian Talmud, the seven commandments are simply enumerated:

> Our sages have said that seven commandments have been prescribed for the Sons of Noah: the first requires them to have judges; the other six forbid sacrilege, idolatry, incest, homicide, theft, and the consumption of a limb taken from a living animal.[58]

The first obligation is absolutely essential. For talmudic Judaism gentiles who wish to approach anything like righteousness must have courts that administer justice. Benamozegh discusses variant rabbinic lists of these seven obligations, including the possibility of adding "be fruitful and multiply," a prohibition on castration, or the forbidding of cross-breeding species and trees.[59] These lists are drawn, not entirely from the immediate context of the aftermath of the flood, but from the wider body of law in Torah which applies to the sojourner, the resident alien, or former inhabitants of the land of Israel. Even those lists which do not explicitly include the necessity of a judicial system include such a requirement implicitly, according to Benamozegh, "as an inevitable result of the very existence of this code."[60] Simply put, the very first and most important requirement for any just human community is that it have a structured legal system for dealing with matters of injustice.

While Benamozegh's overarching project is intended to address issues raised by the Enlightenment, he draws from the wealth of rabbinic thinkers before him who were responding to particular issues vis-à-vis Christianity, Islam, and pressing

55. Ibid.
56. Ibid., 261.
57. Ibid., 262.
58. Ibid., 263 quoting from *b. Sanhedrin* 56b.
59. Ibid., 263–64. Pp. 277–79 report further possible additions according to various rabbis.
60. Ibid., 263.

matters of their day. In all instances questions related to justice and the Noachide are approached specifically and intentionally from within a world committed to the narrative and precepts of Scripture. Novak, Benamozegh, Maimonides, and the rabbinic tradition more generally maintain a concept of natural law that does not circumscribe the demands of the Bible. Just as importantly, it is a version of biblical law that does not require attempts to control a particular national discourse on law and justice, even if from a minimalist position. Rather, the concern is ever to relate in a scripturally faithful way to the reality of encounter with God-fearing people (and at times non-God-fearing people) who are not Jews. Can such a theological movement be taken as appropriate within Christian theological discourse? For any Christian theology that maintains its moorings in Scripture, it must hold some sway.

Novak insists that the Noachide as "natural law" finds its larger meaning in the wider world of Torah and the still larger world of the God that commands. The seven commands of the children of Noah is a biblical law, but there is no way theologically to transform Noachide law into anything other than a limited, preservationist law. The claim is not that there is some sort of ontological condition for God's command which we can abstract from creation and by which we can establish guiding principles. The tradition around Noachide law does insist that humans can reason from revelation and that, because revelation is always spatial, historical, and temporal, it does violence to the biblical narrative to argue that the community that received revelation at Sinai did not exist before it received direct revelation.

To illustrate this thinking narratively, Novak and Benamozegh regularly refer to the following haggadah: "'And he said the Lord came forth from Sinai . . .' (Deuteronomy 33:2)—When the Holy-One-blessed-be-He appeared (*nigleh*) to give the Torah to Israel. He did not appear to Israel alone but to all the nations."[61] This text reports that the Edomites refuse the Torah because it contains the prohibition of murder, the Ammonites and Moabites because the Torah prohibits incest, and the Ishmaelites because it prohibits theft. Novak argues that the greater significance of this text is that there are human preconditions to the commandments. The Israelites, because of their willingness to keep the laws of Noah, were prepared to receive the covenant. When the commandments come to humans, they come to us as "communal creatures, already aware of our communal nature and, thus, ready for the covenant we hope will come to us, but which can never be conjured up by us."[62] Hearing the command of God requires a basic desire for justice.

Implicit in hearing the commands of God is, and always has been, a communal context. Novak claims that we understand this communal context better when we

61. Novak, *Talking With Christians*, 160, quoting *Sifre*: Devarim, no. 343, 396f.
62. Novak, "Karl Barth on Divine Command," 139.

reflect on the Noachide covenant.[63] In large measure the community that was prepared for revelation at Sinai was an Exodus community that kept the Noachide. It had drawn away from Egypt, had minimal legal adjudication, and had recognized the horrors of a state that had power over death and was charged with fostering life. The community to which the Torah was revealed at Sinai had cried out for justice and had been heard. This was a minimal precondition to Israelite reception of God's law.[64]

The Jewish theological conception of the Noachide does not presuppose that we can get behind the noetic consequence of the fall, nor does it assume that "reason," "law," or "justice" are standards abstractable from God or extrinsic from God in any way. Still, Novak insists that Scripture indicates certain basic forms of sociality are necessary but not sufficient conditions for hearing revelation. He asks, "How could one know what a commandment is if one has never had any experience of a commandment *before* the event of revelation?"[65] The biblical account, according to Novak, shows that there is a community that precedes the Sinai revelation, a community that was in place and prepared to hear revelation. It follows then that we *can* reason from revelation, that some of the tools necessary for reasoning from revelation are found in basic preconditions for human community, and that the need for legal reasoning in community is one of the most basic human norms.

As a Mennonite drawn to cross-cultural, interreligious work around peace and justice, I think Novak's account of law—natural, biblical, and otherwise—makes more sense of the biblical and Christian witness. Novak draws deeply on rabbinic sources, Jewish philosophy, and even from Calvinist thinking on natural revelation. He engages regularly with Karl Barth and was a featured speaker at last year's annual Barth conference at Princeton Theological Seminary. Importantly, Novak differs decisively from a great deal of Reformed thinking in insisting that natural law is not to be grounded in orders of creation that can somehow give us insight into God's creative intentions apart from scriptural revelation.

Exegeting the Noah Story Anew

To grasp the significance for Christian theology of Novak's rendering of the Noachide as natural law, close attention to the story of Noah in the wider setting of Gen 1–11 is in order. The story has significant things to say about the law as the form of the gospel.

---

63. Ibid.

64. David Novak, *Natural Law in Judaism*, 185.

65. Novak, *Talking With Christians*, 137.

The story of Noah is dark. It is far removed from the comfortable pastels of the nursery and is instead the color of moonless nights and dark, chaotic waters. The narrative context of the story is the earth's increasing alienation from the Creator God. In Genesis, ever since the first human sinning, the trajectory of divine/human relations has been ever-widening separation, and the grammar in which this alienation is expressed is violence. After Adam and Eve eat of the tree of the knowledge of good and evil, they are cast out of the garden. The woman is at enmity with creeping animals, men and women are alienated from one another with the latter subordinated to the former, and they both become alienated from their bodies which begin to suffer the weariness of work and the pains of childbirth. Death begins its undoing of all things. Men and women are at war with creation itself. Animals become sacrificial game. The ground actively resists creative labor. The land brings forth cursed fruits. This sets the stage for the first murder. Cain comes before God with the bounty of the earth, and we are told that God rejects his offering. There will be no blessing for Cain's labor, and because of this he murders his brother Abel.

After the murder of Abel, God addresses Cain: "Where is your brother?" Cain retorts with a rhetorical question: "Am I my brother's keeper?" Most of us have been taught that the answer to this rhetorical question is yes, we are our brother's keeper. However, Novak insists that the answer to Cain's rhetorical question is "no." To be someone's keeper is to have dominion over them like God has dominion over human beings. The word keeper (šōmēr) "denotes someone who has been explicitly designated by someone else to look after his or her property."[66] Am I my brother's keeper? No, only God is. In fact, to be a keeper presumes that one human being has been given pre-eminence over a brother. This is related, for Novak, to the constant human temptation to "see oneself as God's equal, and as the absolute superior of one's fellow humans."[67] The temptation is in reality the most basic form that idolatry takes so that idolatry is intimately connected to violence and murder.

In the immediate context the text becomes yet darker. It is not entirely clear that Cain knew that he had this kind of power over his brother. In this case Cain might be rebuking God for his distance from creation. Either way, Cain's sin results in further alienation as he is excised from community, exiled from the rest of humanity. From here the story grows darker still.

Humanity as a whole follows the path of murderous Cain. Humans build structures of order, but these are disordered or otherwise lacking. They arrogate themselves as God above other human beings. It is fair to read the much-discussed

66. Ibid., 34.
67. Ibid.

"Elohim" (Gen 6:2) not as male angels or demons, but as "political potentates."[68] Politically sanctioned rape and violence reign.

Then Noah appears. Noah's name means "pleasing," and he is regarded as "blameless in his generation" and as "a man who walked with Yahweh." Rabbinic explanations of the text have posed a very Pauline question: how is it possible to be righteous apart from the law? Textual commentators have focused particular attention on the phrase "in his generation." In one reading Noah is not technically righteous, merely righteous in his own generation. Yet, the three fold repetition of his moral status—"righteous, blameless, one who walked with God"—has led some to ask whether "in his generation" is not an intensifier of Noah's righteousness insofar as he could be righteous in the context of complete moral breakdown. The moral status of Noah's generation is stated succinctly: "Great was human being's evil doing and violence."[69]

The vision of God's judgment is now exceedingly dark. The destruction in Noah is portrayed, not as something that happens through God's active judgment, but through withdrawal. Here we have not a god of firebolts but a God who exits stage left—lights out! In the beginning God had separated light from dark, water from earth, and dry from wet. In the flood these barriers and orders and life-giving distinctions collapse. In a haunting passage we learn the "breath of a breath of life is destroyed."[70] This language echoes the language of Gen 1 where God's breath hovers over the water, giving life to everything. The alienation between God and creation has become almost total. A boat rocks on the murky waters of primordial chaos. A ridiculous collection of animals, clean and unclean, is a microcosm of all things. Here in the boat is the remnant of God's live-giving breath. The ark's cubits and feet and pounds of goods are enumerated by God himself. It is the last place of God's love, breath, and life-giving order in the world. Noah is a man separated out from a world of idolatrous violence, righteous in his generation, preserved from the waters of uncreation.

Once the boat lands on earth, there is a renewed separation between water and a sky that once again bleeds light. Noah brings his thanksgiving offering to God, and just as God smells the pleasing offering from the pleasing man Noah, God comes to a sudden and startling conclusion, proclaiming: I now accept that the human heart is evil from its youth (Gen 8:21).[71] Here God makes a promise to humans. No matter

---

68. Ibid.

69. Translations and references to rabbinic ideals that follow are from David W. Cotter, *Genesis, Berit Olam: Studies in Hebrew Narrative and Poetry* (Collegeville: Liturgical, 2003) 61.

70. David Cotter, *Genesis,* 58.

71. The recognition of this parallel is from Walter Brueggemann, *Genesis: A Bible Commentary for Teaching and Preaching,* Interpretation (Louisville: Westminister John Knox, 1980), 81.

how evil they become, how violent, how murderous, God will never again abandon the world. Furthermore, the text suggests that if one is going to understand God, one will have to return to this story from the beginning. The point is not how God will deal with human sinfulness, but instead, how God has determined not to deal with human sinfulness. Never again will God open the portals of heaven. Never again will God deal with human sin by withdrawal and absolute alienation. Instead, God will deal with human sin by binding ever closer to creation. The rainbow, in the parlance of the Sermon on the Mount, is a promise that rain will fall on the just and unjust. The rainbow is a reminder of God's presence that keeps the waters of chaos at bay. In a sense the entire earth has been marked as an ark, a space of God's protection and care.

This protection and care, this grace, comes to humanity packaged in the form of law—not the violent law of Cain's city, but the gift of a law that can give communal law shape and sign. When one views the baseline morality of the Noachide commands in the context of the story of Noah, human violence is the grammar of alienation from God. Its origin is in "primal" idolatry, a primal idolatry whose most potent expression is murder and the creation of forms of civility in which some people are lords over others. God's command comes to Noah in the form of a call to choose life over death, in what Barth refers to as the most basic form of command. Humans are commanded to live, a command implicit in all other commands, "the command whatever its form always contains the demand that he should live in his acts."[72] God determines to deal with human alienation by a passionate binding of Godself to the world. The immediate form this takes is law: laws regulating human relation with creation, laws that make animals fear humans. Often this basic law has been read as an establishment of legitimate hegemony or a state prerogative over violence.

Law in the aftermath of the flood actually sets its logic against such a reading. God is among humans who presume they have dominion over their fellow creatures. What Judaism calls for in the Noachide is not a statist law or a justification for state-sanctioned violence. Instead, the Noachide demands cultural, legal systems that respond to murder in an organized way. On this reading, Gen 9:6 ("He who sheds the blood of men, by men shall his blood be shed") functions descriptively in a way similar to Jesus' statement "All who take the sword die by the sword" (Matt 26:52).

The vision of a world after Noah is consonant with law as the form of the gospel or the form of divine command. Law, in the rendering of Robert Cover, is paideic (or educative) and celebratory.[73] Without a dynamic relationship with the God of

72. Barth, *CD* 3/4:333.
73. Robert Cover, "The Supreme Court, 1982 Term-Foreword: Nomos and Narrative," *Harvard*

Israel, Gentiles cannot fully participate in the freedom of the Torah or be liberated from the terrors of idolatry. Yet Jewish reflection on Gentile idolatry has always posited that it is different from Jewish idolatry. Gentiles, in order to begin to live free from their idols, must affirm the Noachide. In fact, Novak argues, this more limited sense of "idolatry" is what drives Paul's assertion in Rom 1 that Gentiles "are without excuse."[74] The command most centrally addressing Gentile idolatry is "do not murder." This is a prohibition of a primal idolatry witnessed in Cain presuming to be his brother's keeper.

It is possible for humans to possess a very limited natural knowledge of God, a knowledge of what God is not, from reflection on the disordered state of human society. One's "revulsion at violence and irrationality of injustice leads one to hope that," as the Talmud puts it, "From the negative you hear you can hear the positive."[75] Gentiles who begin to cry out for justice, rejecting murder first and foremost, become questioners who say, "I don't know whether there is true justice or not, but if there is justice, this violent state of affairs could not be it." Even though humans can know nothing about God positively from nature, they can ascertain where God is not and who God is not.[76]

Barth and the Protection of Life

Is there a particularly good way of bridging the gap between Hauerwas's Barthian view against natural law and Novak's embrace of natural law? Barth began his reflections in *Church Dogmatics* 3/4 with the affirmation that humans are commanded to live. The first and last word of ethics is not the sacredness of life but instead the divine command. Barth insists that on an ontological level not even life precedes command. This is a strikingly similar affirmation to Benamozegh's take on the universality of the demands of Torah. Barth insists that because command is more basic than life itself, there is no human being that must live.[77] To claim that one must live is the most primal form of human idolatry. Instead, human life is always a loan and a gift, and yet it is a gift that "presupposes a productive subject, a being capable of

---

Law Review 97.4 (1983) 12–13.

74. David Novak, "Before Revelation: The Rabbis, Paul and Karl Barth," in *Talking with Christians: Musings of a Jewish Theologian*, Radical Traditions (Grand Rapids: Eerdmans, 2005) 114–15.

75. David Novak, "Idolatry as the Root of Injustice," ABC Religion and Ethics, Nov., 2010. Online: http://www.abc.net.au/religion/articles/2010/11/17/3069257.htm (accessed Sept 10, 2014).

76. Novak, "Before Revelation," 124.

77. Barth, *CD* 3/4:324–28.

making for himself a new beginning with his being, conduct and action."[78] Command is the very tether of human life, and because of this life is not sacred in and of itself.

Barth also insists that "the command, whatever its form, always contains the demand that he should live in his acts."[79] Every breath of every human being involves a dynamic interaction with the God who commands. Life is the necessary but not sufficient condition of hearing the command of God, and this life always includes a social element. It is in these natural and historical relations that humans are presented with the encounter that is the command of God. Therefore, while we cannot say that human life is "sacred" or that it creates its own respect intrinsically, it is also appropriate to say that concerns about the dignity of human life are intrinsic to the justice of God, particularly a God who commands that we live.

In fact, it is a disavowal of very basic claims of justice that marks the idolatry of the modern nation-state. These states, Barth insists, seek to sacralize biological life and the imperative to live and become murderous as a result. The individual or state that thinks it must live will ultimately become suicidal. Deified, dehumanized women and men understand life, not as gift, but as a zero-sum game. Moreover, just as is recorded in the stories of Cain and of the Noah generation, primal human idolatry is expressed in the grammar of violence and murder.

Barth links the assumption of a vitalistic life force that is itself sacred to cultures of perpetual war and the creation of regimes that attempt to manage life as a competitive force. The piled high dead at Verdun, Ypres, Hiroshima, The Bulge, and Mauthausen similarly evidence modern humanities' mass suicidal frenzy: "War expresses man's radical inability to be master without merely becoming not only a slave but his own destroyer, and therefore, fundamentally a suicide."[80] Ironically, such suicidal cultures insist that life is sacred, making life and its protection the prime directive for humanity, the basis for all human society and the continual reason for totalizing war against any perceived threat.

Hauerwas clearly believes that the problem with the language of justice and human rights is that at its core it is an affirmation that "humans must live," that human life is sacred and that there is a right to life even if God does not exist.[81] He argues for an alternative to the sacralization of life found in justice language and human rights rhetoric in a retrieval of the language of the martyr. The martyr takes her cue from

78. Ibid., 230.

79. Ibid., 333.

80. Ibid., 452.

81. See Stanley Hauerwas and Richard Bondi, "Memory, Community, and the Reasons for Living: Reflections on Suicide and Euthanaisa," *Journal of the American Academy of Religion* 44.3 (1976) 439–52.

Jesus Christ. Jesus, whose life in God was necessary, made his life contingent. In so doing he was able to take on the legitimacy of the powers.

The structure of Barth's argument, however, seems to be closer to Novak's. "Life" (and by extension human sociality) is necessary for hearing the command of God. Because of this the witness of the martyrs should demand a truer and richer reverence for life (human and animal) than the false idolatry of life as confessed by humanity that believes that it "must live."

Conclusion

To live out this justice as required by Jesus or the command of God is to reject suicidal state violence. Non-Christians and Christians who live in such a way are acting with the grain of the universe, very often in ways that they may not understand as connected to the life of Jesus Christ, the justice of God.

Law is the form of the gospel. Basic moral systems like the seven commands of the children of Noah are not the same thing as the grace and justice that we find ultimately in Jesus Christ. Yet as laws revealed in Scripture and offered in revelatory history, they are related intrinsically rather than extrinsically to Jesus, the justice of God.

When viewing the establishment of basic moral codes in the context of the story of Noah and the rabbinic tradition of Noachide command, we can affirm that basic nomological systems can be a kind of ark that contains God's gracious binding to all humanity. God enters into communal life through the form of laws. Moreover, human violence is the grammar of human alienation from God. The source of this violence is the idolatrous claim that we have dominion over our brothers and sisters and that we are subject to wholly other forms of rationality, law, and adjudication.

Even basic human formulations, such as found in rights language, need not be extrinsic to the justice we find fully in Jesus. It is our job to chasten these standards by living in keeping with the higher standard revealed in Christ, to test and discern whether these basic forms find their larger life in the gracious commands of God and find their fullest human validation in Christ-formed martyrs. Since what is essential is faithfulness to the way of Jesus, there can be a recognizable parallel between discipleship and diverse kinds of secular ethics and worldly wisdom. For this reason the community of God is always open to correction from the outside world insofar as worldly lives and communities can also understand and witness to a life more closely approximating the life of Jesus.

THE BIBLICAL NOAH, DARREN ARONOFSKY'S FILM *NOAH,* AND VIEWER RESPONSE TO *NOAH*: THE COMPLEX TASK OF RESPONDING TO GOD'S INITIATIVE

Robert K. Johnston

Wondering what are the most frequently selected stories in children's Bibles, Stephen Smith turned to Google books and discovered thirty-three such Bibles published between 1831 and 2013. Content analysis of these volumes revealed that two stories proved to be the most popular of the more than four hundred that were re-told—Jesus' birth (the Christmas story) and the story of Noah.[1] The story of Noah was chosen more often than the crucifixion or resurrection, more often than the Prodigal Son, more often even than David and Goliath. Of course, few if any of these paraphrased and simplified Bibles included the biblical ending where Noah is drunk and lying naked on the ground, about to curse his son Ham for shaming him.[2] Nor do they reflect on the excruciating pain Noah and his family surely felt, when shut up in the safety of the ark they realize that thousands of people and animals were being blotted out by the flood—all but eight humans and two animals of each kind. Few if any probably thought to reflect on the fact that everyone, including Noah, was a sinner—that sin entered with Adam and Eve and stained the whole human race.[3] Again, few, I suspect, included the text that says that the Creator was not only "sorry that he had made humankind on the earth," but that "it grieved him [the Creator] to his heart" (Gen 6:6).[4]

---

1. Stephen Smith of OpenBible.info, referenced in *Christianity Today*, May 2014, 16.

2. Darren Aronofsky, quoted in Cathleen Falsani, "The 'Terror' of *Noah*: How Darren Aronofsky Interprets the Bible" *The Atlantic*, March 2014, 3. Online: http://www.theatlantic.com/entertainment/archive/2014/03/the-terror-of-em-noah-em-how-darren-aronofsky-interprets-the-bible/359587/.

3. Cf., ibid., 1.

4. Cf., Darren Aronofsky: "The moment that it 'grieved Him in his heart to destroy creation,' is, for me, the high dramatic moment in the story." Ibid., 2.

How Millions Hear the Noah Story

These retellings of the story of Noah have typically emphasized how animals were rescued following God's command because Noah, a righteous man, was faithful to God and constructed an ark where his family and the animals could ride out the storm. Picture-book stories, children's songs, nursery school decorations, flannel-graph stories, movies, and ceramic collections of Noah and his ark have mostly been presented as comedies, not tragedies, with God protecting a bearded, white-haired Noah, his family, and the animals. Noah and his sons have been pictured as hard at work building the huge ark, only for the animals to come peacefully, two by two. A dove returns later with an olive branch to signal the flood is over, and then a rainbow appears in the sky to signal that God would never let this happen again. The take away has often been: we can count on God to be gracious, and we can, but that is not the whole story.

Representative, here, is the children's song, "Rise and Shine and Give God the Glory, Glory!" a song sung in Sunday schools and at scout camps alike, and one based on an African American spiritual:

Rise and shine and give God your glory, glory!

Rise and shine and give God your glory, glory!

Rise and shine and (*clap once*) give God your glory, glory!

(*Raise hands to shoulder level and sway back and forth.*)

Children of the Lord.

The Lord said to Noah, "There's gonna be a floody, floody."

Lord said to Noah, "There's gonna be a floody, floody."

"Get those children (*clap once*) out of the muddy, muddy!"

Children of the Lord.

So Noah, he built him, he built him an arky, arky.

Noah, he built him, he built him an arky, arky.

Made it out of (*clap once*) hickory barky, barky.

Children of the Lord.

The animals, they came on, they came on by twosies, twosies.

The animals, they came on, they came on by twosies, twosies.

Elephants and (*clap once*) kangaroosies, roosies.

Children of the Lord.

Chorus

It rained, and poured, for forty daysies, daysies.

Rained, and poured, for forty daysies, daysies.

Nearly drove those (*clap once*) animals crazy, crazy.

Children of the Lord.

The sun came out and dried up the landy, landy.

Sun came out and dried up the landy, landy.

Everything was (*clap once*) fine and dandy, dandy.

Children of the Lord.

Now that is the end, the end of my story, story.

That is the end, the end of my story, story.

Everything is (*clap once*) hunky dory, dory.

Children of the Lord.[5]

Millions have grown up wrongly believing that for Noah everything was "fine and dandy" on the "arky, arky," and for those who love God, life is meant similarly to be "hunky dory." As the song suggests, we too are to "rise and shine and give God the glory." Rob Moore, Paramount studio's vice-chairman, put it well, "Most people do have a sense that the Noah story is a short, happy journey where Noah rescues mankind and the animals. They're not thinking, All but eight people die."[6] Here is the story we have countlessly repeated, one that has produced in the minds of millions certain expectations and associations.

But not all have read this story in such sentimental ways. Is life meant to be simply "fine and dandy"? Was it all fine and dandy, even for Noah?

How Young Aronofsky Heard the Noah Story

The filmmaker Darren Aronofsky remembers as a young boy hearing the story of Noah and being filled not only with wonder, but also with terror: "What if I was not one of the good ones to get on the boat?"[7] Would he have been rescued, or would he have been one of the townspeople who were snuffed out? If the latter, surely that would not have been "fine and dandy," as the children's song suggests. Aronofsky says he found "the story scary because I sympathized with everyone who drowned."[8] Here his Jewish context was no doubt influential, but more on that below.

---

5. "Rise and Shine," Online: http://www.scoutsongs.com/lyrics/rise-and-shine.html.

6. Rob Moore, quoted in Tad Friend, "Darren Aronofsky gets Biblical," *The New Yorker*, March 17, 2014, 46. Online: http://www.newyorker.com/services/presscenter/2014/03/17/140317pr_press _release.

7. Darren Aronofsky, quoted in Falsani, "The 'Terror' of *Noah*," 2.

8. Darren Aronofsky, quoted in Robbie Collin, "Darren Aronofsky Interview: The Noah Story is Scary," (April 4, 2014). Online: www.vancouversun.com/entertainment/movie-guide/Noah+great+bi blical+gamble+paid/9698044/story.html.

Later, when he was thirteen and a seventh grader in Brooklyn, his teacher, Mrs. Fried, asked his class to write spontaneously a poem in class. Darren's poem, "The Dove," was written in fifteen minutes and was based on this same Noah story, a story that had obviously remained central in the young teenager's imagination. His poem so impressed his teacher that she entered it in a contest on peace at the United Nations, and surprisingly Aronofsky won. In the poem, the teenager wrote not only about Noah and his good family, but also about the presence of evil, about the screams through the night as people and animals drown, about the dove returning, and the rainbow. He finished the poem:

> Peace was in the air . . .
>
> He knew evil could not be kept away for evil and war could not be destroyed but neither was it possible to destroy peace.
>
> Evil is hard to end and peace is hard to begin but the rainbow and the dove will always live within everyman's heart.[9]

In an interview connected with the movie, Aronofsky said that his childhood poem was about the evil that lives in our hearts and the choice we have about what we are going to do with it. Winning the contest made him realize he might just be good at writing.[10] The poem, one might say, set the young man's trajectory. He became an accomplished screenwriter and director, often continuing to explore this same theme.

The Filmmaker Darren Aronofsky

Whether his lifelong fascination with Noah can be seen as the major catalyst, Aronofsky's career as a filmmaker has certainly focused on characters like his movie's Noah, a point noted by film critic Peter Chattaway. The leading people in Aronofsky's movies are often those "who pursue perfection even to the point of self-destruction," who are "haunted, driven, and so obsessed with [their] task that [they are] prepared to die for it—and to let others die as well."[11] Chattaway, who likes Aronofsky as a filmmaker, labels him "an obsessive director of movies about obsessive people."[12]

---

9. Darren Aronofsky, "The Dove," quoted in "Here's the Poem that 13-Year-Old Darren Aronofsky Wrote about Noah," *Relevant Magazine* (April 1, 2014). Online: http://www.relevantmagazine.com/taxonomy/term/8325.

10. Cf., Darren Aronofsky, in Falsani, "The 'Terror' of *Noah*," 5.

11. Peter T. Chattaway, "First Impressions: *Noah* (dir. Darren Aronofsky, 2014)" (March 20, 2014) 3, 6. Online: http://www.patheos.com/blogs/filmchat/2014/03/first-impressions-noah-dir-darren-aronofsky-2014.html.

12. Peter T. Chattaway, "Of Course *Noah* Isn't 'Biblically Accurate', Nor Should it Be," (October 23, 2013) 1. Online: http://www.patheos.com/blogs/filmchat/2013/10/

Aronofsky's break out movie, *Pi*, is about a mathematician whom others believe possesses the number representing the name of God, and who ultimately cannot take the resultant strain of such perfection. *Requiem for a Dream* focuses on what addictions of all types can do to humans as they are driven by the desire for fulfillment. In *The Fountain*, Hugh Jackman discovers only at the end that "death is the road to awe." *The Wrestler* is about a man who makes devastating choices in his quest for physical perfection, while *Black Swan* is about an obsessive, tortured ballerina who dies at peace after one perfect dance. In most of Aronofsky's stories the main character is one who becomes obsessed with finding or preserving their understanding of innocence or perfection. The results are consistently tortuous.

It was after the success of *Black Swan* (a film that was produced for $13 million and that grossed $330 million in worldwide box office returns as well as garnering five Oscar nominations) that Aronofsky was able to name his next project. He chose his passion—bringing the story of Noah to the big screen, something he had already been working on for some time. Made for $125 million, *Noah* (2014) outperformed even *Black Swan*, garnering worldwide sales of over $359 million. Aronofsky said that, as he wrote the screenplay, he never tried to contradict anything in the Bible: "The film completely accepts the text, the four chapters in Genesis as truth—just like if I was to adapt any book. I'd try to be as truthful to the original material as possible." Of course the filmmaker also went on to say, if there are only four chapters and Noah does not even speak, yet we need to have a two-hour long movie, they also had "to dramatize the story."[13] So, like the paraphrases of the Noah story in children's Bibles, Aronofsky was compelled also to imagine their storyline.

It is important to recognize that as Aronofsky and his co-writer, Ari Handel, began to conceive of their movie they started with the biblical text and asked: "What are the themes and questions that the story's bringing forward that we should be grappling with?"[14] Seeking answers, they read and reread Genesis for more than a decade, looking for those keys which might unlock the story's meaning, while also trying to dramatize it in human terms. As they pondered over the text, they

of-course-noah-isnt-biblically-accurate-nor-should-it-be.html.

13. Aronofsky, quoted in *Rolling Stone* and referenced by Albert Mohler, "Drowning in Distortion—Darren Aronofsky's 'Noah'" (March 31, 2014) 2. Online: http://www.albertmohler.com/2014/03/31/drowning-in-distortion-darren-aronofskys-noah/. Old Testament scholar Walter Moberly writes of "a spare mode of narrating" as typical of Hebrew narrative. Walter Moberly, "On Interpreting the Mind of God: The Theological Significance of the Flood Narrative (Genesis 6–9)," in *The Word Leaps the Gap*, ed. J. Ross Wagner, C. Kavin Rowe, and A. Katherine Grieb (Grand Rapids: Eerdmans, 2008) 63.

14. Ari Handel, quoted in Chattaway, "Noah Interview Round-Up, Co-Writer Ari Handel," 2. Online: http://www.patheos.com/blogs/filmchat/2014/04/noah-interview-round-up-co-writer-ari-handel.html.

concluded that the story actually focused on a series of universal questions, questions basic to all humankind:

> The notion of whether we need to struggle to figure out what the right way to live is, is there goodness and wickedness in all of us, and what do we do about it, what is the right way to treat ourselves and others when they fall short of our ideals of what best behavior is, to treat them with judgment or mercy or some combination of both, what do we need to do to get a second chance and how do we use our second chances when we have them, how do we have hope when there's a lot to be hopeless about, those are universal questions.[15]

For Aronofsky and Handel, such questions suggested that the Bible's Noah story was a fundamental one, one that went deep not only into both our culture and the Judeo-Christian culture, but many other cultures as well. The questions for them transcended all boundaries, though they are rarely raised in most Noah retellings.

Noah, the Movie

Given Aronofsky's own love, yet fear, of the Noah story, and given his own fascination with people obsessed with perfection, it is not surprising that as he grappled with the biblical text, Aronofsky, together with co-writer Handel, found themselves writing a very different kind of biblical epic. In fact, when asked in an interview for *The New Yorker*, Aronofsky said, "Noah is the least biblical biblical film ever made."[16] By this, the filmmaker did not mean that his team had tried to be unbiblical, though that is how his statement was picked up and misquoted in the media. Many news reports and Christian reviewers, including megachurch pastor Rick Warren who had not seen the movie, thought Aronofsky said and meant, "Noah is the least biblical film ever made."[17] Rather, Aronofsky in his remark was trying to distance himself from the predictability of the typical "robe and sandal" biblical drama, from that kind of "biblical film." He wanted as a filmmaker the freedom to dramatize the story anew and to explore a different set of questions that the text more fundamentally suggested. What the filmmakers wanted was not so much a retelling of the story, but a reimagining, one that would invite a new dialogue and spur new questions. They

---

15. Ari Handel, quoted in Michael Dunaway, "On Noah and Faith: A Conversation with Ari Handel," *Paste Magazine*, March 28, 2014, 3. Online: http://www.pastemagazine.com/articles/2014/03/on-noah-and-faith-a-conversation-with-ari-handel.html.

16. Darren Aronofsky, quoted in Tad Friend, "Profile: Heavy Weather, 'Darren Aronofsky gets Biblical,'" *The New Yorker*, March 17, 2014, 46.

17. Emma Koonse, "Rick Warren Blasts 'Noah,'" Misquotes Film's director on twitter," *The Christian Post*, March 18, 2014. Online: www.christianpost.com/news/rick-warren-blasts-noah-misquotes-films-director-on-twitter-116319.

wanted to restore something of the sting of the original story after centuries of pious glosses.

In telling the biblical story of the flood Aronofsky thus filled in the narrative gaps found in the Genesis account, enlarging its context and expanding prior events, augmenting characters (e.g., Methuselah and Tubal-Cain) and inventing new ones to take the plot in new directions (cf., Ila and Naël). Lacking any information about what happened on the ark the filmmaker created a "family drama" in the middle of the story to go along with the "disaster movie" that began the story. Moreover, by altering the biblical ordering of events in the third and final act of the story the filmmakers sought to highlight their understanding of the central theme of the story.

Plot

The filmmakers gave the biblical story a typical narrative arc of three acts, following a brief but significant prologue that sets the story in its antediluvian context. In the prologue both God's perfect creation and the sin and violence that immediately follow are pictured in a series of fast-moving surrealistic and abstract images. The Noah story itself then begins with young Noah and his father, Lamech, in the wilderness. They are descendants of Seth, Adam's son. His father is talking to Noah about the Creator who put the earth under their care. Lamech is about to offer Noah his blessing, when a group of warriors led by Tubal-Cain, a descendent of Adam's son Cain, come upon them and kill Lamech. Having hidden behind some rocks, young Noah escapes with his life.

Fast forward and we next see Noah (Russell Crowe) and his wife Naameh (Jennifer Connelly) living a simple life far from the evils of civilization with their three sons. However, the violent city dwellers are encroaching. After a dream in which he sees creation being destroyed by a flood, Noah travels to his grandfather, Methuselah, a wise, old sage, to ask for advice as to what the dream means. Methuselah both confirms that the dream is from God and provokes a second similar dream. Through these visions Noah understands the Creator as "saying" to him that he is angry with humankind and thus will destroy the whole earth, but "righteous" Noah and his family will be saved with some animals so life can continue.

Meanwhile in Tubal-Cain's city violence and evil are everywhere present. Women are violated, food and water are fought over, and animals are slaughtered. Tubal-Cain believes that humans, those in the Creator's image, have the right to subdue and dominate creation, even as he bemoans the fact that, given Cain's banishment, God has been silent to him as one of Cain's descendants. At the same time, with the help of the Watchers, huge rock-bound fallen angels (cf. Gen 6:1– 4), Noah begins building the ark in which the Creator will rescue his family and every kind of animal. The magical realism of a forest that sprouts from a seed from the original Garden and which provides lumber for the ark and of the animals arriving by twos is both beautiful and filled with wonder. So the first act of this biblical epic ends, a "disaster/action movie" in full swing.

Act two brings with it the surprises we have already mentioned, as the focus shifts to a "family drama" that unfolds inside the ark while the flood takes place. As waters pour forth both from above and from below (cf. Gen 7:11), the family hears cries of desperation from outside the ark (something that the biblical text is silent about). But Noah remains resolute in his commitment to not alter God's judgment by extending mercy to sinful humanity. With Russell Crowe as Noah, viewers find themselves recalling Crowe's previous role as Javert in the movie *Les Miserable*, a ruthless policeman whose commitment to justice and judgment ends up turning him into a brittle and isolated caricature of a man, one whose single-minded obsession for justice leads ultimately to his destruction. Here as well is the paradigm that *Noah* follows. In his single-minded obsession to implement God's justice, Noah turns into a "would-be murderer."

Having seen an image of himself, a doppelgänger, while visiting the violent and sinful humanity of the city, Noah realizes that both he and his family also are sinners; they are no better than the rest of humanity. This leads Noah to decide that God's judgment must not stop with those outside the boat. It must also include his own family. Humanity must no longer have the possibility of progeny, or evil will continue to escalate. In an act that mirrors the story of Abraham's "sacrifice" of Isaac (cf. Gen 22), Noah believes himself to have been asked by God to kill his two baby granddaughters, and with them the possibility of his family being "fruitful and multiplying." From an initial sense of hopefulness for a new world and his family's role in it, Noah comes to believe things are hopeless for humanity. He becomes a misanthrope. Even after Noah's wife, Naameh, and the babies' mother, Ila, plead with him to have mercy and to value life, Noah remains adamant. But when Noah looks at the babies with knife in hand, he finds himself unable to kill these beautiful children. The zealot who is single-mindedly committed to justice finds love and mercy in his heart as the rain ends and the waters slowly subside. But what of the requirements of God's purity and judgment, and the "original sin" that Noah recognizes as also inherent in his family? Noah is tormented.

If in the first act Noah is *saint-like* and in the second an *obsessive* would-be murderer, in the third we find Noah *depressed* and despondent given both his failure to execute what he believes to be God's will and his strong sense of "survivor's guilt," realizing he also is deserving of judgment. After the ark lands, the animals leave, and vineyards are planted. Then we see Noah so drunk on wine that he passes out while naked. After his son Ham finds him in this compromised state, the other brothers come and as the biblical text says, cover their father while not looking at him (cf. Gen 9:23). Eventually, however, with the help of Ila, Shem's wife, Noah overcomes his exile from the family and joins them again. As the movie ends, Noah is wrapping his forearm with the snakeskin relic from Eden (the same relic film viewers saw as the movie opened) and offering a divine blessing over his grandchildren, as a rainbow appears in the sky signaling God's benediction over his creation.

Tone

Such is the plot, one rooted in the biblical text, but also one that fills in its silences. Equally important, however, for an understanding of the movie is the story's point of view or tone. As a filmmaker, Aronofsky is known for his ability to convey meaning through the images and sounds he projects. In *Requiem for a Dream*, for example, this was done through an overpowering number of quick cuts, cuts that caused viewers to almost lose their equilibrium. In *Noah* the movie's tone is again developed not primarily through text, but largely through sight and sound. Particularly important in this regard is Aronofsky's decisions to make Noah's antediluvian world fantastical and to make the story of Noah dark and sobering.

Fantastical

Some viewers have expressed their dissatisfaction with the filmic world of *Noah*. They think it does not always seem believable, but for the filmmakers this is to be expected. The antediluvian world in the opening chapters of Genesis is "otherworldly." It is not like our world and thus should not be pictured as such. Handel comments:

> No rainbows had ever been in the sky, so the physics of the sky and light may have been somehow different [Gen 9:13]. We've got people living a thousand years [Gen 5:27]. We've got fallen beings walking the planet [Gen 6:4], and flaming swords [Gen 3:24], and Leviathans in the water [Gen 1:21]. We really wanted audiences to feel that, and not think that this is a story that takes place in the hills of ancient Judea, in a desert, with someone with sandals and a robe.[18]

Rather than create a familiar world with a white-bearded grandfather caring for a menagerie of animals on a cheerful boat, the filmmakers wanted to have viewers

---

18. Ari Handel, quoted in Dunaway, "On Noah and Faith," 2.

see and hear this story for what it is. They wanted to bring to life the idea that "this was a different world. In some ways, a more primal and mythical world."[19]

We have already spoken of the magical realism of a forest that springs to life from a seed from Eden and of animals that appear suddenly and wondrously from distant realms. But perhaps most representative of the filmmakers' willingness to stretch their viewers' sense of credulity is how the filmmakers imagine the Watchers, or *Nephilim* (Gen 6:4), those giants who in the film help Noah build the ark and protect his family from violence. These creatures have fascinated readers for centuries. Perhaps the most common interpretation of these otherworldly creatures has been to see them as angelic and human hybrids who have no analogy in our world. If so, reasoned the filmmakers, then by definition they must be fantastically rendered. The filmmakers' solution is to make them rock giants, giant lumbering fallen angels encased in rock similar to Peter Jackson's imagining of Tolkien's ents. These Watchers not only add to the otherness of the preflood period, they also help the filmmakers solve problems in the narrative arc. How can Noah and his three sons build such a large ark without help? The *Nephilim* provide an answer. How can Noah and the ark be protected from the violent townspeople who try to save themselves by getting on board the ark when the waters begin to come? The Watchers do the task.

In the Genesis account the *Nephilim* are said to have children with women. Interpreters have struggled as to what this could mean. Handel and Aronofsky choose to take this description metaphorically rather than literally and to see the fallen angels as choosing to love and serve humankind rather than hurt them. In the movie we are introduced to these lumbering giants early in the story when Noah and his family must go through the Watchers' territory on the way to find Noah's grandfather, Methuselah. One of the Watchers tells his son that these creatures were angels of light who were punished by God by being given bodies of earth and rock after disobeying the Creator by helping Adam to live outside the garden. Moreover, humankind, after being helped by the Watchers, turned against them violently and most were killed. Only Methuselah continued to help them.

---

19. Ibid. Old Testament scholar Walter Moberly writes in a similar vein of the Noah narrative not being interested in the "historical": "The narrator reports the inner thoughts and words of YHWH but says nothing about Noah's thoughts or words. . . . Practicalities such as, which animals? what of the living conditions? what sort of food, how much, and how [to] preserve it as edible? . . . are entirely ignored. . . . Humans and animals appear to live in darkness within the ark . . . there is the freshly plucked olive leaf, which shows the waters have subsided. Within the general storyline this makes perfect sense, and is memorable and moving. But the narrator appears to assume that when the waters go down, growing things reappear in the same condition they were in before the waters came; the 'realistic' question as to the likely state of an olive tree and its foliage after a year under the sea cannot be sustained." Moberly, "On Interpreting the Mind of God," 47.

Here is the back story for the Watchers who end up helping Noah by building the ark and protecting him from harm. Although the book of Enoch saw these fallen angels and their giant offspring as the source of much evil and to be judged accordingly, Aronofsky and Handel chose to make them allies of righteous Noah against evil humanity and, as such, ultimately redeemable. When the forces of Tubal-Cain kill the bodies of some of these rock giants who are defending the ark and Noah's family, it is wondrous to see their inner light ascend to heaven even as the rocks fall in a pile. For helping the righteous they are granted a second chance by God. As with humankind, these giants not only experience judgment but grace. Is this biblically correct? One has no idea, but it is as plausible as other conjectures, given the strangeness of the text, and it is consistent with God's character as portrayed biblically.

Dark and Sobering

Secondly, taking his cue from the biblical text where the land is said to be filled with violence and Noah is said to have been both drunk and naked even after the ark again rested on dry land, Aronofsky imagines Noah as a complicated and driven character who is asked to respond to a bleak world filled with violence and darkness. Supporting this choice was Aronofsky's poll of artist friends whom he asked "to return to Genesis and create something in his or her own medium." Aronofsky comments:

> The response was overwhelming. It was interesting that most of them turned their backs on the comedic, folk-tale rendition of Noah and found the darkness in the story. I guess that is because, after all, it is the first apocalypse story. Even though it is a story of hope, family, and second chances, it is also a story filled with great destruction and misery. For every pair that survived, there were countless other creatures on the planet that drowned during the deluge, "innocent" and "wicked" alike.[20]

Atmosphere

Reinforcing the movie's tone is the larger "atmosphere" of the story—the unalterable backdrop of a perfect creation having been betrayed by violence and sin. Here the prelude to the movie which emphasizes humankind's temptation and sin, as well as Noah's subsequent retelling of the fuller story of creation and fall, sets the

---

20. Frederic and Mary Ann Brussat, "Film Review: Noah, directed by Darren Aronofsky," *Spirituality & Practice*, 2. Online: http://www.spiritualityandpractice.com/films/films.php?id=26175.

parameters around which the events of Noah's story unfold. Noah and his family seek to preserve what is left of that perfect creation, and when the waters of chaos come a second time, to usher in its return. In these two "retellings" of creation and fall, as well as in brief flashbacks that Noah has in his dreams, we see in a telescoped manner surrealistic and impressionistic images of both the givenness of a perfect creation and of the indelible effects of sin and violence.

In the shortened opening montage only the escalation of sin and violence is shown leading up to the story's initial scene where Noah as a boy is told by his father, who is about to offer him a divine blessing, that the Creator has given him the responsibility to defend and protect creation. Yet Noah's "blessing" is cut short by yet more violence as townspeople murder his father. In the longer retelling, a story that Noah's father told him and Noah in turn tells his family, we see on the screen the six days of creation, Adam and Eve as children of light, and the snake shedding its skin as it becomes the tempter. Pictured as well is the forbidden fruit, Cain's killing of Abel in silhouette, the Watchers, and the escalation of civilization's violence. Here is the world within which Noah finds himself.[21] It is all he knows of God's judgment and grace, for creation is still recent.

Particularly effective in demarcating the "givens" of this story, and thus of reinforcing God's intention for his world, is the repeated image of a snakeskin that is wrapped around one's forearm.[22] It is first seen on Noah's father Lamech as he attempts to offer a patriarchal blessing over his son, before it is then taken by Tubal-Cain and later recaptured by Ham. Finally, in an *inclusio* that forms the last sequence of the film, Noah, having accepted not only God's justice but also his mercy, takes the skin that Ham has returned to him and wraps it around his forearm so that he might offer a divine blessing over his children and grandchildren as a rainbow appears. In the movie the skin is said to be a "relic," something to remind all that the Creator made animal and humankind (*ādām*) alike and called it "good"/"very good." As Lamech tells Noah while wearing the snakeskin, "May you walk alongside the Creator in righteousness." Here is an allusion to Gen 2. The skin functions, that is, as a symbol of Eden, where Adam and Eve first walked alongside their God.

---

21. For a similar approach, see Jack Miles (*God: A Biography* [New York: Vintage, 1996]) who interprets God in the Bible only according to the knowledge of God presented in the preceding pages. That is, the knowledge that Noah had of God is limited to the introductory chapters of Genesis. All else is yet to be discovered.

22. The analogy is to the phylacteries that Jewish believers wrap around their arms to this day, but rather than being a reminder of the Torah command ["You shall teach them to your children . . . you shall bind them as a sign upon your hand" (Deut 6:8)], the wrapped snakeskin is a reminder of the innocence and goodness of Eden.

Although the imagery and its symbolism seems clear in the film, the snakeskin has caused some commentators to conclude wrongly that the filmmakers were consciously being unbiblical, since in the Bible the serpent image is more often associated with evil.[23] What has been missed by these critics is one of the opening images in the movie where a snake is seen shedding its light skin and emerging as a darker, more foreboding presence. If God's creation was originally perfect, then snakes and their skins were originally good; that is, there was a time when the tempter had not yet entered the snake. This is what is being symbolized. Moreover, Jewish tradition, in wondering how it was possible after the fall for God to fashion skins into clothes for Adam and Eve if there was as yet no killing, sometimes turned to the fact that snakes shed their skins and thus no killing would be necessary in order for skins to become divinely used for clothes. Thus, what Aronofsky used as a "relic" to remind Noah and his family of God's presence with us and his grace in our lives was a snakeskin from Eden, presumably a remnant of that "perfect" snakeskin that God used to clothe Noah's forbearers.

Character

Noah's dark tone and antediluvian context shape much of the movie's meaning, as does its rootedness in Gen 1–5, but ultimately it is not these that carry the central power and meaning of the story. Rather, it is the character of Noah himself (and thus, the movie's title). As the movie portrays him, Noah is a righteous man who becomes a zealot, taking God's plan into his own hands in an act of hubris and forgetting that God's revelation of his righteousness to Noah has included both God's justice and mercy. Noah becomes obsessive in his commitment to God's judgment of sin, someone psychologically in tune with the heroes of Aronofsky's earlier movies, *Pi, The Wrestler,* and *Black Swan.* Noah becomes a tortured soul who believes the human race must end in order that God's creation not be destroyed again by sin. He chooses not to help the young Cain-ite woman, Na'el, whom Ham chooses for a wife, when she becomes caught in an animal trap, even though it means her certain death, and he even plans to kill his own grandchildren in order to be obedient to God's desire for justice. Ending up in the third act a lonely misanthrope even after being unable to kill the babies, someone who simply drops out of the world, Noah is only brought back to a life of faith by God's continuing grace as mediated through his family who continues to love and care for him.

---

23. Cf., Brian Godawa, "The Subversion of the Serpent in Aronofsky's Noah," (April 4, 2014). Online: http://www.godawa.com/movieblog/tag/noah-movie; Brian Mattson, "Sympathy for the Devil," (April 2, 2014). Online: http://www.drbrianmattson.com/?offset=1396360800000.

In reimagining this human side of the Noah saga, Aronofsky forces us, in the words of Rabbi Marc Gellman, "to abandon what scholar Herman Gunkel called 'the sacred inattention with which we read the Bible.'"[24] His retelling of the character of Noah raises questions that are rarely asked. Can one obey "God" too much? Could threatening to kill one's own kin so as to extinguish the human race ever be thinkable? (One has only to think of Abraham and his sacrifice of Isaac.) Why did not Noah argue with God about saving more people as Abraham and Moses did? (This is a question found in multiple Jewish commentaries on Noah.) Aronofsky paints a stark portrait of what we are capable when we believe God is telling us to do something. Surely the recent worldwide "fundamentalist" turn has added verisimilitude to his imagining.

The original vision that Noah had in the first act involves both death and life, judgment and mercy. It is a vision centered in water that renews, even as it destroys. The discussion that Noah has with Methuselah is particularly revealing. Having traveled through the territory of the Watchers (the lumbering rock-people) to find Methuselah, Noah tells him of his apocalyptic vision/dream. Methuselah responds saying he knows what Noah saw, because Methuselah's own father, Enoch, had warned him that, if humankind continued down its destructive path, the Creator would annihilate them. Such a vision from the Creator had involved for Enoch the fiery destruction of humankind for its wickedness, but Noah corrects him, saying he saw water—"death by water and new life." After Methuselah gives Noah a drink of herbs that causes Noah to have a second similar vision—one of creation, of the snake, and of animals swimming to the surface of a large ocean and boarding what looks like a wooden vessel—there is a continuation of the conversation about water and fire, with Noah telling his grandfather that while fire consumes all, water cleanses.[25] It separates the good from the bad. The visitation ends with Methuselah "blessing" Noah by giving him a seed from the original Garden from which will come the lumber for the ark. This man of God tells Noah to trust his dream as being from the Creator. "You must trust that he speaks in a way that you can understand. Remember Noah, he chose you for a reason."

On his way home, as Noah and his son again pass through the Watchers' territory, Noah sees unthinkable violence, but also the beauty of a flower that blooms magically from a barren landscape. Here the filmmaker gives viewers reinforcement of the divine message to Noah, this time in an image. There will be judgment, but

24. Marc Gellman, quoted in Peter T. Chattaway, "The Jewish Roots of—and Responses to—Noah," (March 31, 2014) 10. Online: http://www.patheos.com/blogs/filmchat/2014/03/the-jewish-roots-of-and-responses-to-noah.html. The original interview was published online: http://www.chicagotribune.com/features/sns-201404011700-tms-godsqudctngs-a20140403-20140403,0,2157523.story.

25. Cf. Isa 43:1–3.

also new life that will miraculously bloom from the void. Arriving home and telling his wife Naameh of his second vision, she inquires, "Did he speak to you?" Noah responds, "I think so."

By the end of the first act, however, Noah's humility has turned into an iron will, even as he fails to hold onto the tension of judgment and grace inherent in his memory and experience. However clear the initial divine visions, or significant their reinforcement from Methuselah, or powerful the symbol of the flower in the void, the focus of Noah's two-fold, divine charter becomes singular as the ark is being built. "Righteousness" is reduced to "judgment for sin." When Noah ventures out into the Cain-ites' cities where violence and evil are everywhere present, his commitment to carry out God's judgment clouds his memory of the concomitant mercy and blessing that God promises through his own family. Seeing his doppelgänger also living in the city and participating in the barbaric and violent ways of his neighbors, Noah realizes that he and his family are also sinners, are also deserving of God's judgment. Convinced that Adam and Eve's "original sin" has tainted all humanity irredeemably, he projects that God wants humanity to die out. There will be no more children.

Driven by an overdeveloped sense of justice that is no longer tempered by mercy, a struggling and flawed Noah becomes more angry and violent as the story progresses. Yet God is not through with Noah. Noah announces his terminal plans for his family only for the unexpected to happen. Having also gone for help to Methuselah, one still in touch with the Creator, Naameh reveals that the Creator through the old sage has miraculously helped Shem's wife Ila to be able to conceive, and she is now pregnant. Beside himself with rage, Noah tells his family that he hopes the baby is not a little girl or he will have to kill it. As the women and Shem plead with Noah, viewers sense Noah's struggle, but he remains adamant. Noah's sense of righteousness has diminished from the Creator's balance of judgment and mercy to a steely-eyed condemnation of humanity's violence toward creation and creature. Again, to quote Rabbi Gellman, Noah "understands the flood but not the ark."[26]

We have already spoken of Noah's character in the third act, where reduced to a misanthrope, Noah flees life and all that is beautiful. However, the beauty of his new family, the "flower" amidst his void, ultimately proves his salvation. Not only is there sin, violence, and the degradation of creation, but God has given his family new life through Ila and her twin girls. It does not happen immediately, but in time Noah joins his family in tending their new garden as a rainbow fills the sky offering a divine benediction.

---

26. Gellman, quoted in Chattaway, "The Jewish Roots of—and Responses to—Noah," 11.

The Movie's Sources

From the earliest days of Christianity, Noah has almost always been portrayed as a saint amongst sinners, someone who remains righteous in the midst of a wicked society (Heb 11:7). This was the summons addressed to early Christians in pagan Rome, but the Jewish tradition has treated Noah somewhat differently. Early rabbis wondered about Noah, for he seemed to lack human concern. How could he not object to what amounted to genocide? One rabbi has God saying to Noah, for example, "I lingered with you . . . so that you would ask for mercy for the world!"[27] Unlike Abraham and Moses, Noah seems simply to have accepted God's judgment. As one scholar puts it, for the Jew "righteousness is all about what you do for your fellow man. And Noah does NOTHING for his fellow man. . . . He executes God's commandment to the letter."[28] Among most Jewish commentators, Noah is found wanting for he failed to protect human life. The name "Israel" after all, means "he who wrestles with God." Noah lacked this spiritual audacity. Aronofsky, himself a Jew, grew up understanding Noah in this way. He and his writing partner, Ari Handel, took from this Jewish tradition the need to ask questions of Noah, and the movie we have described above develops this more complex interpretation of his character.

The movie also deals with the Jewish tradition in more fundamental ways. The movie adopts both as its methodology and its style the Jewish exegetical tradition of midrash of which its questioning of the character of Noah is but one example.[29] Discussing their use of this midrashic tradition, Handel commented in an interview:

> The exact meaning of "midrash" is complicated, but it basically is commentary. In the Jewish tradition, you look at a text in the Bible, and there are clues there, subtle details that raise questions. And they're there for a reason, the thinking goes. They're there to make you ask those questions. They're there for more stories to tell, and to invent, and to imagine, that would shed light on those questions. And these midrash interpretations aren't meant to be absolutely, exactly what happened. They're meant to be hypothetical, what may

27. *Zohar Hadash Noah, 29a*, quoted by Rabbi Michael Leo Samuel who is quoted by Chattaway, "The Jewish Roots of—and Responses to—Noah," 13. Rabbi Samuel's original article was published in the *San Diego Jewish World*, April 4, 2014. Online: http://www.sdjewishworld.com/2014/04/04/noah-departs-many-ways-biblical-narrative/.

28. Shmuley Boteach, "Hollywood 'Noah' is Kosher, Says Celebrity Rabbi," March 27, 2014, quoted in Chattaway, "The Jewish Roots of—and Responses to—Noah," 6. Rabbi Boteach's original article was published in the *Times of Israel*. Online: http://www.timesofisrael.com/hollywood-noah-is-kosher-says-celebrity-rabbi/.

29. Walter Moberly writes that the spare mode of Hebraic narration affords commentators "many opportunities for the interpretative imagination to expatiate about that on which the text is silent—opportunities of which classic midrash made the most." Moberly, "On Interpreting the Mind of God," 63.

have happened, to illuminate an aspect of the story, and those take place in dialogue with other midrash and other commentaries. It all takes place within the grounding of not contradicting the text in any way, but within that context it's looking for other interpretations and trying to understand things more deeply.[30]

Along the same lines Aronofsky and Handel are quoted by Jack Jenkins as responding to another interviewer by saying that they pulled heavily from Jewish rabbinic midrash. As Jenkins explains, "Rabbis essentially add stories to the biblical/tanakhical narrative for educative effect. These stories aren't meant to be given the same authority as Scripture, but are instead designed to both resolve problems of interpretation as well as expose aspects of the holy narrative that would be otherwise difficult to grasp."[31]

This long-standing tradition, in the words of Jewish scholar Jacob Nuesner, "did not write *about* Scripture, they wrote *with* Scripture."[32] Midrash suggested one way the story might have happened.

These midrashim on the biblical account of Noah include sections of the pseudepigraphal books of *1 Enoch* and *Jubilees*, both which have extended depictions about the "sons of God," now called the "watchers," and their involvement with the flood (cf. *1 En* 6:1– 2, 7:1– 8:3, 10:4,11– 12, 19:1; *Jub* 4:22, 5:10). There also are a large number of commentaries by rabbis over a six-hundred-year period which wrestle with the enigmas of these antediluvian texts. In these Jewish commentaries we find, for example, discussions of the snakeskin's use as clothing, the suggestion that the ark was a place of enforced chastity, discussions of how it was possible to build the ark, how Noah was mocked by others, how Noah heard God speak through a series of nightmares—think of Jacob hearing God speak in a dream, or Abimelech, or the dreams of the two prisoners where Joseph was confined, how the clothes God gave to Adam were stolen and ultimately handed down to Noah, how the luminous mineral zohar provided light on the ark, how Tubal-Cain was a villain, and how Noah was only righteous "in this generation." Aronofsky also extended the midrashic tradition with such other suggestions as Noah suffered from "survivor's guilt" and that Tubal-Cain killed Noah's father, Lamech. In this way Aronofsky's movie is in itself an example of contemporary midrash.[33]

30. Ari Handel, quoted in Dunaway, "On Noah and Faith," 1–2.

31. Jack Jenkins, "Sorry Conservative Christians, You Don't Get a Monopoly on Noah," (April 2, 2014), quoted in Chattaway, "The Jewish Roots of—and Responses to—Noah," 7. Jenkins' original article was published in *Think Progress*. Online: http://www.thinkprogress.org/culture/2014/04/02/3422173/conservative-christians-noah/.

32. Jacob Nuesner, *Midrash: An Introduction* (New York: Aronson, 1994) x.

33. For an overview of Aronofsky's movie as Midrash, see Chattaway, "The Jewish Roots of—and

As with others writing midrash, the movie's storytellers felt no need to be overly literal in their depiction. Their goal was to remain true to the core meaning of the text while exploring its questions, corners, and edges. As one might expect, this has caused some Christian critics, particularly those committed to a largely historical approach to the text, to have multiple questions: Why in the movie does the ark land on the beach and not on a mountain? How could Tubal-Cain stow away on the ark? Why are the second and fourth days of creation conflated in Noah's recounting? Why does Methuselah constantly crave berries? (Perhaps as someone still linked through Enoch to creation, he loved the plants given to him?) What was the strange birthright ritual with the snakeskin? Was the movie's Naameh meant to be Tubal-Cain's sister (Gen 4:22)? Why the inclusion of Ila's barrenness or the invention of Na'el? Should not there have been three wives of Noah's sons boarding the ark, not just one? Is Naameh's rejoicing that Ila's twin daughters was a sign that God had also provided wives for Ham and Japheth a sufficient explanation? But such questions or their answers are not the filmmakers' concern. They envisioned their task not as a photographic reproduction of the text, but a midrashic, thick depiction of it.

Rather than being a liability, the filmmakers' choice of both mining the midrashic tradition of Noah and extending it through their own reimaginings is largely responsible for the strength of the movie's storytelling. Given the fact that millions of the movie's viewers grew up knowing only its sanitized, Sunday school version, that is, having only an "arky, arky" in their imaginations, the movie, as Alissa Wilkinson comments, forced viewers "to 're-see' [the] story anew, to once again sit on the edge of our seats and wonder what will happen next. That's hard to do with such a familiar story, and this is done well, while still respecting and hewing to its source material, as well as it can."[34]

The Movie's Theme: What Does "Righteousness" Mean

Noah, the movie, treats sin with the seriousness that it deserves. The second sentence of the film states, "Temptation led to sin." Immediately we see on the screen the forbidden fruit being eaten, then the first murder by Cain, and then Lamech being killed. Throughout the movie there are flashbacks to Cain's murder of Abel, to continued violence, and to the degradation of creature, humankind, and creation. Sin is ubiquitous, even in Noah and his family. In a scene that reflects what Aronofsky himself describes as humankind's "original sin," Noah goes into the city to find wives

Responses to—Noah."

34. Alissa Wilkinson, "Noah," *Christianity Today*, March 27, 2014, 3. Online: http://www.christianity today.com/ct/channel/utilities/print.html?type=article&id=117572.

for his sons only to be immersed in its darkness and pervasive sin.[35] But rather than simply reject his neighbors as sinners, Noah comes to realize, as he sees his doppelgänger also residing in the city, that he too is filled with the same corruption, that he too and his family are sinful.

Returning to the ark, Noah tells Naameh that there will be no wives for his other two sons because the people of the city are evil. Then he surprisingly adds additional reasons his sons should remain unmarried—because his three sons themselves are also sinful, because even Naameh is sinful, and Noah finishes by declaring his own sinfulness. This totalization of humanity's sin causes Noah to wonder, thus, if any should escape judgment, even his own family. Would not his family and their descendants only sully the new world? So without God's direction, and contrary to God's earlier revelation in Noah's water-filled dream, Noah decides that his family should die out, that they should be the last generation.

Though sin is universal in Aronofsky's rendering of *Noah*, it would be wrong to conclude that this is the movie's theme, the perspective from which the movie's story is told. Sin is only the background. Rather, the movie *Noah* has for its subject matter how a righteous God and his righteous follower Noah will respond to the violence and sin they encounter. The movie has as its central question what "righteous" means, given the ubiquity of sin.

Aronofsky states that he found it significant in the biblical text that God not only "was sorry that he had made humankind on the earth" and wanted to "blot out" human beings, but that "it grieved him in his heart" (Gen 6:6–7). In other words, there was in the character of God, in his righteousness, both justice and mercy. "The pain of that (the decision to blot out most of humankind), the struggle of that, must have been immense. To basically go from creating this beautiful thing to watching it fall apart, and then doing this horrible thing where you have to try and start again."[36] So the filmmakers took this large cosmic idea, the proper balance of justice and mercy, and structured their film around it.[37]

Here is the key question of *Noah* according to Aronofsky:

35. Cf. Gordon Wenham, "Original Sin in Genesis 1–11," *Churchman* 104 (1990) 324. Wenham labels Gen 6:5 as one of most "devastating analyses of the human condition in Scripture."

36. Darren Aronofsky, quoted in Sarah Pulliam Bailey, "Q&A: 'Noah' director Darren Aronofsky on justice vs. mercy," Religious News Service (March 24, 2014). Online: http://www.religionnews.com/2014/03/24/interview-director-darren-aronofsky-on-justice-vs-mercy-in-noah/.

37. Cf. Gerhard von Rad, *Genesis: A Commentary* (rev. ed.; Philadelphia: Westminster, 1973) 153: "We see, therefore (already in the primeval history), that each time, in and after the judgment, God's preserving, forgiving will to save is revealed. . . What is described, therefore, is a story of God with man, the story of a continuously new punishment and at the same time gracious preservation, the story, to be sure, of a way that is distinguished by progressive divine judgment, but that, nevertheless, man could never have traveled without continued divine preservation." Cf. also Carol Kaminski, *Was Noah Good? Finding Favour in the Flood Narrative* (New York: Bloomsbury, 2014) 6–23.

What does it mean for a creator, a patriarch, to consider destroying something that he made and loved? What does it mean to be in that position, where your heart is grieved by the situation but you still feel that it's necessary? That's really where the Noah story starts, is God thinking of destroying something he loves? (And how) can we relate to that on a human level?[38]

Aronofsky found in God's complex righteousness—both God's justice and mercy—a paradigm for his main character, Noah, as well. He comments:

We wanted to get that grief, that struggle, and stick it into Noah, so we can understand as people what it must have felt like. What would hurt more than to do—in vague terms—what Noah is about to do? Which for us was an exact metaphor for what the decision was, what the Creator went through. But he chose love! He chose mercy, which for us is the exact same story as the story in the Bible, just put into human terms.[39]

In response to questions from Cathleen Falsani published in *The Atlantic*, Aronofsky spoke about the movie's theme, Noah's (and God's) righteousness:

Even if you subscribe to the idea that Noah is all good (which he's not, he's just righteous—which doesn't mean good in theological terms, it means a balance of justice and mercy), why go through this act of destruction if the next story is Babel, which is about how man's hubris once again needs to be smited?

So why go through this? What is the reason for it? To me, that's what's powerful about it. It's meant as a lesson. It's poetry that paints images about the second chance we've been given, that even though we have original sin and even though God's acts are justified, he found mercy. There is punishment for what you do, but we have just kind of inherited this second chance. What are we going to do with it?[40]

This is the film's question that Noah himself must answer.

When Noah's wife, Naameh, goes to Methuselah for counsel and help, she asks about the apocalyptic vision Noah had, and why there is little mercy in Noah's response. Methuselah responds in two ways. First, he counsels, "The vision came to

---

38. Darren Aronofsky, quoted in Dunaway, "On Noah and Faith," 3. Cf. von Rad, *Genesis*, 122: "The Yahwistic story of the Flood is planned very skillfully. It began with the narrator's letting us share in the reflection about God's grieving heart and letting us learn directly from God's mouth the resolve of judgment. At the end of the narrative the Yahwist again takes us up into the immediacy of the thoughts in God's heart. And as in the prologue, so here we are faced with the Yahwist's very own words."

39. Darren Aronofsky, quoted in Bailey, "Q&A: 'Noah' Director Darren Aronofsky on Justice vs. Mercy."

40. Darren Aronofsky, quoted in Falsani, "The Terror of 'Noah'," 2. Cf. Gerhard von Rad, *Genesis*, 124: "The biblical story of the Flood has been made a witness to the judgment and grace of [the] living God."

Noah. The choice is his."[41] But he also signals to Naameh the centrality of grace, responding to Naameh's pain over Ila being barren by healing the young woman's infertility. As the person most identifiable as someone who walks with God, Methuselah gives Naameh, but also we as viewers, the clear message—to walk with God is to be concerned not only with God's justice, but also to experience divine mercy and grace.

In interviews the filmmakers again and again describe their movie's theme. When, for example, the website HollywoodJesus.com asks Handel what "righteousness" is in the context of the story, he repeats, "Righteousness is the correct balance of justice and mercy."[42] This is the painful lesson Noah struggles to learn. When Naameh and Ila plead with Noah to have mercy on their babies, they never question that God has spoken to Noah or that he is to be an expression of God's justice. Instead, they recognize there must be more to righteousness than simply a heightened sense of right and wrong. There must also be love. Such paradoxical thinking is tragically foreign to Noah as it is to many of the film's viewers; love and justice seem mutually exclusive. Thus, when Noah looks at his granddaughters with knife in hand and the clear intent to kill them so as to be obedient to God's just command, and yet cannot do it, for all he saw was "love," Noah believes himself to be a failure. He believes he has failed to act righteously. His depression and drunkenness naturally follow. It is only through the continued love and respect of his family and God's continuing, gracious favor that Noah can finally reconcile his actions with his God-given vocation. Though at the beginning of the movie, Noah believes God has called him to be an agent of justice, by the end he finds both through his family's love and the divinely given rainbow that "justice" must also encompass "mercy." Both are part of God's understanding of righteousness.

The Movie's Effect

When drawing illustrations for a book, one has two choices. The artist can simply try to replicate what is described on the printed page—think of the simple line drawings in the 1970 edition by MacMillan of C. S. Lewis's Narnia series, or any number of other children's stories, or one can attempt a conversation with the original text that was its inspiration, even while drawing something that has its independent life and

41. This comment is reinforced as the story comes to its climax. Ila says to Noah as he is about to kill her twin babies, "The choice was put into your hands because he wanted you to decide if man was worth saving."

42. Ari Handel, quoted in Chattaway, "Noah Interview Round-Up: Handel," 3. The original interview by Jacob Sahms was published by HollywoodJesus.com. Online: http://www.live.hollywoodjesus.com/?p=12329.

significance—think of Leonard Baskin's massive pen and ink drawings that accompany Richard Latimore's translation of *The Iliad of Homer* in 1962.[43] The illustrations for the former seem banal when removed from the context of the original text and add little if anything to it. The drawings of the latter, on the other hand, can stand on their own terms, even as they invite careful scrutiny and open out for dialogue when set alongside the original story.

Aronofsky's *Noah* is a clear example of the second illustrative approach, even if the movie studio tried in its publicity to suggest the movie was faithfully adhering to the first. In their press release prior to the movie's release, Paramount Studios labeled the film "a close adaptation of the Biblical story" hoping to cash in on the lucrative market that Mel Gibson's *The Passion of the Christ* had uncovered. They even created a trailer that was shown at numerous Christian conferences that emphasized Noah's heroic, solitary stand against evil, not hinting at anything of his dark complicated character.[44] To seal their sell the studio set the second half of this trailer to a worship song by the Christian musician, Kim Walker-Smith, a song that had no relationship to the movie. In short, the studio in its attempt to garner a profit failed to trust the movie it had produced to capture the imagination and respect of its audience. It tried, instead, though they would of course argue with my language, to suggest that the movie *Noah* was merely another banal, illustrative movie that sought to reproduce the words of the Bible. They failed to understand that the film might function both to invite conversation with the original text and to have its own independent power and meaning.

Better, surely, for the trailer would have been Patti Smith's haunting lullaby, "Mercy Is," a song she wrote for the movie for Noah's father to sing to him as a boy, and for Noah to later sing to his children:

> Mercy is as mercy does, wandering the wild. The stars are eyes watching you, a breath upon a cloud. Two white doves, two white wings, to carry you away, to a land in memory, a land in memory. The sky is high, the earth is green, and cool below your feet. So swiftly now, beneath the bough, your father waits for thee, to wrap you in his healing arms, as the night sky weeps. Two white doves, two white wings, to carry you away, for mercy is a healing wind that whispers as you sleep, that whispers you to sleep.

Here is the heart and soul of the story: a heavenly father waiting for Noah, waiting to wrap him in his healing arms, even as the night sky weeps. Here as well is

43. Cf. C. S. Lewis, *The Lion, the Witch, and the Wardrobe* (New York: Macmillan, 1950) and *The Iliad of Homer*, trans. Richard Lattimore, illus. Leonard Baskin (Chicago: University of Chicago Press, 1962).

44. See Onine: http://www.patheos.com/blogs/filmchat/2013/07/church-groups-get-their-first-glimpse-of-noah.html.

what Noah is called to do in response to God's righteousness, something his father had provided him, and now something his own children and grandchildren need from him. The movie asks the question how will Noah respond to God's initiative of righteousness which includes both justice and mercy?

Though the studio failed to understand what they themselves had created (or better, though the studio failed to understand what their filmmaker had created), audiences immediately understood what kind of movie *Noah* was. Not only did the movie gross over $350 million dollars in ticket sales, it caused viewers to open up their Bibles and to put what they had seen and experienced into conversation with the Genesis text. Had the movie been faithful to the biblical text? *Noah* sparked a massive spike in Bible reading, something few could have predicted. This was the moviegoers' response to Aronofsky's portrayal of Noah's response to God's divine initiative given in a sinful world.

Using statistics available now that the biblical text is increasingly accessed on line, You Version reported on Twitter that on the weekend that *Noah* opened, people opening their Bibles to Gen 6 increased by 300 percent in the United States and by 245 percent globally. Bible Gateway saw a 223 percent increase over the previous weekend when the movie was released, and Google also noted the increase. Similarly, You Version reported that on the opening weekend of *Noah,* almost 400,000 people read or listened to the Noah story on their app, the highest number of people exploring that passage that they had ever experienced. Commenting on this massive spike in interest in reading the Noah story in the Bible, Patton Dodd, the editor of the site On Faith, said "Movies like *Noah* are an invitation into stories like Noah. Whatever else the film does . . . it makes you wonder what the story of Noah is about, why it holds so much power, and what it might have to say to us today."[45] Rather than simply repeat what the story "says," Aronofsky's movie sought instead to suggest what it might "mean," even what it might "mean to me." In doing so, it offered a gift to its viewers—insight into a God who has revealed himself to be righteous, a God who balances justice and mercy and calls us to follow him in response to his righteous ways.

Some Concluding Reflections

Can this case study provide insight into how Christians should respond to the divine initiative? The example we have considered is purposely multilayered, as is life.

---

45. Patton Dodd, quoted in Morgan Lee, "'Noah' Movie Sparks Massive Spike in Global Reading of the Bible's Book of Genesis," *The Christian Post*, April, 4, 2014. Online: http://www.christianpost.com/news/noah-movie-sparks-massive-spike-in-global-reading-of-bible-book-of-genesis-117334/.

What we are considering is viewers' response to Darron Aronofsky's response to Noah's response to the divine initiative. Though complex, our response to the movie *Noah* is nevertheless illumining. Let me close by offering several reflections based on the discussion above:

1. The topic is messy, as I have indicated. In considering humankind's response to the divine initiative, we cannot simply limit ourselves to only two "players"—God and "me," for "I" am also defined within community(s) and the Transcendent is also immanent both in creation and creature. The topic is a mediated one.

2. It is a mistake to equate religion's popular piety, or even its dogma, with God's initiative among us. Like Noah, believers too often skew the divine message so as to hear what we wish to hear (in this case, an "arky, arky" for us and our family and judgment for "them").

3. The God of Scripture is always contextually heard in particular ways. This was so for Aronofsky. His Jewish experience made him sensitive to that which most Christians have overlooked. The reader's/viewer's personality and social context always matter.

4. It is, therefore, always dangerous to think that our understanding of God's revelation is synonymous with God's revelation. Here was Noah's mistake, but it is also our mistake as we engage in biblical interpretation today. Our judgments are fallible, as Rick Warren found out.

5. Though Scripture has a common "author"—God, its multiple human authors make it dangerous for us to limit reading one text only in light of another. In our present example, to read Noah only in light of the book of Hebrews is a mistake. There is not a single, overarching biblical theology, but rather multiple, complementing biblical theologies.

6. Aronofsky has rightly understood that the story of Noah, like all biblical stories, makes demands on its readers/viewers. It suggests that as God's followers, Christians are called to the difficult task of finding the right balance of justice and mercy. God's "righteousness" can be equated neither with a sentimental love nor a matter-of-fact justice.

This example of viewer response to the movie *Noah's* response to the biblical Noah's response to the divine initiative reinforces the observation by William Dyrness that Scripture functions more like a musical score than a blue print.[46] Kevin Vanhoozer changes the metaphor to that of a drama to be enacted, as does Marva

---

46. William Dyrness, "How Does the Bible Function in the Christian Life?" in *The Use of the Bible in Theology: Evangelical Options*, ed. Robert K. Johnston (Eugene, OR: Wipf & Stock, 1997) 171.

Dawn.[47] Regardless of the artistic metaphor, what is evident in this filmic example of OT storytelling is the power of the arts to focus meaning and invite participants to re-engage the divine initiative as God speaks through the retelling of Scripture. The call on Noah's life is but a particular example of the Christian's larger calling to respond to a "righteous" God who desires all humankind to follow God in righteousness.

47. Kevin Vanhoozer, *Faith Seeking Understanding: Performing the Drama of Doctrine* (Louisville: Westminster John Knox, 2014); Marva Dawn, "Practical Theology—Lived Spirituality," in *For All the Saints*, ed. Timothy George and Alister McGrath (Louisville: Westminster John Knox, 2003) 137–53.

RESPONSE TO JOHNSTON

Paul Scott Wilson

I am pleased to respond to Robert Johnston's excellent reflection on the movie *Noah*. To do so from the perspective of homiletics seems particularly appropriate since moviemaking and preaching are parallel arts when the Bible provides the basic text. The title of this symposium, "Encounter With God: the Human Response to the Divine Initiative," fits Johnston's paper at several levels. It is a record of director Darren Aronofsky's encounter with the Noah story, of Noah's encounter with God, of viewers' encounter with the movie, and in a less precise or more teasing way, Johnston's own response it.

Eric Auerbach in his *Mimesis* famously described Abraham's journey with Isaac to sacrifice him on the mountain as "fraught with background." Abraham must sacrifice his son, yet the text says nothing about Abraham's thoughts and emotions, Isaac's questions, or their conversations as they journey to the place of impossible calling. The phrase "fraught with background," was Auerbach's way of describing the omission of narrative detail not central to the story and the inclusion of details laden heavy with meaning. It also signaled spaces in the emotional and psychological landscape that the viewer might enter in the process of discerning religious truth.

The Bible story of Noah is also "fraught with background," and the movie renders those empty spaces in unique ways. When I first read Johnston's paper, I had not yet viewed the movie. I recall a minister who was a keen moviegoer. As soon as a movie came out, he would view it in the theatre and then in his Sunday sermon give a complete summary, the whole plot. I stopped wanting to attend both the movies and the church. Johnston by contrast makes *Noah* more interesting by his comments. He engages the movie with rich research that helps us to understand why the writers and director made the choices they did. They added fantastical characters, the Watchers or Nephilim who help build the ark and thus help answer the realist's question how Noah on his own was able to construct such a large ship. The director took the Noah story at face value and ventured that it belonged in a time prior to our own laws of physics: people living a thousand years, flaming swords, Leviathans, and fallen people walking on earth. To this the director and writers added their own imaginative details: seeds from Eden grow amazing trees for the ark, animals wondrously are drawn to the ark from distant lands, and the entire story of Noah's family. The director makes three acts with Noah's character going from righteous in Act One to rigid moralist in Act Two through depression and eventually to giver of mercy in Act Three.

Johnston is obviously intrigued by *Noah*. He borrowed Clifford Geertz's term "thick description" (*The Interpretation of Cultures: Selected Essays* [New York: Basic, 1973]) to describe the movie's inventive technique, calling it "an illustrative approach" to the Bible story. The director engages in a kind of midrash or commentary, meant to answer interpretative questions and to invite dialogue. Johnston makes the movie more layered with rich meaning by the information he provides. He even points out the differences between publicity trailers of the movie intended to appeal to churchgoers and those for the wider public.

For Aronofsky the theme had to do with what is righteousness given "the ubiquity of sin"? How are the Creator and a righteous Noah to respond to violence and sin? The answer Johnston finds in the movie is that judgment and mercy must be balanced. In Act One, as the quotation from Rabbi Gellman insightfully notes, Noah "understands the flood but not the ark." By the end Noah discovers, as co-writer Ari Handle says of the theme, "Righteousness is the correct balance of justice and mercy." As Johnston puts it, "to walk with God is to be concerned not only with God's justice but also to experience divine mercy and grace."

By the end of the paper I was deeply grateful and wanted more, the same way that fine sermons may leave people wanting more. Specifically, I wanted to know more about Johnston, partly because the glimpses we have of him are so likeable. His infectious love of this movie comes through plainly, and one has a sense that some of the theology reflects his own. Part of the subtitle of his paper is "Viewer Response to *Noah*." Viewer response is represented not least by Johnston answering questions raised by movie critics, like why the snakeskin appears in *Noah*, or why the Watchers are agents of good in the movie when they are agents of evil in the book of Enoch. Viewer perspectives are also reflected in the reports of increased reading of the Bible after *Noah*'s release. For the most part Johnston responds to viewer questions and criticisms by explaining or otherwise defending the director. His own questions, critiques, or applications of the movie are hard to find in the version of the paper I received. At one point Johnston asks, "Could threatening to kill one's own kin so as to extinguish the human race ever be thinkable?" The question begs reflection on what *Noah* says to contemporary society that at times seems to flirt with similar behavior. What critical pushback does Johnston offer?

Regarding a second point for conversation, I wonder if moviemakers and their commentators do not face more challenges than most of us in avoiding what Derrida and others call binary opposition, particularly in the light/dark dichotomy that can have racial overtones. Deconstruction has us say things we did not intend. I wonder if the medium of light on which movies depend makes avoiding this more difficult. Consider how the term "dark" is used in this paper. Aronofsky is quoted as saying that the number of artists he asked to render the Noah story "turned their backs on the comedic, folk-tale rendition of Noah and found the darkness in the story." This focus on darkness in itself is interesting as an indicator of our postmodern times, where Derrida's "trace" that acts as a kind of shadow or absence has become the main event. God's saving action with Noah is the typical focus of the church, but in the movie it is seemingly less central than the deaths. The director in his language about the movie uses darkness negatively, as a way to speak of God's judgment and/or the human deaths in the story. Johnston picks up on this. He employs a subheading "dark and sobering" under which he gives a brilliant explanation of the snakeskin in the movie as a symbol of blessing: "opening images in the movie [show] where a snake is seen shedding its light skin and emerging as a darker, more foreboding presence. If God's creation was originally perfect, then snakes and their skins were originally good; that is, there was a time when the tempter had not yet entered the snake." In this quotation "dark" is again negative, symbolizing evil and sin. Is it wise to employ the term "dark" in this way, given that it evokes its opposite, implying a hierarchy of light equals good and dark equals bad?

As a teacher of homiletics, I wonder if there are lessons from *Noah* that Johnston might offer to preachers? Preachers often narratively fuse new elements to the biblical text in ways that make it a different text, thereby seeming to distort the Word of God. Sermons sometimes fuse a text with the contemporary world in a manner like the drawing of a rabbit/duck, both present but only one recognizable at a time. I advocate that preachers make movies of the text with their words, so I find it surprising to be asking this: When a biblical text becomes a literal movie, is it legitimate to expect it to communicate the Word? Johnston and the director may be right in interpreting the Genesis account in terms of righteousness as a balance of good and evil, but this falls short of what I understand to be the gospel of God's saving action that the church is commissioned to preach.

Both the sermon as a genre and the movie *Noah* are expressions of midrash, putting contemporary stories alongside the biblical text for interpretative purposes, yet there is a difference. Ideally the sermon retains the text as an image of itself, and this need not be true of the movie. In *Noah* the Bible text is significantly altered, not least by the addition of psychological motives, characters, and drama. When it introduces cartoon-like Watchers, and when the world in significant ways no longer resembles our own, can the God that world represents be taken seriously so as to meet the needs today of the poor, hungry, imprisoned, or lame? It would be interesting to devise a theology of biblical moviemaking in dialogue with a theology of the Word.

CORINTH, CALVIN, AND CALCUTTA: TRINITY, TRAFFICKING, AND TRANSFORMATION OF *THEOLOGIA*

Paul C. H. Lim

Before I launch into the substantive part of our conversation, I would like to thank the organizers of this marvelous conference on "Theological Interpretation of Scripture," where we get to think theologically about Scripture and reflect scripturally about theology, all with a keen awareness of the historical context of our life within church and academy in a global setting. It is, as far as I can tell, intentionally interdisciplinary and intensively communal, the very type of work I had wished my training would have afforded, but as an early modern English historian trained at a setting such as Cambridge, interdisciplinarity was often regarded as a graduate students' pipe-dream which, once you got a tenure-track job was best filed away in the dustbin of academic "could-have-beens" and "should-have-beens."[1] Therefore, I mean it *all very seriously* when I express my gratitude for *allowing* me an academic-cum-ecclesial context to think about my threefold passion: Scripture, historical theology, and contemporary context within which my faith seeks understanding (*fides qaerens intellectum*).

I have entitled this "Corinth, Calvin, and Calcutta: Trinity, Trafficking and Transformation of *Theologia*," not merely for alliteration but more importantly because these words encapsulate my role as a pilgrim *en route* to the City of God, especially as a theological educator.

Second Corinthians 3:12–18

As the theme of this conference is "Human Encounter with God," I would like to think of the biblical portraiture of the consequence of human encounters with God, as outlined in 2 Cor 3:12–18.[2] Paul juxtaposes two powers of transformation as a

---

1. For an exemplary approach to interdisciplinary historiography, see Theodore K. Rabb and Robert I. Rotberg, "History and Religion: Interpretation and Illumination," *Journal of Interdisciplinary History* 23 (1993) 445–51; and Julie Thompson Klein, *Crossing Boundaries: Knowledge, Disciplinarities, and Interdisciplinarities* (Charlottesville: University of Virginia Press, 1996).

2. For a helpful contemporary treatment of the theme of human transformation in response to

result of encountering God. First, in 2 Cor 3:7–15 Paul speaks of the encounter of God that led to Moses' shining, glorious face on Mount Sinai (cf. Exod 34:29–35), which required an active veiling of the face of Moses, for it was inordinately "radioactive," thereby causing fear in the hearts of the Israelite community, including Moses' own brother Aaron. Second, Paul speaks of a less spectacular but far more quotidian event and with a greater number of people affected. Paul does indeed affirm the salvific efficacy of that particular modality of encountering God for Israel, with Moses as the mediator of revelation and redemption. Moreover, as we see in Rom 9–11, Paul had a great soteriological aspiration couched in the uniquely eschatological language, as we see, "Then *all* Israel will be saved" (Rom 11:26). Therefore, it behooves us at this point to register a caveat that, rather than seeing 2 Cor 3 as an example of Paul the anti-Semitic supersessionist, one must see this as a case of the divine power for human transformation, first for the Jewish community and second for the newly emerging Christian community whose Scripture—at least at this time—was Israel's Scripture.[3]

How should we read 2 Cor 3? For Thomas Aquinas the hermeneutical connection between Moses and Jesus was analogous to figure and fulfillment. In his lectures on 2 Corinthians, he noted that Christ fulfilled "in truth what Moses delivered in figure, because all things happened to them in a figure."[4] Then he cites three concrete examples from redemptive history to illustrate how this was so: first, the death of Christ and the rending of the "veil of the Temple"; second, the Pentecost event was seen as a hermeneutical move, from "carnal" understanding to "spiritual" understanding in matters of faith; and third, this removing of the veil was proleptically shown when he opened the mind of the Emmaus disciples so that they could "understand the Scripture" as to what was written about Christ in the Tanak (Luke 24:45).[5] He does emphasize the glory of the old covenant which had Moses as the mediatorial figure. A few paragraphs later Thomas will use the word "veil" (*velamen*) in a negative sense to speak of the blindness of those who still hover around the figures of the Law without letting them lead to the fulfillment in Jesus. Still, in

divine initiatives, see Paul B. Duff, "Transformed 'From Glory to Glory': Paul's Appeal to the Experience of His Readers in 2 Corinthians 3:18," *Journal of Biblical Literature* 127 (2008) 759–80.

3. Bruce Longenecker, "On Israel's God and God's Israel: Assessing Supersessionism in Paul," *Journal of Theological Studies* 58 (2007) 26–44; N. T. Wright, *Paul and the Faithfulness of God* (Minneapolis: Fortress, 2013) 806–10.

4. Thomas Aquinas, *Super II Epistoloram ad Corinthios Lectura*, trans. Fabian Larcher, par. 105. Online: http://dhspriory.org/thomas/SS2Cor.htm#33. Last accessed 19 September 2014.

5. Ibid. On the theme of "participatory exegesis," in which Thomas is engaged, viz., doing biblical exegesis as a way of helping the readers to participate in the "life divine" by the invitation of the Triune God, see Matthew Levering, *Participatory Biblical Exegesis: A Theology of Biblical Interpretation* (Notre Dame, IN: University of Notre Dame Press, 2008) 36–62.

paragraph 103 Thomas acknowledges that the "splendor of his face" was a direct consequence of Moses' encounter with God, an entirely positive thing. Furthermore, Thomas reiterates the point that what was faulty was not intrinsic to the old covenant ("not that the Old Testament is veiled"). Instead, their hearts were veiled in that they could not see *through* the veiling of Moses.[6] Thus the veiling of that glory was for the benefit of the people.

If on the one hand, this glory was concentrated in one figure, Moses, and many contemporaries of Moses could only encounter the divine glory reflected in his face in a veiled fashion, with the Jesus' advent Paul declared that now that the veil has been removed many carry *with them* the glory of God. We need to take a moment to reflect deeply on Paul's point. Let us assume that he is not being anti-Semitic in his reading of his own people's history of salvation. Then at least what he is trying to do is show the breathtakingly beautiful widening of the scope of the glory of the One in whom all of our veils are taken away. Calvin does indeed acknowledge that "the law is in itself bright," yet the true "splendor" of it all is possible "only when Christ, appears to us in it."[7] Neither Thomas nor Calvin is denying the salvific efficacy of the Law as expressions of divine grace for that particular dispensation (*dispensatio* as Augustine was wont to use this word to denote different epochs of human encounter with God).[8] Yet what they do want to show—and understand precisely is Paul's point—is that with Christ the lunar light of the Law is eclipsed by the solar brilliance of Christ.

The other aspect of this encounter of the divine is the freedom it brings. In v. 17 Paul offers an interesting juxtaposition of the Lord and the Spirit and the sense of liberty it affords the believer who sees her identity wrapped up in the story of the One who "gives life to the law—by giving us his Spirit."[9] Here Calvin makes a very Trinitarian hermeneutical move to better make sense of the work of God. As the patristic theological maxim goes, when God works all the persons of the Trinity work in different ways for the same purpose, thereby making their "external work indivisible."[10] So here in this passage, if God the Father gave the Law, God the

---

6. Aquinas, *Super II Epistoloram ad Corinthios Lectura*, par. 110.

7. John Calvin, *Calvin's Commentary on the Bible: 2 Corinthians*, at 3:15. Online: http://www.studylight.org/commentaries/cal/view.cgi?bk=46&ch=3. Last accessed 17 September 2014.

8. On Augustine's use of the term *dispensatio*, see *De Fide et Symbolo*, par. 6, 8, and 9. See also *Outward Signs: The Powerlessness of External Things in Augustine's Thought* (Oxford: Oxford University Press, 2008) 126–27. Cary defines *dispensatio* as used by Augustine as "all of God's activity in history on behalf of our salvation and especially of course the Incarnation and historical life of Christ."

9. Calvin, *Calvin's Commentary on the Bible: 2 Corinthians*, at 3:17.

10. "Opera trinitatis ad extra indivisa sunt." On Aquinas's view of this maxim of Trinitarian theology and how it is influenced by the Cappadocians and Augustine before him, see Bruce D. Marshall, "What Does the Spirit Have to Do?" in *Reading John with St. Thomas Aquinas: Theological Exegesis*

incarnate Son came to fulfill it, and now we see that God the Holy Spirit takes residence in the lives of NT Christians to bring closer to completion the work of cosmic transformation, one human life at a time.

Aquinas gives authenticity to the freedom that is given to us through the ministry of the NT. Yet it is (1) *pnuematologically grounded,* (2) *relationally sustained,* and (3) *eschatologically anchored.* It is pneumatologically grounded because one gains freedom through the understanding the Spirit gives of the "OT without a veil." Thomas has that confidence precisely because the same Spirit is the author of the OT; thus, the author can be the best interpreter of the authorial intention. This freedom is relationally sustained as believers continue to see the "glory of the Lord as though reflected in a mirror" (3:18). It is in that sustained act of seeing the glory of the Lord that the ripple effect of one's own transformation into glory occurs. This is an entirely gratuitous act, which is responded to with a renewed sense of free will and freedom. It is also eschatologically anchored. One gets the sense that this assimilation/transformation is a movement along an asymptotic curve, i.e., it gets very, very close but does not actually touch it. Put differently, while we are transformed assuredly from a life of bondage and fear—this is how Calvin primarily sees the language of freedom—into a life of freedom and joy, and while we are transformed to be more and more like the image of Christ who perfectly images God the Father (2 Cor 4:4), the asymptotic curve of our transformation would not lead to an ontological fusion, even when one acknowledges deification/*theosis* as a definite eschatological possibility/reality.[11]

For Calvin this freedom within the context of the ministry of Christ was not given primarily to ministers, *pace* Erasmus. The foregoing threefold aspect of the freedom we saw in Thomas Aquinas' lectures on this passage is also found in Calvin's exegesis. He writes:

> . . . that the whole excellence of the gospel depends on this, that it is made life-giving to us by the grace of the Holy Spirit. . . [so that] the image of God, which had been effaced by sin, may be stamped anew upon us, and that the

---

and Speculative Theology, eds., Michael Dauphinais and Matthew Levering (Washington, DC: Catholic University of America Press, 2005) 68–69.

11. In his *Commentary on John* at 15:9 Thomas explicitly articulates a doctrine of *theosis*: "The Son did not love the disciples in either of these ways. For he did not love them to the point of their being gods by nature, nor to the point that they would be united to God so as to form one person with him. But he did love them up to a *similar point*: he loved them to the extent that they *would be gods by their participation in grace* ["ut scilicet essent dii per participationem gratiae"]—'I say, 'You are gods' (Ps 82:6)." Online: http://dhspriory.org/thomas/John15.htm. Last accessed on 20 February 2015.

advancement of this restoration may be continually going forward in us during our whole life, because God makes his glory shine forth in us by little and little.[12]

First, Calvin interprets the role of the third person of the Trinity primarily as "life-giving," making the Law and the gospel come alive. Note also the language of the "image of God" which Paul links christologically in 2 Cor 4 by calling Christ "the image of God." For Calvin as well, the freedom that believers enjoy now is not merely pneumatologically grounded, it is also relationally sustained. This i*mago Dei* is "stamped anew," and this restoration will continually move forward, sustained by the relational tie between the triune God and the believing community. Finally, note the eschatological anchor of Calvin's discussion of this drama of transformation resulting from the human encounter with God. He writes that "the advancement of this restoration" will be occurring all the way through one's life, with eternity as goal. At the end of the chapter both Aquinas and Calvin offer helpful insights into the eschatological goal of our transformation. For Aquinas there is a "triple degree of knowledge" among the followers of Jesus, which can be seen as three concentric moves from the outer circle to the inner center. The outermost circle is a move from natural knowledge to knowledge of faith. The middle circle would be the move from the clarity of the knowledge of the OT to the clarity of the knowledge of grace in the NT. The final circle is a move from the clarity of natural and scriptural knowledge of God to the "clarity of eternal vision." For Calvin this contemplation of the glory of God is never static but always dynamic: "That it is not befitting, that it should be a dead contemplation, but that we should be transformed by means of it into the image of God."[13] Furthermore, it is not only dynamic but also eschatologically grounded. This work of transformation into the *imago Dei* is "not accomplished in us in one moment, but we must be constantly making progress both in the knowledge of God, and in conformity to His image."[14]

We have seen how Paul's second letter to the Corinthian community sought to underscore the reality of transformation of the human self, society, and the vision of salvation with the rhetoric of the *image of God*, both as the link between humanity and God and the embedded identity matrix of Christ as the One who, as fully human and divine, was the perfect *image of God*. Further help is provided by a closer look at Calvin, particularly his theological interpretation of Scripture found in his *Institutes*, where he delves deeply into the question of *who* exactly images God and what possible difference it might make in the way we interact with one another.

12. Calvin, *Calvin's Commentary on the Bible: 2 Corinthians,* at 3:18.
13. Ibid.
14. Ibid.

Calvin and His *Institutes*

Calvin is a figure whom theologians bypass at their own intellectual peril, in the same way that Augustine is a figure that one must go *through* and not merely *around*. Thus Karl Barth, as he was lecturing on Calvin in 1922, declared that this formidable figure was a "waterfall, a primitive forest, a demonic power, something straight down from the Himalayas . . . strange, mythological; I just don't have the organs, the suction cups, even to assimilate this phenomenon, let alone describe it properly."[15] For this section I will highlight a powerful and poignant paragraph, *Institutes,* III. vii.6, that beautifully hints at the transformative potential for true human flourishing that can happen as a result of the human encounter with God.

When I teach history of Christianity in the Reformation era each spring, I assign this reading and *always* ask about this lengthy quotation in the final exam, encouraging the students to wrestle with the implications of this section on the "Nature of the Christian Life." That has been my pattern since arriving at Vanderbilt eight years ago.

Before we get to the quotation, let us rehearse a few first principles laid out in the sections preceding III.vii.6. Because of space limitations, a few bullet points will have to suffice.

1. Dialectical tension between the *sensus divinitatis* and the radically curtailed limits of natural theology.

2. The way Calvin cuts through the Gordian-knot of the problem of knowledge, both of self and of God, in a way that is christologically grounded with a Trinitarian orientation.

3. Human knowledge, if defined as a collection of information that governs the mental and physical activities of human faith, hope, and love, has an incurable penchant for distortion. True human knowledge can only be achieved by someone whose power and purchase of ethical rectitude and moral perfection can be transferred to those who do not share it. True divine knowledge can only be initiated and sustained by God. The only one who can embody that simultaneity is the incarnate Christ, true and righteous God-Man.

4. God the Holy Spirit leads the individual follower of Jesus and the community of disciples to keep in step with the divine purposes and trajectory of God's work.

---

15. Karl Barth, *Revolutionary Theology in the Making: Barth-Thurneysen Correspondence, 1914–1925* (Richmond: John Knox, 1964) 101.

It is within this context that Calvin shares his keen insight on the only hope for true intercommunal flourishing. Rather surprisingly, Calvin anchors this discussion on something universal, the *imago Dei* in every person. We will see how he grounds the universal mandate for human rights and ethics on something that is truly *given* to all, although that recognition might not be readily made, even within Calvin's own life and certainly within the Calvinist tradition.[16] I do not say this to destabilize or destroy the heuristic that is found in the quotation below, but rather as a way of reminding us that all of us do indeed have feet of clay, irrespective of what metals make up our torso.

I will quote the text at length and offer a four-point discussion of Calvin's Trinitarian communal ethic:

> Love of neighbor is *not dependent upon manner of men but looks to God.* Thus, The Lord commands all human beings without exception 'to do good.' Yet the great part of them are most unworthy if they be judged by their own merit. But here Scripture helps in the best way when it teaches that we are not to consider what men merit of themselves but look upon *the image of God in all men, to which we owe all honor and love.* . . . Therefore, whatever person you meet needs your aid, you have no reason to refuse to help him. Say, 'He is a stranger'; but the Lord has given him a mark that ought to be familiar to you, by virtue of the fact that God forbids you to despise your own flesh [Isa 58:7]. Say, 'He is contemptible and worthless'; but the Lord shows him to be one to whom God has designed to give the *beauty of His image.* Say that you owe nothing for his service; but God, as it were, has put him in his own place in order that you may recognize toward him the many and great benefits with which God has bound you to himself. . . . Assuredly there is *but one way* in which to achieve what is not merely difficult but *utterly against human nature: to love those who hate us, to repay their evil deeds with benefits.* . . . It is that we remember not to consider men's evil intention *but to look upon the image of God in them,* which cancels and effaces their transgressions, and with its beauty and dignity allures us to love and embrace them.[17]

The first and obvious point in this passage, indeed in all of Calvin's theology, is that all human ethical actions and virtue formation are predicated on the encounter that was *initiated by God.* Indeed all neighborly love—the horizontal axis of charity—must have divine *ḥesed* as the "alpha and omega," both beginning and the end of

16. In this regard, Calvin serves as a precursor of the theological moves made by Jean-Luc Marion, *Being Given: Toward a Phenomenology of Givenness*, trans. Jeffrey L. Kosky (Stanford: Stanford University Press, 2002), and the Radical Orthodoxy school. See J. Todd Billings, "John Milbank's Theology of the 'Gift' and Calvin's Theology of Grace: A Critical Comparison," *Modern Theology* 21(2005) 87–105.

17. John Calvin, *Institutes of the Christian Religion*, ed. John T. McNeill, trans. Ford Lewis Battles, 2 vols. (Philadelphia: Westminster John Knox, 1960) III.vii.6. Emphasis added.

our journeys.[18] Calvin writes that neighborly love should not depend on the "manner of men," i.e., what type of ethical merit they have to warrant that love. Instead, it has to have a Godward direction; it "looks to God." Note here also Calvin's ruthlessly realistic perspective on the human condition; he and his followers did not believe in "total depravity of humanity" for nothing! Judged by their own merit, hardly anyone would qualify as deserving of the radical embrace of the Other. This is where Calvin's "totalizing vision" of humanity comes in. We are all, in varying degrees, afraid of any totalizing discourse, especially in postmodernity.[19] This Calvinian "totalizing vision," however, has an interesting dialectical tension. On the one hand, this totalizing vision of Calvin vis-à-vis humanity has a clearly negative valence—the "T" (total depravity) of the (in)famous Calvinist TULIP! Nevertheless, this overwhelmingly negative assessment finds an internal balancing act when he talks about "the image of God in all men, to which we owe all honor and love." Note two things here: the universality of the scope of the *imago Dei* and the obligatory nature of the presence of the *imago Dei*. You "owe" honor and love to all humans, if for nothing else than the mere fact that they are image bearers of the triune God.

If one were to put the foregoing observation in contemporary ethical parlance, it might be as follows. The basis of Calvin's deontological ethics is *not* found in the order of redemption but in the order of creation. It is quite clear that he is not referring to the *imago Dei* of only those who have saving knowledge of the triune God, nor is he referring to a particular group of Christians, be they ordained priests/pastors or elders. So he writes, "whatever person . . . needs your aid." To be sure, he does make a slight bit of differentiation when he accentuates the ethical responsibility toward "those who are of the household of faith." And yet the preponderate thrust of the argument in *Institutes* III.vii.6 is that the basis of all neighborly action is the common thread of creation seen in the *imago Dei*. As one ponders the theo-political, socio-economic, and creedal-cultural implications of what we have been discussing, it becomes dizzyingly sweeping and inescapably binding on all aspects of our creaturely existence.

As if he anticipated the retort of his readers, Calvin accentuates the theme of the ethically and morally obligatory nature of the *Imago Dei* in all human faces. He argues that there is only one way to achieve something that is not merely incredibly hard, but more bluntly, against human nature, i.e., loving those who hate us and to repay their evil deeds with benefits. That is to look not at the intention but at the

---

18. On Calvin's view of *hesed* and a *theocentric* view of self, society, and salvation, see Ellen F. Davis, *Wondrous Depth: Preaching the Old Testament* (Louisville: Westminster John Knox, 2005) 21–23.

19. See, *inter alia,* James K. A. Smith, *Who's Afraid of Postmodernism? Taking Derrida, Lyotard and Foucault to Church* (Grand Rapids: Baker, 2006).

image! One way to look at this sentence is to see it as Calvin's own *midrash* on Jesus' Sermon on the Mount. Calvin agrees that the teaching of Jesus about turning the other cheek and loving your enemy is not only hard but simply counterintuitive. Yet he does not balk at this ethical demand by Jesus. Instead, Calvin proffers the universality of the *imago Dei* as *the only way* to make good on this command by Jesus, the perfection of the *imago Dei* himself. Here I must register some quibble. *How* exactly does the "other's" transgressions get cancelled and effaced by noticing the *imago Dei* in them? And *what* kind of intrinsic "beauty and dignity" can one find in the *imago Dei* itself when it seems deeply marred, so much so that it was the fountain of the transgressions that are morally so abhorrent? Lastly, how does the loving embrace actually occur?

Just to be an *agent provocateur*, what about the case of Michael Servetus, burned at the stake in Geneva on 27 October 1553, with at least some modicum of influence from Calvin?[20] If indeed the scope of this deontological ethics of Calvin was universal, how does one deal with the particularistic scope of Calvin's Christian theology and praxis? What of Calvin's followers, say the Dutch type, who ended up extirpating the land belonging to a group of Africans in the southern part of that continent and who used theological justification to create an Apartheid State? As I mentioned earlier, these questions are *not* intended as a way of destabilizing or destroying the credibility of Calvin's teaching. Yet one can only wonder at the gap between the sublimity of this rhetoric as seen in the quotation above and the reality of how this has been carried out. One clue occurs within Calvin's own text. In fact, in III.7 Calvin says that the gist of the Christian life is "self-denial." Seen in that light, denial of my priorities and positions—as he says "utterly against human nature"—is the work that the individual Christian herself simply cannot carry out. As Calvin makes abundantly clear from the outset of Book III (where he speaks about the application of redemption wrought by the Holy Spirit), the one agent, indeed the only one, who can carry out the work of participation into life divine was not the moral agent himself/herself, but the Holy Spirit, "the Lord, the giver of life," thus truly God. In other words, Calvin's view on participation-unto-*theosis* or more simply, sanctification, was that it was God the Spirit who initiates, woos, and comforts, and it is

---

20. Interpretations of Calvin's role in the "Servetus Affair" have often served as a mirror revealing the predilections and perspectives of the historians themselves, and they are a legion. Arguably the most even-handed approach, especially for the way that "affair" was appropriated in Enlightenment discourses, is Irena Backus and Philip Benedict, "Introduction," in *Calvin and His Influence, 1509–2009*, eds. Irena Backus and Philip Benedict (Oxford: Oxford University Press, 2011) 10–12; see also Ernestine van der Wall, "The Dutch Enlightenment and the Distant Calvin," 203–7 in the same volume.

the human agent—in response to the call of the Spirit—who acts, delights, agonizes, and takes up the cross.

Behind the beauty of III.vii.6 of the *Institutes* lurks a haunting and salutary warning for all sojourners unto the City of God. *How* do I see the *imago Dei*? To answer that, I will now take readers to Calcutta, hopefully having picked up enough hermeneutical cues from Corinth and Calvin.

Calcutta

If Scripture and tradition are the two important sources for religious authority—at least for me, what about the contemporary horizon upon which I must see the hand of God at work?[21] That leads me to the third "C" of the title, Calcutta (now known as Kolkata), the seventh largest city in India, perhaps best known to many as the city where Mother Teresa embodied the ethical teachings of Paul or John Calvin (perhaps she showed considerably less interest in Calvin than Paul).

Currently I am writing a book provisionally entitled *Evangelical Rescue? Global Christianity and Human Trafficking*, and for the purpose of research I spent a good deal of last summer in Seoul, Korea, in Kolkata and Delhi in India, and in Philadelphia, Boston, and New York. All the foregoing places are big cities with big problems. Kolkata stood out among them, partly because of that to which I was exposed. My hotel was not far from one of the major brothels in Kolkata, and I did ethnographic research on three BAMs (business as mission) organizations which were employing or hoping to employ formerly trafficked sex workers for production of goods, whether baked goods, saris/scarves, jewelry, stationeries, or tote bags.[22] Another group of people with whom I worked are what I would call "evangelical freedom fighters," those who work (or have worked) for organizations such as International Justice Mission or Justice Ventures International, rescuing one life at a time, as they seek to implement a series of changes and bring about redemptive elements in the global justice system. It was truly life-transforming, to say the least.[23]

---

21. With "tradition" I am adopting the two-source concept of tradition—Tradition I and Tradition II—from Heiko Oberman. See *The Dawn of the Reformation* (Edinburgh: T. & T. Clark, 1986) 279–89.

22. The best book on the overarching theme of economic development and socio-cultural-political freedom remains Amartya Sen, *Development as Freedom* (New York: Anchor, 2000). There is a growing literature on BAM's; the most foundational sources are, *inter alia,* Michael R. Baer, *Business as Mission: The Power of Business in the Kingdom of God* (Seattle: YWAM, 2006); and C. Neal Johnson, *Business as Mission: A Comprehensive Guide to Theory and Practice* (Downers Grove, IL: InterVarsity, 2009). See also the list provided on the www.businessasmission.com website: http://businessasmission.com/library/books/.

23. On these organizations and other antihuman trafficking endeavors, see John Schmalzbauer, "Whose Social Justice? Which Evangelicalism? Social Engagement in a Campus Ministry," in *The New Evangelical Social Engagement*, eds., Brian Steensland and Philip Goff (New York: Oxford University

I had given a talk at Cornell University earlier this year entitled "Trinity and Trafficking," in which I raised the questions, *since* this God of eternal and triune harmony allows trafficking of human beings with the *imago Dei* to continue, what are my responsibilities and does that change my theology in any way at all? When I gave that talk, I had not been to Kolkata, Delhi, or Seoul. One of the things that the BAMs prohibited me from doing—which made entirely good sense, actually—was taking photographs of the workers there. The rationale is as simple as astute: these women had earlier been objectified against their wishes as their bodies were ravaged roughly twenty times a day, the average figure. Therefore, their managers will not allow them to be objectified now, even in the much softer form of their pictures being taken.[24] On my first visit to a certain factory, I happened to come at the time of their chapel service. About sixty faces of sunken cheekbones, hollow eyes, and quite tired-looking women emerged from their workstations for a brief reprieve from their labor. Some of them sang joyfully, some even lifted their hands, as a white "chaplain" of the factory with multiple tattoos—I lost count after a few tries—led them in this time of devotion. But most of them just sat there, seemingly enjoying a time to reflect on their lives, fleeting though they may be, but uneventful most certainly not! The simplicity, sincerity and sadness/serenity that met my gaze upon many of the women's visage blew me away. What hope is there? They *do* have hope, don't they? Their lives are better, aren't they? The beauty of the *imago Dei* in them was truly powerful to lead me to embrace them, figuratively for sure, as we with our unveiled faces are being transformed into the greater likeness from glory to glory. This sounds sublime, but *how/where* do we see it?

It has been the problem of sight that has tripped many a pilgrim *en route* to the City of Eternal Joy. I do not *see* God at work! I don't *see* Christians living out their faith! One can see a pattern here. The apostolic rejoinder notwithstanding—we walk by faith, not by sight—a relatively incurable human penchant is to substitute sight for faith, or worse yet, use sight (the absence thereof, really) as the defeater for faith. I can easily imagine the allure of the "Faustian bargain" stripping away all the layers of belief, especially since I wondered about the very same thing, walking as I did at late night in the downtown slum areas of Kolkata. There I encountered more people sleeping in the streets than I have ever before, watching as I did each day in the alleys

---

Press, 2014) 51, 54, and 60–61; and David Swartz, "Global Reflex: Global Evangelicals, Human Rights, and the New Shape of American Social Engagement," 229 and 231–32 in the same volume.

24. Siddharth Kara, *Sex Trafficking: Inside the Business of Modern Slavery* (New York: Columbia University Press, 2010); Kevin Bales and Ron Soodalter, *The Slave Next Door: Human Trafficking and Slavery in America Today* (Berkeley: University of California Press, 2009). One of the most powerful collections of the stories told *by the slaves* themselves is *To Plead Our Own Cause: Personal Stories by Today's Slaves*, eds. Kevin Bales and Zoe Trodd (Ithaca, NY: Cornell University Press, 2008).

and shacks near one of the red light districts, where I experienced the simultaneity of inexpressible stench and the inimitably exhausted looks of creatures, canine and human alike. Where do I *see* the fingerprint of God here? *How* do I discern the patterns of divine presence and purposes of the Triune amid such stench, squalor, and abject destruction of *shalom*?

When Calvin says that *all* people have the *imago Dei*, does that include the pimps, thugs, and other despicable vultures who prey on the vulnerability of young girls, boys, and women, only to toss them to the lower dogs when they are no longer usable? If so, then *how* does my action toward them change? It is quite easy, rightly so, to see the *imago Dei* that needs further restoration and beautification in the faces of the formerly trafficked victims. But what do I do with the moral revulsion I felt when I stared in the face of a pimp and a madam? To borrow the language of Calvin, how on earth do I look past "men's evil intentions, but look upon the image of God in them"? How in heaven's name should the presence of the *imago Dei*—in all human beings, mind you!—"cancel and effect their transgressions" because of the intrinsic "beauty and dignity" which will inexorably "allure" and lead us to "love and embrace them"? I mean, with all the theo-rhetorical flairs notwithstanding, is Calvin serious? More pressingly, should we take this seriously? If so, *how* does one take this interpretive valence seriously? Especially as I have been on the journey to research this growing evangelical interest in and commitment to global justice and efforts to eradicate sex trafficking, how does Calvin's teaching provide the *right type of moral impetus* to bring about restorative justice for the perpetrators and unconditional embrace and mercy for the trafficked victims?

Transformation of Theologia

These and other questions lead me to the final section of the paper: "Transformation of *Theologia*." Indulge me in a one-paragraph encapsulation of the thrust of the argument thus far. From the section on 2 Cor 3, we have seen that the human encounter with God will ineluctably lead to the participation—in the Platonic and Thomistic sense—of the Christian communities and individuals into life divine/triune.[25] That transformation is pneumatologically grounded, relationally sustained, and eschatologically anchored. In other words, just as the "Lord is the Spirit," it is the Spirit that grants the restoration of the free will, thus freedom. Further, the work of the Spirit is always to lead the believing individual/community to further "contemplate the

25. On this theme the best accessible source is Rudi A. te Velde, *Participation and Substantiality in Thomas Aquinas* (Leiden: E. J. Brill, 1995). See also Najeeb Awad's contemporary application of this Thomistic idea of participation in "Thomas Aquinas' Metaphysics of 'Relation' and 'Participation' and Contemporary Trinitarian Theology," *New Blackfriars* 93 (2012) 652–70.

Lord's glory," the glory of Jesus Christ. There is that eschatological, asymptotic curve of human transformation with "ever-increasing glory" (*lit.* "from glory to glory").

From the section on Calvin we encountered a sublimely capacious text which calls readers to a life of discipleship of a radical embrace, based not upon color, culture, creed, or cash-value, but because of the christologically grounded reality of the *imago Dei,* as an order of creation and not of redemption. Put differently, we are not called to love the *imago Dei* of those whose lives are on a different trajectory because of the benefits of their redemption "in Christ." Conversely, we are called to a life of seeing the *imago Dei* in all persons irrespective of who they are, what they do, where they have been (immorally or unethically!), etc. The challenge of taking this Calvinian deontological ethics seriously is not in the challenge itself as much as in the vector of praxis. How does one apply this in a real life context?

That led me to the next section of applying the powerful teaching of Calvin to my recent work in Kolkata. It is absolutely easy to see the *imago Dei* beautifully displayed on the faces of those who are at work in eradicating trafficking of all sorts. But what of the victims? Worse yet, what about the devilettes who are indefatigably at work in destroying even the vestigial elements of the *imago Dei*, both within them and within their victims, as they are henchmen dehumanizing the sex workers into seeing their participation in the sex industry as making them mere objects of commodification, exploitation, and gratification of the customers' desires?

With this survey in mind, it is necessary to raise pressingly practical, ecclesial questions. *How* do I teach this in my local congregation? Further, *how* do I instantiate this contextualized, globalized view of self, salvation, and Savior within my context of theological education? Simply put, what is the ultimate cash value of this question about the "transformation of *theologia*"?[26]

From the Corinthian text I learn that abject pessimism has no place in the life of the individual Christian or a community of the followers of Christ. God *is* at work in our world. The triune God who said "Let there be light" (cf. Gen 1:3 and 2 Cor 4:6) into creation is the One-in-Three who continues to shine that light in our hearts. Consequently, even in theological education, especially in our context of shrinking enrollment, endowment, and educational imagination, it is a salutary reminder that eschatological optimism must foreground our present endeavors. There will invariably be the taut tension between felt reality and unseen hope. Yet this text teaches me that we "with unveiled faces" do get to see the "glory of the Lord," but with a crucial caveat. Paul adds a key phrase: "as though reflected in a mirror." It is a cognate of the word that he used in 1 Cor 13:12: "For now we see in a mirror." In both these

---

26. The best text on this issue is Ed Farley, *Theologia: The Fragmentation and Unity of Theological Education* (Philadelphia: Fortress, 1983).

instances Paul uses the words "mirror" and "mirroring" in two important ways: (1) the image reflected shows a good proximation of reality on the other side of the mirror; (2) yet it is not the reality itself but only an image. In other words, while we get to witness the glory of the Lord, it is provisional and not complete, relational and not autonomous. It leads us to an ironic juxtaposition of eschatological hope and epistemological humility.

I have been hit hard with the context of Calvin's *Institutes*, especially given my own institutional context. Vanderbilt Divinity School's self-designated appellation is *Schola Prophetarum*. There are some inherent potential perils for a school that calls itself the school of the prophets. You see, prophets were often, by definition, minority-cum-marginal voices speaking truth to power. But what happens when there is, what I would call, a "prophetic mainstreaming"? When the prophetic voices are no longer marginal, vying to be heard, but are now the regnant voice and paradigm, with relatively uncontested hegemonic control? How do we mind the marginalia? Whose status of *imago Dei* is questionable within the context of Vanderbilt Divinity School?

Switching gears a bit for the sisters and brothers in an ecclesial context, how do I teach this in my church? One way is to point out that this radical embrace of the other *is* "utterly against human nature," a truly Calvinian realism here! The other—and this is not explicitly in the text but my hermeneutical leap of faith—is to point out that any human act (from the standpoint of Calvin, the radical Augustinian) such as "look[ing] upon the image of God in them" has to be a synergistic act. In other words, recognizing the *imago Dei* in the unlikeliest of them has to be an act that is initiated, sustained, and perfected with the Holy Spirit clearly in view. Without that divine aid recognition of true human dignity is simply impossible. We look *up* to God as we look *around* to the *images of God* in our neighbors or enemies, whether in our pursuit of evangelism, community justice, or antihuman trafficking campaigns. This is much easier said than done, but that should not lead us to shy away from saying it.

From the context of Calcutta and the complicating global realities that inexorably impinge upon the way we do/are church and academy, challenges toward transformation of *theologia* are innumerable. I will mention a few for our conversation. When I was teaching at Gordon-Conwell (2001–2006), my primary focus was in systematic and historical theology, slightly off-target from my graduate training in history of Christianity. One of the acronyms I coined while there was "RWCV"— Real World Cash Value—of any particular doctrine *du jour*! As a way of anticipating the arc of their pastoral ministry, I was encouraging students to ask the requisite "So what? Who cares?" questions that might be in the hearts of many polite parishioners and on the tongues of a few less-than-polite folks in their congregations. Knowing that such (de)pressing realities are around us, only a Skype call away, would have to influence the way we think about the object(ive) of our *theologia*. By *theologia* I do not mean to restrict it to the stuff that constitutes theological education. It has also to include the church, for the church is the place in our world where most people can look for some *theological* guidance and perspectives.

Realizing the ubiquitous nature of global poverty and the ingenious exploitations of human agents as the *given condition* of our present-day, late-modern, capitalistic world, should not all our endeavors—academic or ecclesial—be funneled to our present-day concerns? Can I parse Sanskrit verbs while Rotterdam is burning?[27] Can I talk about intricacies of Nestorian Christology while members of ISIS might be hunting down Syrian Christians *right now*? I am not suggesting that all our efforts must be presentist. My training as a historian at a place such as Cambridge simply would not allow that to take root. Yet historians can also become antiquarians in their desperate efforts to avoid activist agendas.

As you can see, I have raised far more questions than provided answers, a discursive practice entirely warranted, even awarded in academic institutions, but perhaps duly warned against, even excoriated in ecclesial institutions. I am well aware of that. Therefore, I want to finish this paper with a note of apology-cum-gratitude for the ministers of the good news in the mix: apology for not analyzing the local congregational context better and gratitude for indulging a lover of the gospel of Jesus Christ for a bit. My faint hope, however, is that this theological provocation has gotten you to think a bit outside the box in our collective efforts to see the *imago Dei* in all of us, including myself.

27. This memorable expression comes from Nicholas Wolterstorff, *Until Justice and Peace Embrace* (Grand Rapids: Eerdmans, 1983) 162.

RESPONSE TO LIM

Jonathan M. Wilson

I thank Dr. Lim for this important paper which challenges the academy and the church to look to earlier church leaders as exegetes and ethicists who have much to say to our century and its issues. Lim's paper is a timely theological reflection on the ethical conundrums faced by godly advocates in the redemption of victims of the sex industry. "Corinth, Calvin and Calcutta" interprets 2 Cor 3:12–18 with Augustinian lenses focused on Aquinas and Calvin. Its focus is the ethic based on Calvin's premise that all human beings bear the *imago Dei,* which poses the conundrum: How does one find the *imago Dei* among pimps?

As stated in the opening and closing paragraphs, the goal of the paper is that it will engage across theological disciplines and across the boundaries between the academy and the church. I am writing a dissertation at the Lutheran School of Theology of Chicago on German Lutherans in the late eighteenth century, and I am also the pastor of a local Evangelical Covenant church. As an example of the dialogical nexus to which this paper and this symposium are aimed, I bring both of my roles to my response.

The Pastor Responds Concerning the Trinity

The paper's chief purpose is to establish the role of the Holy Spirit in the recognition of the *imago Dei* even in the person who is actively wicked. The paper offers a summary of Trinitarian functions in the human drama of transformation: "if God the Father gave the Law, God the incarnate Son came to fulfill it, and now we see that God the Holy Spirit takes residence in the lives of NT Christians to bring closer to completion the work of cosmic transformation, one human life at a time."

Especially in light of the book Lim has recently published on the Trinity and ethics,[1] I propose that if a discussion of the triune God's three persons is germane to this paper, then it should be more fully developed. Mine is a pastoral perspective that appreciates the necessity for a guarded approach to the presentation of Trinitarian doctrine. Perhaps terms employed by Augustine, Aquinas, and Calvin can

1. Paul Lim, *Mystery Unveiled: The Crisis of the Trinity in Early Modern England*, Oxford Studies in Historical Theology (Oxford: Oxford University Press, 2012).

be introduced into this summative framework. The NT picks up the theme of the Hebrew Scriptures that the law is God's Word and identifies the Son himself as *ho logos*, as in John 1 when the Christ as the incarnate Word is described as the one by whom all things are created and sustained (see also Col 1). The partial revelation of God's Word in Torah is thus encompassed by the fullness of Christ as *ho logos*.[2] This is how I would understand what Calvin meant in saying that we see the law in its true splendor "only when Christ appears to us in it." As one who stands in a corner of the long shadow cast by Luther, may I in addition suggest that the Son as Word also functions as a personal transforming principle, inasmuch as the Son as *ho logos* is fully present now in the preaching and the sacraments.

The History Scholar Responds Concerning John Calvin

Among the reformers Calvin's *imago Dei* ethic is not unique.[3] Having said that, those of us from outside the formal boundaries of Calvinism will agree that Calvin is often right, and he is right in his ethics to pursue the inescapable logic of the Sermon on the Mount. Neither is it unique that Calvin would approve the death sentence of the heretic Severtus. In the twenty-first century most would disapprove of putting heretics to death but would find slave-traders to be wretches. That is our world, not that of the Reformers.

In his commentary on John 8 Calvin wrote, "But let us remember that, while Christ forgives the sins of men [*sic*] he does not overturn political order, or reverse the sentences and punishments appointed by the laws."[4] Most of the chief reformers understood that there must be teeth in the civil government's enforcement of law; in some cases the reformers wanted those teeth sharpened into fangs. For Calvin a criminal—whether a heretic, a witch, or an adulterer—must be dealt with based on ethics concerned with the protection of society. Far from being inconsistent, in Calvin those who criminally transgress their ethical responsibility to the *imago Dei* in others ought to be held accountable to the community. All the mainline reformers reflect Augustine's influence in their views that the civil law must have teeth.[5]

---

2. Gail R. O'Day, *The Gospel of John*, The New Interpreter's Bible 9 (Nashville: Abingdon, 1995) 519.

3. See Martin Luther's "Freedom of the Christian," in *Martin Luther's Basic Theological Writings*, ed. Timothy Lull (Minneapolis: Fortress, 1989) 585ff.

4. Online: http://www.puritanboard.com/f44/john-calvin-death-penalty-adultery-61432/ (accessed 9/21/2014).

5. Augustine, *City of God*, Book 1, Chapter 21. Cf. Martin Luther, "On Secret and Clandestine Preachers" in *Luther's Works*, ed. Conrad Bergendoff (Philadelphia: Muhlenberg) 40.379–394.

The Academic Pastor Responds Concerning Finding the Imago Dei

Now to the central issue: Can Calvin's ethical directive of finding the *imago Dei* in all people apply to human traffickers? The paper's questions are rhetorical and leave the reader to wrestle, which as Lim points out is laudable in the academy but often excoriated in the church! I respond that as a pastor I am stirred by Lim's story and personal turmoil, while the scholar in me wonders if the ethical conundrum is really as complex as the paper intimates. I propose that the paper has already built into itself resources that speak to its troubling questions.

First, one could look to other premises in Calvin. Looking to Calvin in line with Aquinas and Augustine we might ask, if the ethics of the *imago Dei* entail accountability to the community, what roles can the sword of government (Rom 13) have in rectifying the misery of human trafficking. Christians can be advocates not only on the streets and in safe-houses, but also in legislatures and police headquarters.

The paper mentions the "T" in Calvinism, total depravity. Another petal on the tulip can be resourced for the *imago Dei* conundrum, and that is the "U" of unconditional election. It is here we find that grace is so amazing it can even save a wretch like John Newton, a slave trader who was converted to faith, composed the lyrics to "Amazing Grace," and eventually worked for slavery's abolition. The face of a human trafficker shows me a wretch—like me. My faith that such as a wretch as myself has been saved solely by the grace of God allows me to see that possibility in any other, and so I am called to proclaim the good news without distinction.

Second, when it comes to finding the *Imago Dei* in the actively wicked, there is still another resource already spoken of in the paper: Mother Teresa. She was not a Calvinist and her chief ministry was not among victimized sex workers and their morally wretched enslavers. However, she is someone whose life, as the paper says, "instantiated and embodied the ethical teachings of Paul or John Calvin."

In her book *Where There is Love, There is God*, Mother Teresa writes, "No one can love as God. He has made us in His image. He made us. He is our Father." Later in the same volume she states, "Love, to be true, must hurt." And then, "Knowledge of God, love of God, service of God—that is the end of our life—and obedience gives us the key to it all."[6] I propose that Mother Teresa's answer to the question of finding the image of God in another, no matter how wretched, is that you do it by doing it. This is the challenge of the Sermon on the Mount.

As a pastor I admire Lim's commitment to on-site advocacy on behalf of victims of the sex trade in Kolkata, and I honor him for his moral courage in looking their exploiters in the eye; he does not lean on the conundrums that arise from his

---

6 Mother Teresa, *Where There is Love, There is God* (New York: Doubleday, 2010) 9, 147, and 260.

turmoil as an excuse to stop doing. The protestant scholar looks to John Calvin and protests that such things Lim has already accomplished in Kolkata are only possible by being infused into the life of God through the grace and power of the Holy Spirit. To this the evangelical pastor responds "Yes."

HERE AM I: MOSES AND THE MEANING OF OUR BODIES

Brian Bantum

The question of the body has been a pernicious one from the very beginning. As Jews began to discern the significance of a certain prophet, their own bodies would become new problems to be puzzled out, resisted, and reflected upon. The invisible God had become a visible Word. God has a body! Of course, we know the controversies that would embroil the church as it sought to articulate how this was possible and what the implications were for disciples to understand who they ought to be and what their bodied lives were for.

Judith Butler, in the preface to her groundbreaking and still influential work, *Bodies that Matter: On the Discursive Limits of Sex*, reflected on beginning to write a book intended to consider the materiality of the body. The problem, she found, was that "Not only did bodies tend to indicate a world beyond themselves, but this movement beyond their own boundaries, a movement of boundary itself, appeared to be quite central to what bodies 'are.' I kept losing track of the subject."[1] Butler would go on to consider gender as a perpetually moving boundary. Ultimately her work would offer a notion of gender grounded on the idea of performativity, or identity as constructed more by the meanings pressed upon a body rather than inherent or essential identities latent within particular bodies, whether male or female.

This paper will return to Butler's original question and from an explicitly theological point of view ask the question, "*Why* do our bodies matter?" More specifically, given the context of our conversations during this conference, "How do our bodied lives respond to encounters with God's initiative?" In this endeavor I will look at the account of Moses to consider liberation and human response.

Why Moses? The story of Israel is the story of humanity's response to God as a people made out of nothing, refusing God in the garden, refusing their life with one another and with God, and ultimately journeying from place to place in and out of a promised land. Israel's life is constituted by life with God. Within this story perhaps one of the most fundamental turning points in Israel's story is the

---

1. Judith Butler, *Bodies that Matter: On the Discursive Limits of "Sex"* (New York: Routledge, 1993) ix.

Exodus story. Moses' life signifies both God's recognition of Israel as children of God and God's desire that these people be free. Apart from Abraham and Sarah it could be argued that there are fewer individuals more significant in Israel's life and self-understanding.

Moses, like Jesus, is also appropriated and deployed to signify a vision of Christian life. How do we live deeply into this transformative encounter with God? In rather fascinating ways interpretations of Moses display how Christians have sought to answer this question. Alongside their Christology, interpretations of Moses display how various theologians imagine their own lives and the lives of those they teach as inhabiting the transformation of encounter with God. In considering Moses' response to God, I will first briefly describe three historical invocations or interpretations of Moses and his calling to liberate the people of Israel from Egypt. In these interpretations we see also the questions and commitments contemporary to each writer. My question for each focuses on the framing of bondage and liberation and how Moses' participation in God's work displays particular visions of Christian life that explicitly or implicitly locate the body within visions of bondage or freedom. To get a sense of the various approaches and implications of these approaches, I will examine three figures and by extension their traditions: Gregory of Nyssa of the Cappadocians, John Calvin in the Reformation, and slave spirituals/preaching of eighteenth and nineteenth century American slaves. In these accounts we begin to see several tensions emerge that are inherent in the Exodus narrative. What is the relationship between Israel and Egypt, and what does Moses' movement from Israel to Egypt and back again reflect? What is significant in Moses' marriage to Zipporah, the daughter of the Midianite priest? Lastly, what is the significance of Moses' response to meeting God at the burning bush?

Gregory of Nyssa and Moses as Transfigured Humanity (Our Bodies are Bodies and Souls in Tension)

Fourth-century theologian Gregory of Nyssa read Moses through a hermeneutic of spiritual virtue. For Gregory, Moses was an allegory of Christian personhood who would ultimately discern that "none of those things apprehended by sense perception and contemplated by understanding really subsists."[2] Moses' life is caught between the profane and barren idolatry of Egypt and the spiritual truth of Israel. For example, in Gregory's reading of Moses' fight with the Egyptian, Moses does not

---

2. Gregory of Nyssa, *Life of Moses* (New York: Paulist, 1978) 60.

merely fight for his people but displays the struggle of idolatry against true religion.[3] Here Israel is less a people than a sign of true understanding.

Towards this true understanding Moses is one whose life becomes a sign of proper perception and cultivation of a rationality that pursues virtue, disciplining the body and refining it. Gregory's comment on the fullness of this personhood is worth quoting at length:

> What does the history say about this? That *Moses the servant of Yahweh died as Yahweh decreed, and no one has ever found his grave, his eyes were undimmed, and his face unimpaired.* From this we learn that, when one has accomplished such noble actions, he is considered worthy of this sublime name, to be called *servant of Yahweh*, which is the same as saying that he is better than all others. For one would not serve God unless he had become superior to everyone in the world. This for him is the end of the virtuous life, an end wrought by the word of God. History speaks of "death," a living death, which is not followed by the grave, or fills the tomb, or brings dimness to the eyes and aging to the person.
>
> What then are we taught through what has been said? To have but one purpose in life: to be called servants of God by virtue of the lives we live. For when you conquer all enemies (the Egyptian, the Amalekite, the Idumaean, the Midianite), cross the water, are enlightened by the cloud, are sweetened by the wood, drink from the rock, taste of the food from above, make your ascent up the mountain through purity and sanctity; and when you arrive there, you are instructed in the divine mystery by the sound of the trumpets and in the impenetrable darkness draw near to God by your faith, and there are taught the mysteries of the tabernacle and the dignity of the priesthood.
>
> And when you, as a sculptor, carve in your own heart the divine oracle which you receive from God; and when you destroy the golden idol (that is, if you wipe from your life the desire of covetousness); and when you are elevated to such heights that you appear invincible to the magic of Balaam . . . and when you come through all these things, and the staff of priesthood blossoms in you, drawing no moisture at all from the earth but having its own unique power for producing fruit.[4]

Gregory's vision of the body is not strictly dualist, where the body needs to be escaped. But the body does need to be controlled, directed, and intermingled with the miraculous so that it can transcend its earthly contingencies so that even death is a "living death." The body in this regard becomes an icon, a window to a deeper or higher reality, to borrow from Eastern Orthodox icon theology. For Gregory, Moses' body is a profound display of this transformation and this journey where the

3. Ibid., 57.

4. Ibid., 135–36.

ordinary acts of eating and walking, and the ordinary elements of wood, bread, and water become infused with the miraculous.

In this vision there are earthly realities that must be consumed by fire, which must be defeated and killed in battle. These are the realities of the pagan, the Egyptian, and those who fashion golden calves and idols out of wood. Gregory sees Moses' virtue in fundamental opposition to these cultural artifacts. Interestingly, Gregory rarely points to the physicality of the tabernacle or the staff but always beyond them to a transcendent spiritual reality.

Why is this important as we consider *why* the body matters? I am certainly drawn to the language of our bodies conforming to the archetype and where the "staff of priesthood blossoms in me," but how do we know what aspects of our material life are idolatrous? For Gregory the body is a window, a necessary one into a deeper truth of our personhood. The materiality of our body and our world is but a series of perpetual decisions, opportunities to see and choose freely, and insofar as we choose rightly we illumine the truth of who we are and conform more thoroughly to the image of the One who created us. The materiality of our body and our life is thus necessary but ordered. That is, the material is always indicative of the spiritual. The promised land of Gregory's interpretation is less physicality and geography that requires one's feet to traverse from one point to another. Rather, Gregory imagines bondage, wilderness, and freedom within the body. Put differently, the body is the land upon which one lives and experiences the freedom of one's creatureliness.

Jean Calvin and Moses as a "Geography of Freedom" (Our Bodies are Body and Soul in Tension of Citizenship/Belonging)

While the ancient interpreter Gregory saw spiritual analogies in both the patterns of bondage and redemption in the Exodus moment, John Calvin's Reformation interpretation of Moses and the Exodus moment expressed not only notions of spiritual freedom but highlighted the larger tensions of political freedom and national belonging. Historian John Coffey argues the Exodus was a formative moment in the imagination of Christians who were trying to understand the significance of political power and freedom, whether it be Constantine or the Puritans. Here, proper worship is made possible through the intervention and involvement of God. For Coffey, these were examples of "deliverance politics . . . a species of historical providentialism. It specified one of the ways in which Providence operated in the affairs of nations. God was the Deliverer of Exodus. A God who acted within human history to bring freedom from oppression and slavery."[5]

In the context of a theological and socio-political landscape where pseudo-nationalistic theologies were dividing and subdividing Europe, Calvin sees Moses as more than an allegory of spiritual versus bodily need. Moses is one who was torn from his people and eventually returns to lead them to a new land where they may worship freely and truthfully. Such notions of belonging are highlighted in Calvin's narration of Moses' renunciation of his Egyptian mother and the embrace of his true people.

> And it came to pass in those days, when Moses was grown. Now did that faith which the Apostle celebrates begin to shew itself, when Moses, despising the pleasures and riches of the Court, chose rather to suffer the reproach of Christ, than to be accounted happy apart from companionship with the chosen people. Nor was it only love for his nation, but faith in the promises, which induced him to undertake this charge, by which he knew that he should incur the hatred of all the Egyptians. For although he did not immediately resign his wealth, and honorable station, and influence, and power, this was, as it were, the preparation for divesting himself of all these deceitful allurements. Whence the Apostle says, "he refused to be called the son of Pharaoh's daughter." (Heb 11:24)[6]

Calvin's attention to the cultural tension is peculiar among interpreters of Exodus and Moses. It serves to highlight Calvin's understanding of faithfulness as not only a spiritual reality but a "companionship with the chosen people." Moses' decision to turn to Israel was an embrace of a community, a political reality that was opposed to the tyranny of Pharaoh. To return to Coffey's analysis, this interpretation was connected to Calvin's political and theological struggle against the Pope: "Calvin's reading of Exodus was both Christological and political. In *The Institutes*, it served as a model of temporal liberation from 'intolerable tyranny of the Pharaoh' and as a type of the spiritual deliverance wrought by Christ when he freed his people from the 'fatal tyranny of the devil.'"[7]

In this respect, Moses is a harbinger of freedom that establishes a place free from the persecution and idolatry of Egypt and leads them to a promised land. Calvin reads Moses as being groomed and educated for this purpose so that his time in Midian is a period of preparation for the task before him. "Therefore God in

---

5. John Coffey, *Exodus and Liberation: Deliverance Politics from John Calvin to Martin Luther King Jr.* (New York: Oxford University Press, 2014) 8.

6. John Calvin, "Commentary on the Harmony of the Law, Vol. 1" in *Calvin's Commentaries* (Grand Rapids: Baker, 1996). Online: http://www.ccel.org/ccel/calvin/calcom03.i.html, (Exod 2:1–10).

7. Coffey, *Exodus and Liberation*, 29.

a manner withdrew him, that he might gradually render him fit and equal to undertake so difficult a task. For the experience of forty years in such a laborious and ascetic mode of life, did not a little avail to prepare him for enduring any hardships; so that the Desert may well be called the school in which he was taught, until he was invited to his more difficult charge."[8]

The difficult charge before Moses would be leading his people through the desert, serving to inculcate them once again with the Law and draw them into the fullness of the promised land. Calvin's interpretation of Moses highlights an understanding of the body as a communal reality and one which requires material conditions to thrive. In the upheaval of the Reformation what emerges is not only a theological innovation but a mode of theological reflection deeply tied to a geographical vision, a place of freedom wherein one's belonging to God was displayed and enacted. Moses' body signifies a journey of belonging and citizenship where he moves from his true people to an idolatrous people, to a "school" of preparation outside the city, only to return to his people and lead them to their true land. The end of this journey towards liberation is a life with God upon a new land, where "[God] now again sets [Israel] apart, (*sanctificat,*) and promises that he will be their God. In these words their peculiar election, as well as its perpetuity, is asserted; since to be accounted the people of God means the same as to be by especial privilege received into his favor and to be called by adoption to the hope of eternal salvation."[9]

Regarding assessment of Calvin and the larger arc of Reformation invocations of the Exodus, Coffey says, "The Reformation had been sold as an assault on 'popish bondage.' Now there were Protestants demanding freedom from regal tyranny and clerical taskmasters. Using the liberation narrative of the Exodus, they had reimagined Protestant politics."[10] This political imagination is exemplified in Calvin's interpretation of Moses as one who properly discerns his people and forsakes the idolatry and oppression of Egypt to lead Israel to a *place* of communion with God.

Moses' body is one that is set between competing claims upon it. His faithfulness is displayed in his proper discernment of where true liberty lies and in his participating in God's redeeming work to draw God's people into that space of faithfulness. For Calvin this work of drawing Israel into faithfulness was the overarching "harmony" of the law wherein God's people abided with God fully. Moses' freedom is not exemplified in being away from tyranny but in his being in harmony with God's law. How can we begin to understand Moses as a political body, one that mediates and establishes boundaries where true law can reign? The subsequent story

---

8. Calvin, "Commentary on the Harmony of the Law" (Exod 2:11–15).

9. Ibid., (Exod 6:7).

10. Coffey, *Exodus and Liberation,* 55.

of Moses' leadership of Israel through the wilderness is a further unfolding of this essential observation regarding Moses and his witness.

African American Interpretations of Moses and Exodus (Our Bodies are Bound to Others, Circumscribed and Oppressed, but our Bodies are Meant to be Free)

Gregory of Nyssa's interpretation of Moses centered largely on the interrelationship between Moses' body and his soul, creating a profound allegory of Israel's bondage to Egypt as the soul's bondage to the body. While retaining a certain measure of Gregory's suspicion of the body and the temptations of idolatry, Calvin pressed this analogy as a broader indictment of socio-political structures that prevented proper worship and communion with God. In Calvin's estimation Moses was one who discerned who he belonged to and was used by God to help Israel again see who they belonged to.

Even more than belonging, freedom was a place beyond Egypt, a promised land where the elect could live into their covenantal identity. Calvin's interpretation illuminates the interrelationship between the political and quasi-national tumult of the Reformation as well as the theological scaffolding of Puritan movement to America and the subsequent colonial manifestations that a theological promised land would become. The political ramifications of the Reformation theological vision required a space in which to worship freely. Proper worship and doctrine were created around bodies. Here upon the boundaries of the promised land doctrinal posts were erected to delineate who was in and who was out. In this regard it could be said that the political was bound to the intellectual or contemplative life akin to Gregory. Here the body was not only one's own body, but a body politic, a people whose lives were constrained within a harmonious law and who were careful to police the boundaries between the elect and those who were not. The body was the community.

But to remain here is problematic. America and American Protestantism were a direct descendant of these interpretations, with their own myths bearing an eerie resemblance to the Exodus narratives, a people oppressed, fleeing miraculously across a great sea to establish a place where they could worship faithfully and be the people of God. Yet within this seemingly redeemed space those who were free to worship also became free to enslave. At the least their spiritual/political freedom was not severely encumbered by the enslavement of the Africans.

While Gregory would imagine enslavement as the soul to the body and Calvin as a people who are not free to worship, the African slaves in America were a people bound to masters in a daily, brutal comprehensive reality. The entirety of their lives and bodies were stripped down and laid bare for economic and personal consumption. In the midst of this some slaves miraculously came to see the Christian God as their God. As they did, the story of Exodus became one of the central stories in African American Christian imagination.

Invocations of the Exodus began in the earliest Christian expressions of black slaves in the United States. The figure of Moses and Pharaoh's drowning were prominent themes in Negro spirituals as "Their songs and sermons emotionally transported them into experiences that transcended the boundaries of geography and chronology."[11] The identification of Moses and enslaved Israelites was more than an analogy of hope. Moses was an existential presence. This could be attributed to a dynamic sense of the Spirit or to the way in which the presence of ancestors was a real presence carried with slaves across the Atlantic. Either or both of these realities animated slaves' reading of the Bible's patriarchs and matriarchs. In either case the spirituals that sang of Moses' participation in God's work called the possibility of God's redeeming work into an eschatological presence, which allowed slaves surreptitiously to disrupt their master's operations and simply to survive the terror that was their daily life. To see even brief excerpts of the spirituals is to see the obvious connections with escaping the bodily realities they faced even as God met them in the midst of their trials. For example,

> "Go Down Moses"
> *Go down Moses*
> *Way down in Egypt land*
> *Tell ole Pharaoh*
> *To let my people go.*
> "Wade in the Water"
> *See that band all dressed in red*
> *God's a-going to trouble the water*
> *Looks like the band that Moses led*
> *God's a-going to trouble the water.*

The invocations of Moses in the spirituals are expressed powerfully by Absalom Jones, an early African American preacher whose preaching viewed Moses as a participant in God's redemptive work literally to draw people out of enslavement. This participation, unlike the spiritual allusions of Gregory or the political inferences of Calvin, is a direct allusion to those who actively participated in "going down" to the South in order to bring slaves from the South to the promised land of the North.

---

11. Gary Selby, *Martin Luther King and the Rhetoric of Freedom: The Exodus Narrative in America's Struggle for Civil Rights* (Waco: Baylor University Press, 2008) 41.

Jones would recall Moses and the Exodus in an interpretation of the slaves' place in history. "The history of the world shows us that the deliverance of the children of Israel from their bondage is not the only instance in which it has pleased God to appear in behalf of oppressed and distressed nations as deliverer of the innocent, and of those who call upon his name."[12] Jones's interpretation highlights not only the liberative hermeneutic of African American Christianity but also a deep sense of God's *presence* with them in their condition. This reality of presence was not only a comfort but a promise of what God would do among the black slaves in America. Historian Albert Raboteau observes, "The story of Exodus contradicted the claim made by defenders of slavery that God intended Africans to be slaves. On the contrary, Exodus proved that slavery was against God's will and that slavery would end someday."[13] Here notions of spiritual freedom and a bodily/political freedom were profoundly interconnected. The body was made to be free from more than the economic and political manipulations of bodies for profit and abuse.

African American interpretations of Moses were grounded within a radical identification with the bodily reality of enslavement. To suggest that this is to differentiate between the spiritual or political identification described by Gregory or Calvin would be to miss how African American Christian slaves radically united the spiritual and the bodily in their theological imagination. African American Christianity was not merely an appropriation of the teachings of the slavers' preachers but a complex interpretation of the biblical witness that saw a God who worked on behalf of the slaves and met the oppressed in the reality of their affliction.[14] While they saw their personhood diminished, crushed, and used at every turn of their daily life, in the Bible they read of God's desire for freedom and God's participation to make that desire come to fruition. Moses symbolized the freedom to exist in a space—to occupy the same land but in a new way. Citizenship was not an alternative place but a rebirth of full citizenship within one's "native land."

Yet in the midst of these moving declarations of freedom are also accounts of how this notion of liberation was circumscribed even as it was expressed. Minister Jarena Lee described her call to ministry and the resistance she received from other

12. Albert J. Raboteau, *Canaan Land: A Religious History of African Americans* (New York: Oxford University Press, 2001) 41.

13. Ibid., 44.

14. The tension between accommodation and activism has been a constant one in African American Christianity. For some important discussions of these tensions see Hans A. Baer and Merrill Singer, *African American Religion in the Twentieth Century: Varieties of Protest and Accommodation* (Knoxville: University of Tennessee Press, 1992); C. Eric Lincoln and Lawrence H. Mamiya, *The Black Church in the African American Experience* (Durham: Duke University Press, 1999); and James H. Cone, *Martin and Malcolm and America: A Dream or a Nightmare* (Maryknoll, NY: Orbis, 1995).

African American pastors.[15] In this way, we see how freedom could be argued for in one respect and a limited vision for black women still maintained. Similar patterns of misogyny were common in later civil rights movements such as the SCLC's resistance to Ella Baker as director.[16]

A movement which read the Exodus text so personally and experientially and yet could not discern the widest implications of that liberation requires us to ask how Moses' life and the Exodus of Israel could be read more expansively. How do we respond to God's initiative in the most expansive way possible? I want to consider more carefully Moses' body as a fulcrum of liberating response. What is the relationship of our body to our personhood and our anthropology?

Re-Interpreting Moses' Body

While Christian traditions have offered a variety of interpretations of Moses, connecting his life to a broader vision of what Christian life encapsulates and is oriented towards, these various interpretations have relied upon allegorical theological interpretations divorced from the historical moment of Moses' and Israel's life. By history I mean not only the descriptive process of narrating events but rather history as a mode of self-location, what Hendel calls the creation of a cultural memory.[17] This memory is bound to discerning the significance of the moment one occupies, where one is situated in the world.

Exodus and Moses' life are a testament to the space Israel occupies in the world, and they wrestle with the multilocality of its identity. Such an identity is not simply the story we tell of ourselves but the complicated way our bodies get mapped upon and entangled within competing narratives. Gregory saw Moses the servant of God, while Calvin saw the redemption of the elect and more broadly the establishment of social space to display this election. The American slave saw a liberator and people whose bodies were unfettered and moving to a literal promised land.

In a way I am saying simply that these interpretations of Moses are contextual. Of course, this is nothing new. More particularly I want to suggest that these readings have flattened Moses. Exodus' description of Moses presents us with a *spatial* Moses, a Moses that inhabits the world as a son of two mothers, the husband of a non-Israelite, the father of Gershom whom he names as a signification his own

15. See Jarena Lee, *Spiritual Narratives*, ed. Sue E. Houchins (New York: Oxford University Press, 1988).

16. For more on Ella Baker see J. Todd Moye, *Ella Baker: Community Organizer of the Civil Rights Movement*, Library of African-American Biography (Lanham, MD: Rowman and Littlefield, 2013).

17. See Ronald S. Hendel, "Cultural Memory" in *Reading Genesis: Ten Methods* (Cambridge; New York: Cambridge University Press, 2010).

foreignness. Put differently, these various interpretations resist the complication of multi-locality that the reader encounters in the Exodus story. Moses' story highlights an ambiguity that he must move through in being used by God. This process is a bodily process that takes him in and out of homes, into and out of relationship with people. These realities serve to form him in ways that we cannot understand as intellectual commitments. They are realities grafted onto his body. In this way his moving through these spaces becomes a bodily enactment and announcement of God's presence and activity in the world.

To account for Moses' body as significant in the liberative story of Exodus we must attend to the movement of Moses through the various presences narrated in the beginning of the Exodus account. These often conflicting realities constitute an "ambiguity of being" (Merleau-Ponty) that is tied to an "ambiguity of our body." Merleau-Ponty's work in *Phenomenology of Perception* helps us to recall the mystery inherent in our own bodily lives.[18] Noting such physical anomalies as phantom limbs, he points to the failure of the body to recognize itself in some cases and to the fact that there are limits to what we can know even as our body is the conduit through which we gather knowledge of the world and of ourselves. This gap becomes an inherent mystery interior to our bodily lives. He says, "What allows us to center our existence is also what prevents us from centering it completely, and the anonymity of our body is inseparably both freedom and servitude. Thus . . . the ambiguity of being in the world is expressed by the ambiguity of our body, and this latter is understood through the ambiguity of time."[19] In this way the body is constituted by an estrangement and an intimacy with itself, but this inherent ambiguity is not only a matter of how our consciousness is tied to an incomplete knowledge of our body. Ambiguity is a deep recognition of the ways in which we are unaware of how our bodies have been formed in and by the world. One's self-understanding is the process of uncovering the layers of identity knit into us through concrete bodily practices as well as through our place in a given social moment. These threads are not always known and must be perpetually discovered, rendering our bodily lives always ambiguous.

Slave/Oppressed

Slavery is not simply about the limitation of a people's movements and the exploitation of their bodies for labor. Slavery encompasses a complicated nest of interconnections and fragmentations between those who enslave and those who are enslaved.

18. Maurice Merleau-Ponty, *Phenomenology of Perception* (New York: Routledge, 2012).

19. Ibid., 87.

As sociologist Orlando Patterson observes in his groundbreaking work *Slavery and Social Death*,

> The slave is violently uprooted from his milieu. He is de-socialized and de-personalized. This process of social negation constitutes the first, essentially external, phase of enslavement. The next phase involves the introduction of the slave into the community of the master, but it involves the paradox of introducing him as a nonbeing.[20]

Moses enters a world as an Israelite slave marked for death. These children are not human beings, but tools for controlling an alien population within their boundaries. He is born in the bosom of the bonded, his life oriented towards perpetual servitude and the enclosing of his life within the boundaries of Egypt's idolatrous ambitions. Israel's enslavement constituted the enfolding of their entire notion of personhood and belief within the confines of servitude towards Egypt and their gods. From the killing of infant males to using women as tools for nursing children, the slave's identity was perpetually bound to its service to Egyptian aspirations and need.

This reality inscribes upon Israel a disoriented identity where,

> Institutionalized marginality, the liminal state of social death, was the ultimate cultural outcome of the loss of natality as well as honor and power. It was in this too that the master's authority rested. . . . The slave came to obey him not only out of fear, but out of the basic need to exist as a quasi-person, however marginal and vicarious that existence might be.[21]

If slavery dictates the significance or insignificance of every moment in the slave's life, agency personhood is only possible within confined moments of resistance or acquiescence.

In Moses' life we see moments of subtle resistance in the midwives' rebellion of inaction, allowing firstborn males to be born under the guise of "the Israelite women's strength," and in Jochebed, Moses' mother, sending Moses away in the basket. To claim her own humanity and the humanity of her child she must sever their kinship. Even as she miraculously receives him again to nurse him, he cannot be her child but belongs to another. The deaths that slavery exacts are not only individual but social. Even in Israel's freedom from Egypt their hearts and hope cannot escape an imagined prosperity of enslavement. When the Israelites are ultimately free but

---

20. Orlando Patterson, *Slavery and Social Death: A Comparative Study* (Cambridge: Harvard University Press, 1982) 111.

21. Ibid.

wandering in the desert, their enslavement confines their notion of freedom as they expressed their desire to return to their masters, who at least fed them.

The conflictual reality of life as a slave takes on deeper complications in Moses' life. Moses himself would walk among his fellow Israelites, but as an "Egyptian." We are told "he went out to his people and saw their forced labor. He saw an Egyptian beating a Hebrew, one of his kinsfolk. He looked this way and that, and seeing no one he killed the Egyptian and hid him in the sand" (Exod 2:11–12). While Moses had been adopted by those in power, he continued to identify with Israel and with their oppression. Moses' identification with his people thus renders his bodily presence in the halls of Pharaoh a disruptive presence. Moses' body is a presence of the "nonbeing" whose proper place is in the slave quarters, and yet he walks with the protection and security of one raised within the walls of power. This paradoxical presence undoubtedly explains the Pharaoh's intense anger about Moses' murder of the Egyptian overseer. Moses had revealed his true "nature" and violated his precarious standing within the walls of power. The Pharaoh's demand for Moses' death was a recalling of Moses again to his prior state of "nonbeing," one who should have died in the Nile.

Moses is inextricably bound to these people whose lives had been utterly depersonalized, the entirety of their lives oriented around erecting structures of devotion for gods who were not theirs. Moses, an Israelite child, raised within the cultural space of Egyptian privilege, was not indifferent to those who looked like him. His presence in the palace or in the street was a sign of the conflicted interconnections that emerge between oppressors and the oppressed and the limited options available when seeking to speak one's full personhood.

Oppressor/Empire

When his mother sets him in a basket in the reeds and he is discovered by the servants of the Pharaoh's daughter, his enslaved body is enfolded by arms of power. His body, even while being nursed by his mother, now speaks of authority and possibility when he walks through the halls of his adoptive mother. While scholarship is divided on whether Moses was an actual historical figure and whether he was seen as an Egyptian or Israelite by other Israelites, the text depicts a tension in Moses' self-awareness and his reception by Israelites. On the one hand, he begins to see his fellow Israelites' suffering and will go so far as to murder one of their overseers who was abusing two of them. Yet these two men do not see Moses as one of their own, but another, one who is not like them. We find in Exod 2:13–14a: "When he went out the next day, he saw two Hebrews fighting; and he said to the one who was in the wrong, 'Why do you strike your fellow Hebrew?' He answered, 'Who made you a ruler and judge over us? Do you mean to kill me as you killed the Egyptian?'"

The Israelites' response to Moses is instructive. While Moses' occupation of the palace is a precarious one, his movement into the streets of his enslaved brethren does not take him "home." Moses displays a sense of connection even when he is not recognized by those to whom he belongs. Yet the Israelites' rebuke of Moses signals that Moses walks through the streets as a sign of Israel's enslavers. In their eyes he is not the oppressed but the oppressor whose body and life is nourished by the suffering of his brothers and sisters, mother and father. "Who made you ruler and judge?" they say to Moses, questioning his place among them.

Though Moses exhibits concern for the plight of "his" people, his murder of the Egyptian also demonstrates his formation within the halls of power. An enslaved Jew would understand explicitly both the danger such an act would pose for the murderer and also the effect such an act would have upon the community. An act of violence against an overseer is a profoundly political act that would be met with retribution to ensure the slaves would not pursue further acts of defiance. In the American slave system similar acts of retribution towards the community would be exacted upon the community of slaves (including whippings, reducing of rations, and extra work) to ensure the community would self-police any acts of resistance.

Moses' act against the overseer demonstrates not simply a heart for his people but an experience that remained detached from the realities of his kin. Could we say that his "initiative" in that moment was born not of the slave quarters but the palace? In the palace he had the power to determine himself, to choose or to not choose. There, an overseer would be his subordinate, one whose life was subservient to Moses. When Moses kills the Egyptian, perhaps he sees one who is, at best, equal to him, and as he engages his body with the overseer Moses inserts his body within the bodily contestation of presence, seeking to make himself present to Israel. As he does so, he uses his body as one who belongs within echelons of power. His body is his to determine, a privilege no Israelite dare assert so publicly or so violently.

This ambivalence is evident again in Exod 3:11 when God commands Moses to return to Egypt, but now as an Israelite: "But Moses said to God, "Who am I that I should go to Pharaoh, and bring the Israelites out of Egypt?" Interpretations of this hesitancy could certainly emphasize Moses' humility, believing he does not have the requisite skills or power to fulfill what God is asking of him, but Moses continued protestations can also be read as exhibiting a cultural alienation from Israel, his people. While he understands himself as an Israelite, he was not raised eating their food, praying their prayers, or speaking their language. His rebuttal to God, "Who am I?" is less a confession of humility than a confession of his own privilege and lack of connection to his own people. This cultural alienation can be seen further in his continued questioning of God's commands:

> But Moses said to God, "If I come to the Israelites and say to them, 'The God of your ancestors has sent me to you,' and they ask me, 'What is his name?' what shall I say to them?" (Exod 3:13)
> But Moses said to the Lord, "O my Lord, I have never been eloquent, neither in the past nor even now that you have spoken to your servant; but I am slow of speech and slow of tongue." (Exod 4:10)

Moses demonstrates an ambivalence concerning his belonging among the people as he reveals his ignorance even of God's name and his inadequacy of speaking his people's language.[22] Since Moses was educated within the halls of the palace, he was unfamiliar with the physical plight of his people and untrained in the faith of his mother and his father. What will he call this God who comes to him? How will he convince them? Where his privilege as a citizen of the empire makes possible the use of violent agency, it also renders him strangely unfamiliar with an identity of faith that marked his mother's people.

Foreigner/Alien

Moses' body as oppressed and oppressor would eventually conflict as he saw two of his people harassed, but when he killed the Egyptian, his people did not recognize him. Moses fled the danger of that irreconcilable space; he was threatened with death. As Moses entered the wilderness he escaped death only to discover more profoundly the loss of place. So Moses came to occupy a third space; having fled the enslavement of his people and the privilege of the royal class, he became a shepherd and the husband to Zipporah, a Midianite priest's daughter.

As Moses abandoned the cloth of royalty and the shackles of his enslaved people, he donned the marks of a shepherd and lived among people who existed beyond the reach of Egypt's power. Among the Midianites he again resided within a space of power, but the reach of this power was limited to sheep and family. Moses was again immersed among a people who, while familiar with Egypt and Israel's gods, remained a distinct people. Israel's freedom and hope was recapitulated through the

---

22. Recent scholarship has suggested that the reference to Moses' eloquence is evidence of a speech impediment. However, lack of eloquence and slowness of speech could also be associated with one who is not familiar with another people's language, or at the very least, the particular dialect of a people. While Israel and Egypt certainly shared a language that allowed them to communicate, Israel maintained their cultural language grounded in the language of their Scriptures. Moses' ignorance was not in communicating generally but communicating the theological language God was giving him to speak.

middle space of Midian. (Joseph had been sold to the Midianites who sold him to Potiphar.)

With the Midianites Moses entered an exilic life for forty years. While he seemingly found a home among them, we see in the birth of his son an alienation remained: "[Zipporah] bore a son, and he named him Gershom; for he said, 'I have been an alien residing in a foreign land'" (Exod 2:22). Moses' self-imposed exile did not diminish his lack of a sense of place (whether among Israel or the Egyptians). Exilic existence is not simply a matter of citizenship but encompasses the entirety of one's life where, as cultural theorist Edward Said suggests,

> For an exile, habits of life, expression, or activity in the new environment in-
> evitably occur against the memory of these things in another environment.
> Thus both the new and the old environment are vivid, actual, occurring to-
> gether contrapuntally. There is a unique pleasure in this sort of apprehension,
> especially if the exile is conscious of other contrapuntal juxtapositions that
> diminish orthodox judgment and elevate appreciative sympathy. There is also
> a particular sense of achievement in acting as if one were at home wherever
> one happens to be.[23]

Moses' son is the naming of his own perpetual dislocation that both abides with the Midians, while also remembering the conflicted peoples of his homeland.

The Body of the Encountered

As God encounters Moses in the burning bush, God calls a man whose bodily life is inextricably bound to three women: Jochebed, Pharaoh's daughter, and Zipporah. These women and their peoples are woven into Moses' tastes, his accent, his eyes, his nose, and his gait. God encounters a man who has found his home in many places and yet feels homeless in the midst of them.

It is this displaced body that God will send. In the face of the burning bush, God tells Moses to take off his sandals "for this is holy ground." In Moses' journey from land to land, into and out of peoples, he is again brought into a new place. God's purposes and presence are not abstract ideas but the ground he feels between his toes. Taking off his sandals allows Moses to feel beneath his feet the promise of God's home, to bring his personhood, his feet which have trod within so many homes, into a new relation.

As Moses' interchange with God unfolds, God tells Moses what he will do and Moses, out of his displacement, responds that he cannot. Still, Moses remains upon

---

23. Edward Said, "Reflections on Exile," in *Reflections on Exile and Other Essays* (Cambridge, MA: Harvard University Press, 2000) 186.

the ground that is his home, each promise extending itself, enfolding Moses within the surety of who God is rather than who Moses is not. Moses seems so uncertain of what to call God, of how he will speak to Israel and what he will say and whether they will believe him. Yet in this uncertainty, in this displacement that finds homes in many places and yet is never at home without God's word addressing them, Moses comes to embody the deepest truth of Israel's identity. He is one whose life is constituted utterly by God's calling. He is sustained by the provision, wisdom, and compassion of those whom God places in his life, and his identity is tied to his mission. Upon leaving that holy ground, Moses' body inhabits not only a variety of cultural curiosities but the liberating promise of God.

This necessary relationship and yet distinction underlies the heart of Jewish existence. Jewish philosopher Michael Wyschogrod writes concerning Israel's existence, "Israel is not a body foreign to the divine will and to Torah. God dwells in Israel. He dwells in the midst of its uncleanness. He envelops Israel."[24] Wyschogrod goes on to differentiate this dwelling as similitude. Israel's identity is both bound to God and different from God. This presence is a *real* presence. In this way Moses' body is both bound to these various peoples and distinct from them. His liberating presence is a refusal of Egypt's idolatry, which collapsed the divine and the Pharaoh, and a rebuttal of Israel's position as slaves and subjects to this foreign god. God's coming to Moses in the wilderness of his Midianite life is an embodiment of God's movement towards Israel, even in their enslavement, to recall them to an existence bound not to land or idolatrous enslavement but to God's presence among them, even under their very feet.

The Meaning of Moses' Body

Why does Moses' body matter? Why do our bodies matter? In seeing the depiction of Moses in the book of Exodus, we begin to see the display of a bodied life that does not diminish the cultural realities or histories of a person or a people. The particular body cannot be separated from the cultural realities that entwine to form one's personhood. Moses' identity is entwined with the faithful acts of three women who risk in order to preserve life. His body is bound to the varying accents of language, food, and belief that make him seemingly disqualified for the redemptive work to which God is calling him, but it is these very embodied limitations that are inhabited and enlivened by God's presence. Moses' body matters because it is the point which marks what was and what will be, what is not and what is possible. His bodily

---

24. Michael Wyschogrod, *The Body of Faith: God in the People Israel* (San Francisco: Harper & Row, 1989) 213.

presence matters because it measures the reality of God's abiding as not merely an intellectual exercise but a presence that requires our feet to touch the ground.

Our bodies matter as well because any notion of one's personhood that seeks to balance a false dichotomy of body and soul or idea and material ultimately resists the mystery that our bodied lives present to us, that in God's encountering us, mystery encounters mystery. Our souls discern and perceive through biological systems that are themselves networked in ever-complicating ways. Our ideas about who we are or who God is are irrevocably bound to the ways in which our bodies are formed through relationships, food, family, and the myriad of practices that constitute our cultural space. With Moses we are confronted with a body that is not a faithful Israelite, a man raised within the Empire and who lives in exile among the foreigners only to be encountered by his mother's God. As Moses picks up his staff and journeys into the heart of Egypt, his body carries with it signs of its entrance, exit, and return. As he walks through the streets of Egypt and into the palace, he need not speak words in order to communicate that God is working in their midst. His very presence declares something that his words will eventually confirm.

Gregory of Nyssa calls us through Moses to contemplate upon the good and thus usher our body towards life even beyond death. Calvin sees in Moses one who could faithfully arbitrate between faithfulness and idolatry. Black slaves read Moses as indicative of God's liberative work in the world and as participating in their bodily freedom. While these are all undoubtedly significant aspects of Moses' witness in Exodus, to interpret the significance of Moses' body is to discover not only a spiritual or political significance but also to see how our response encompasses the totality of our bodily life and experiences. Culture, more than the coalescence of food, language, and customs, is the clay which forms our personhood and the ears through which we hear and see the One who encounters us. To see Moses is to see the various ways our experiences, alienations, transgressions and liberations coalesce and become transformed within our lives.

In light of the Exodus account of Moses what is the human response to encounter with God? Perhaps we can now say it is a response of confession. A response to being encountered by God's divine initiative does not leave the mystery or historical realities of where our feet have been. In God's encounter with us we are confronted with the ways we at once occupy the house of Pharaoh and the slave woman's quarters, and we realize our bodies are mysteries and that we are forever strangers in our own land. The meaning of our body is this perpetual reminder: it beats even as it is beaten, even as we act out of an unknowing that haunts us. To be encountered by God is to be met in a place, in a body. In that encounter the entirety of our bodily life is enfolded within God and oriented towards God's purposes. Our response is to be confronted by the unknown ways our lives are being entangled and transfigured in this redeeming work, even while we embrace the ambiguities of our own bodies and the bodies of others, and the ways we are perpetually perpetrator, perpetrated, and alien.

TRANSCRIPTS OF THE TRINITY: READING THE BIBLE IN THE PRESENCE OF GOD

Cheryl Bridges Johns

We live in a world intolerant of silence. It seems that there are no silent spaces. Our cars are filled with sound coming from the radio or a blue tooth device. Children ride in mini-vans equipped with movies on small screens that are built into their seats. Our homes are often a cacophony of sound with multiple televisions and stereo systems playing simultaneously. We shop with canned music playing in the background. While we sit and wait for an appointment, we can use our smart phones to access music, movies, and audible books. All these things and more make it safe to say that at the dawn of the twenty-first century we are absolutely addicted to sound.

However, for all our love of sound and determination to fill every moment with noise, there is a deep silence no one seems to mind. It is what James Smart called a "strange silence."[1] In 1970 he warned, "The voice of Scripture is falling silent in the preaching and teaching of the church and in the consciousness of Christian people, a silence that is perceptible even among those who are most insistent upon their devotion to the Scriptures."[2]

I often wonder what Smart would say today. If in 1970 U.S. Christians were neglecting the Bible, their silence is nothing in comparison to ours. Today the strange silence is no longer strange. It is normative. Rarely do we hear the Bible read in public places. Christian speech is not seasoned with reference to biblical texts. Parents do not quote Scripture to their children. Within the walls of our churches discipleship programs and preaching are flavored with biblical texts, but few people are involved in direct study of the Bible. Congregations have little tolerance for the public reading of passages of Scripture. As a whole, Americans, in the words of Gary Burge, "are in danger of losing the imaginative and linguistic world of the Bible."[3]

It is a strange irony that, as more and more translations of the Bible are available and there are more forms of electronic delivery of the biblical text, the rate of biblical illiteracy continues to rise at an unprecedented rate. The American Bible Society just

1. James Smart, *The Strange Silence of the Bible in the Church* (Philadelphia: Westminster, 1970).
2. Ibid., 15–16.
3. Gary M. Burge, "The Greatest Story Never Read: Recovering Biblical Literacy in the Church," *Christianity Today*, August 9, 1999, 45–49.

released its latest study on "The State of Bible" (conducted by the Barna Group). This study revealed disturbing data. In 2014 there are just as many Americans skeptical of the Bible as there are engaged with the Bible. Nineteen percent of Americans saw the Bible as inspired Word of God and read the Bible at least four times a week. On the other hand, 19 percent of Americans indicated that they believed the Bible to be just another book, merely a collection of stories.

The survey noted that Bible ownership remains strong (88 percent), with the average household owning 4.7 Bibles. However, only 37 percent of Americans read the Bible once a week or more. Millennials (18–29) had very different views of the Bible than do all American adults. Fewer millennials see the Bible as sacred, and 39 percent of them never read the Bible (as compared to 26 percent of all Americans).[4] These statistics reveal that Bible reading is not an "ordinary practice" among many people.

To further complicate matters, the Bible is often used as a weapon in the so-called culture wars. Both the religious right and the left are captive to certain visions of Christianity that are more culturally scripted than biblically narrated. In this context the Bible loses its distinctive "otherness" as Word of God. Statistics regarding millennials reveal how this generation is the collateral damage in these wars. This generation looked for elders, but they found warriors. As a result they are leaving established religion. They come from families and churches that have been torn apart by the shrill rhetoric of both the right and the left. These refugees of the cultural wars are growing in number. They are the "post foundationalist" or the "post evangelical, the "spiritual but not religious." Like all refugees they have stories to tell about their reasons for leaving the faith. Moreover, many have hopes and dreams of a new land. One only has to read their blogs to realize how deep runs their disenchantment and how deep runs their longing for something more.[5]

Some of these young refugees have their Bibles with them, and they are searching for new ways of reading the text. As one millennial noted, they are looking for "a textual hermeneutic that moves beyond the trench lines and polarization of the mainline/evangelical cold war."[6] Phyllis Tickle shares this concern for this generation of what she calls the "scriptural innocents." She sees their lack of biblical knowledge propelling them in one of two directions: "to seek ever more eagerly for structural engagement" with the Bible, or else a "propelling of Scripture itself farther and far-

---

4. Online: http://www.americanbible.org/features/state-of-the-bible-research-2014.

5. Example of "post evangelical" millennials can be seen in the blogging by Rachel Held Evans (rachelheldevans.com) and Micah Murray (micahjmurray.com).

6. Tim Conder and Daniel Rhodes, *Free for All: Re-Discovering the Bible in Community* (Grand Rapids: Baker, 2009) 47.

ther into the attics of life where all antiques are stored for a respectful period of time before being thrown completely away."[7]

The Bible as a Disenchanted Text

The scientism and foundationalism of modernity created a Bible quite different from the one read by our ancestors. Our modern Bible—the one read by conservatives and liberals alike—is more of a historical document than the lively oracles of God. In the short space of this paper it is impossible fully to explore how this came to be. Suffice it to say that the Bible has not survived well in the Enlightenment project. It has suffered the fate of most everything else, namely becoming an object and a commodity.

N. T. Wright makes the point that "the Enlightenment (whose leading thinkers included Hume, Voltaire, Jefferson, and Kant) was, in fact, for the most part an explicitly anti-Christian movement."[8] I would want to temper Wright's view of the Enlightenment by noting the earlier contributions of Northern humanists such as Erasmus, who worked to keep faith and reason together. However, I agree with him that the Enlightenment project as a whole offered a different vision of the cosmos than does Christianity. This vision, namely that the universe operated out of natural laws that could be understood and harnessed for the betterment of life, gradually stripped the world of any supernatural dimensions.

The Enlightenment project not only transformed how we image the cosmos, it radically altered how human beings relate to the world. Enlightenment humans are rational, thinking subjects who can know, study, analyze, and master the world. This "turn to the subject" can be summed up in the dictum of Rene Decartes: *cogito ergo sum*—"I think, therefore I am." Wright rightly notes, "The Enlightenment insisted on reason as the central capacity of human beings."[9]

There is much to praise in humankind's transformation into the rational subject. It empowered humanity to seek out solutions to the world's problems. It enabled people to explore the depths of nature, harnessing its laws thereby generating some of the world's greatest inventions. It created a healthy sense of individual identity and freedom, thereby paving the way for the development of democracies and belief in human rights.

---

7. Phyllis Tickle, *The Great Emergence: How Christianity is Changing and Why* (Grand Rapids: Baker, 2008) 116.

8. N. T. Wright, *The Last Word: Beyond the Bible Wars to a New Understanding of the Authority of Scripture* (New York: Harper, 2005) 91.

9. Ibid.

However, rational power is intoxicating. Over the course of centuries we came to believe that all the world's woes could be solved through reason and science. What little of the sacred or the supernatural survived was relegated to the private realm or reserved for the naïve, the poor, or the superstitious.

During the latter part of the nineteenth and the early twentieth century, Christians, especially those engaged within the academic academies, felt the pressure to bring faith into the modern world of scientific inquiry and reason. At this time science was the model for all disciplines. It was felt that those engaged in the disciplines of Christian theology and biblical studies had to become more scientific or be left behind.

During most of the twentieth century theologians and biblical scholars eagerly arose to the challenge of gaining admittance to the scientific academy. What is often missed, however, is that this great effort to be scientific led to the rise not only of Protestant liberalism but also the rise of Protestant fundamentalism. Both fundamentalism and liberalism in their basic approach to the study of the Bible bore the modern burden of what Max Weber described as "disenchantment."[10]

The modern world made it possible to reduce the world to its "factual essence," and both fundamentalists and liberals understood their quest to be finding and supporting the "facts" of their faith. Biblical scholars turned to the Bible in order to find "proof" or "evidence" to support their understanding of the world. In this quest the Bible became a critical player in modernity's obsession with its own power.

For liberals a search for the "factual" meant a turn toward the higher criticism of the German universities. This model emphasized a so-called "neutral objectivity" and a commitment to science in naturalistic evolutionary terms.[11] Under this guiding vision the Bible came to be understood as a collection of human documents revealing the evolutionary layers of history and interpretation. The Bible's robust reading of the world and its vivid eschatology was consumed within the eschatology of the Enlightenment, namely one that emphasized a reading of history as human progress. It is a view that Wright aptly describes as "we know better now."[12]

Conservatives during the early twentieth century rejected the "new science" of the German model. This science with its "speculative hypotheses," they argued, was not a true science. Darwinian evolution was unscientific because it was based upon mere hypothesis.[13] Instead, conservatives entrenched themselves in the earlier Baco-

10. http://anthropos-lab.net/wp/wp-content/uploads/2011/12/Weber-Science-as-a-Vocation.pdf.

11. Mark Noll, *Between Faith and Criticism: Evangelicals, Scholarships, and the Bible in America* (Grand Rapids: Baker, 1991) 32.

12. Wright, *The Last Word*, 96.

13. George Marsden, "Everyone's Own Interpreter? The Bible, Science, and Authority in Mid-Nineteeth Century America," in *The Bible in America: Essays in Cultural History*, ed. N. Hatch and M.

nian model of science as objective and empirical analysis. In addition, conservatives embraced the science known as "Common Sense Realism," an approach that argued that the world could be known directly and through careful observation it could be studied. It is the science of what Thomas Reid called "self-evident first principles."

For early twentieth-century conservatives such as Charles Hodge and B. B. Warfield, the Bible was inspired, but moreover it was a book that could *scientifically be proven* to be valid. It is out of this scientific ethos that they developed the doctrine of Scripture known as inerrancy. Inerrancy's basic premise is that in the original autographs the Bible was penned without error. This lack of error was *proof* of divine inspiration. As factual, the Bible could be demonstrated to be true. This was the burden of fundamentalist science, a burden of scientific inquiry, gathering facts that provided proof of the Bible's authenticity.

Within the fundamentalist version of the Bible there was little room for the supernatural or the mysterious. The fundamentalists believed that these things left the earth with the death of the apostles. In fact, conservatives such as Warfield distained the supernatural as much as or more than did the so-called secularists. For Warfield the Enlightenment eschatology of "we know better now" caused him to mock the old superstitious beliefs in miracles. He lamented how an ingrained belief in magic still tinged the thought of people in an age that understood "the true forces of nature."

The conservatives believed that Scripture was all the church needed as witness to Christ. It was a perfect, scientific record of truth that, if read with a reasonable mind, would cause people to come to faith.

Even though the Bible was shown to be "scientifically valid," by the end of the twentieth century fewer conservative Christians were reading this text. During this era the Christian (biblical) worldview movement arose as an attempt to address the increase in biblical illiteracy. The movement's proponents did not ask basic questions as to why people were no longer reading the Bible. Instead they dug their heels deeper into modernity. Barna's book *Think Like Jesus: Make the Right Decision Every Time,*[14] was, in many ways, a last ditch effort to shore up the modern project. Barna suggested that the problem today is how few people know how "to think like Jesus." Barna's Jesus is much more like the Greek philosopher Plato than the Jesus of the Bible. For Barna, Jesus knew the core principles of the law and the Scriptures. When faced with opposition or a decision, he drew from the reserve of principles. For Barna and others in the biblical worldview movement believers are to read the Bible

Noll (New York: Oxford University Press, 1982).

14. George Barna, *Think Like Jesus: Make the Right Decision Every Time* (Brentwood, TN: Integrity, 2003).

so that they can see the world through a biblical lens, having in mind the principles contained therein. In spite of their best efforts the biblical worldview movement failed to stem the rising tide of biblical illiteracy.

It is increasingly clear that the Bible of modernity—the scientific, objective text of facts and principles—is failing to draw Christians into its pages. It seems that this Bible has little power to enchant the lives of believers. There is a great need for a new Bible. By "new" I do not mean a different Bible or even another translation of the Bible. By "new" I mean that we need a Bible that moves beyond the world of facts and proof and worldview, principles, and application. We are in need of a Bible that has the power to reintroduce words like "holy" and "sacred" into our relationship with the text. We need a Bible that is Scripture. We are in need of a Bible that speaks as the subject, as otherness and not one that is merely the object of our inquiring minds.

We have come to the end of the modern Bible. Presently there is apathy in Bible reading, and U.S. Christians are entering what many are calling a Great Dark Age of biblical illiteracy. On the other hand, there is a hunger among the millennials for enchantment, for wonder, for beauty, for mystery, for the glorious, and for the dangerous. Now is the time for us to reclaim a reading of the Bible that would offer these things to this rising generation. If we do not claim the Bible as living Word of God, if we continue down the evangelical, modern, scientific fundamentalist road, our children and grandchildren will find the Bible to be a relic of a past and not a present living reality.

As a way forward I want to offer a vision of the Bible as an extraordinary means of knowing God and having God's life transcribed into us. In order to capture this vision I will discuss what may be described as an "ontology" of the Bible. By ontology I do not mean a way of interpreting the Bible but a way of identifying the nature and purpose of the Bible. It is my understanding that the Bible as Spirit-Word is a sanctified vessel that creates extraordinary space that takes readers into extraordinary time. Furthermore, it is my understanding that human beings as spirit-flesh are created and endowed with the capacity to be transformed into the life of the text. We read the Bible in order to become what Charles Wesley called "transcripts of the Trinity."[15]

15. *The Poetical Works of John and Charles Wesley*, ed. G. Osborn (London: R. Needham, 1869) 3:86.

The Bible in Life and Mission of God

In both the modern liberal Bible and the modern conservative Bible God is not intimately related to the text. Both camps see the Bible primarily as an artifact of history. For conservatives the Bible is a pristine, perfect record of God's inspiration. For liberals the Bible is a multilayered record of humanity relating to God. Both groups have divorced the great marriage between Spirit and Word.

It is important that the divorce between God's life and the Bible be healed. The true home of the Bible is found in the life of God. More specifically, it is found in the economic life of the Trinity and God's mission of restoring the creation. Scripture has been given the power of mediating the powerful work of God on the earth. Scripture is an agent of God's mysterious work through Jesus Christ in the restoration of all things.

This economy of God is not merely information about God. It is how God desires to be known. In other words, God's mission is to reconcile God's life with our life. It is God's mission to bring us into fellowship with him and to have his life transcribed into ours. Scripture plays a critical role in this mission. By the Holy Spirit the Bible mediates the presence of God. This view of Scripture's power calls for a robust pneumatology, one that our modern view of the Bible lacks.

As the time of his death approached, Jesus made it clear to his disciples that his presence would not cease upon his leaving them. The Holy Spirit would cause the Word to remain in them and would make known to them the mysteries of God. Furthermore, in the coming of the Holy Spirit the life of God would become the home for the people of God. The oneness, the wisdom that is in the triune life, would be extended to others. It is the Holy Spirit who is "God's outreach toward the world," making it possible for humanity to participate in the life of God.

The Bible should be understood as married to the work of the Spirit. By the power of the Spirit the Living Word is made present in human history. By the power of the Spirit the real, living presence of Jesus works in the world. The Bible in this marriage becomes Spirit-Word. The same Spirit who filled the incarnate Word fills the written Word. Just as Jesus did not minister apart from the work of the Spirit, so too the Bible does not speak apart from the work of the Spirit. The Bible does not have the ontological status as the incarnate Word. It is not divine, but Scripture has its own genuine reality, one that is fit to enter into the divine service.

This pneumatic ground of Scripture within the mystery of God's economy frees the biblical text from the confines of history. It becomes more than an artifact. By the power of the Spirit Scripture becomes an agent of God's reconciling mission. By the Holy Spirit the Bible is not a static repository of information. Rather it is pregnant with meaning, and in the words of Jackie Johns, "the Bible is pregnant with the eternal life of God."[16] By the Holy Spirit the Bible allows us to behold the glory of the only begotten Son. As we read the Scriptures we can testify with John that we have seen him, the only begotten of the Father.

The Bible as Sanctified Vessel

John Webster understands the Bible existing primarily as a sanctified vessel. For him the sanctification of the Bible is "the process in which the limitless freedom of God, the human element of the Bible is given its own genuine reality that is molded to enter divine service."[17] The Bible is thus "Holy Scripture." The biblical texts are human documents written by human hands, but these documents are placed into service for divine purposes. The action of the Holy Spirit not only made sacred the writing of the text but extends into the complex histories of literary tradition, the redaction of texts, and the compilation of texts. Likewise, the Holy Spirit anointed the process of canonization and interpretation of the texts. This work of the Spirit continues throughout human history as the church has read, studied, preached, and taught the Scriptures. Such a view of the sanctification of the Bible goes far beyond the idea of inspiration of the original writers. Instead, it requires a robust pneumatology that covers the entire span of God's saving actions in history. The Bible is thus an ordinary/extraordinary book. It is like no other. It is very much a human document written by human hands, and it reveals a very messy human history. But the Bible is also a divine document, sanctified and commissioned for service in the economy of God. The Spirit of God takes this human document and sanctifies it for service. The Spirit of God fills this document, making it alive and radiating with the presence of the triune God.

The Bible as Sacred Space

Because the Bible is alive, radiating with the power and presence of God, whenever the Bible is read (corporately or individually), the text becomes an avenue for the creation of sacred space. This space represents the convergence of Word, Spirit, and humanity. In this convergence the text is much more than a historical record caught within the framework of linear time. Something more profoundly mysterious is at play. Performance of the Bible creates a thin space where the veil between the supernatural and the natural worlds becomes transparent.

16. Private conversation, Fall 2014.

17. John Webster, *Holy Scripture: A Dogmatic Sketch* (Cambridge: University of Cambridge Press, 2003) 27.

This space is the very life of God drawing near to dwell with humanity. It is a perichoritic space wherein God's Spirit reaches out to draw us into the triune life. In this space the Word literally dances around us, convicting and transforming. In this space the Spirit-Word becomes the bridge between the mysteries of God and the mysteries of the human spirit. The Spirit-Word becomes the pen through which, in the words of John Wesley, God "transcribes his life in our own."[18]

In this dimension of biblical space, time is drawn as a vertical line as well as a horizontal one. We may call this dimension "eschatological time," for within its realm the eternal breaks into the temporal. The Bible becomes an icon or a portal wherein "light from the future streams into the present."[19] As Steven Land has noted, the Bible creates a divine fusion of time. In this fusion of space and time the past draws near and the future bends toward the present.[20] Reading the text is, therefore, an eschatological experience, a transtemporal journey that brings participants into the eternal presence of God. This space is thus sacramental, offering within its borders the efficacious power of transformation. It is abounding with real presence.

This space created by the Spirit-Word is both deeply personal and corporate. God's life as "being in communion" necessitates that our experience of that life is shared in communion. The Spirit-Word creates a community because God's life is communal. Because this community is not bound by temporal time and space, it includes those who were first witnesses to the Word as well as those who are now standing in the presence of that Word.

It is impossible to plumb the depths of scriptural space. It is as deep and as wide as God. It is as multidimensional as eternity. It is transforming space, alive and radiating the power of the Holy Spirit. It does not politely offer to us ways to think like Jesus or principles to live by or a biblical worldview. The Bible offers a truth that seizes us, captures us in its holy power. Like the realm of the Holy of Holies, sacred scriptural territory is both wonderful and dangerous. It is wonderful because in it we find the delights of the triune life offered to us out of God's ecstatic self-giving. It is dangerous because this space offers to us God as the living subject.

The Reader as Spirit-Flesh

You may ask, "How can any human being manage such a text?" "How can people interpret its meaning?" Operating out of the flat, two- dimensional mind of

18. John Wesley, "Preface to Notes on the New Testament," The Works of the Rev. John Wesley A.M. (ed. Thomas Jackson; London : J. Mason, 1829–1831) 14:238.

19. Nickolai Berdyaev, *Slavery and Freedom* (New York: Scribner, 1944) 261.

20. See Steven J. Land, *Pentecostal Spirituality: A Passion for the Kingdom* (Cleveland, TN: Centre Pentecostal Theology, 2010).

Enlightenment rationalism we cannot know and understand the Bible. A new vision of the text requires a new vision of the reader, one that moves beyond human beings as merely "thinking machines."

The good news is that we were created for the multidimensional, sacred world of the Bible. Just as the Bible is ontologically defined as Spirit-Word, humans are spirit-flesh. We are ontologically fitted for communion and union with the divine life. Furthermore, our mortal flesh can house the sacred presence of the triune God. Just as God chose to fill the ordinary text of the Bible, even with its human authors who lived in messy ordinary times, with the power of the Living Word, so too God chooses to fill us with his treasures.

Created in the image of God humans are made in a perichoretic pattern that is a dance of the personal and the corporate, the temporal and the eternal. We are made, as John Ziziolous describes, "beings in communion."[21] We have a relational ontology that reaches outward in both vertical and horizontal dimensions. We are designed to house the life of God. We are designed to have communion with each other.

Humans can be set apart as sanctified vessels. Just as the Bible is sanctified for use in conveying the life of God, so too we can be sanctified vessels fit for the presence of God. The Bible is both a sanctified vessel in itself and an agent in our sanctification. In other words, God uses his sanctified Word to sanctify his people. Being transformed by the Word, we are prepared to receive more of the Word. Thus the Bible takes us from deep to deep, from glory to glory. The deeper we go into the Word the more we are able to radiate the life of God. We are ordained to be what Charles Wesley called in his hymns "transcripts of the Trinity."

> Father, Son and Spirit hear
> Faith's effectual, fervent prayer,
> Hear, and our petitions seal;
> Let us now the answer feel
> Mystically one with thee
> Transcript of the Trinity
> Thee, let all our nature own
> One in Three, and Three in one[22]

---

21. John Zizioulas, *Being as Communion: Studies in Personhood and the Church* (Crestwood, NY: St. Vladimir's Seminary Press, 1985).

22. *The Poetical Works of John and Charles Wesley* 3:86.

LIVING WATER IN JOHN 4:7–30

Paul Scott Wilson

Serving a drink of water is no big deal. It happens in roadside restaurants almost automatically. You sit down, look at the menu, have some conversation, and the waitress comes over. She wears a nametag that has been put on and taken off so many times that half the name of the restaurant is worn off where she grips it. "Liz" is her name. "How are you today, dear?" She says it so naturally and it rolls off her tongue so quickly that she must have long forgotten she is using intimate language to address strangers, or else she knows that honey on the lips makes sweeter tips. She is hurried, she does not wait for an answer, as she fills the glasses with cold water from her aluminum pitcher, "Have you decided yet what you want?" Serving a drink of water is no big deal. Liz probably does it a hundred times a day.

A lot of people pay no real attention to Liz. She is one of a sea of waiters and waitresses in roadside restaurants across the land. Some of us might not notice the crepe soles of her shoes are worn down at the sides and heels, the dark rings under her eyes, or that she has on her left upper arm, just visible below her sleeve, a tattoo of a ball and chain with a red rose. Most people are probably too busy with the menu, or hungry, or tired from the highway to notice such things, but when Jesus comes in and sits at an empty table, he notices, he sees her. "I've been looking forward to a tall glass of water," he says. "If you want water, we've got plenty of it," she says, "Know what else you want?" He looks directly into her eyes, and she is startled by something she sees in him, or that he sees in her. He says, "If you knew the gift of God I have for you, you would ask me for living water. Chicago water is good. It is good water, but it has its limits. 'Everyone who drinks of this water will be thirsty again, but those who drink of the water that I will give them will never be thirsty. The water that I will give will become in them a spring of water gushing up to eternal life.'"

Apparently serving a drink of water can be a big deal. I wonder how many people we meet in a day need the cup of water Jesus offers? I see a lot of people in a day, and I wonder. Does the driver of the bus that sideswiped a car need Jesus' cup of water? What about the greengrocer couple from Korea who keep the shop open from seven to eleven to better the lives of their children? What of the single mom on the subway or my dentist? What about the man sitting on the sidewalk with the empty Starbucks cup? All I have to do is add the water, but how do I—how do we do that? Do we quote Scripture? Do we pray? Offering a drink of water is a bigger deal than we thought. This is why so many students at our theology schools spend so much on education—to find out how to offer a simple cup of water. We have hermeneutics, systematics, homiletics, ethics, historical, pastoral, and constructive theology to tell us this one simple thing. How do I serve the drink of living water that will become in others a spring of water gushing up to eternal life?

John Skoyles is the poetry editor of *Ploughshares* magazine and the author of the recent memoir *A Moveable Famine.*[1] A former girlfriend of his from thirty-five years ago had read some of his poetry in *The New Yorker* and emailed him. In the course of their exchanges he told her about his memoir that he had written mostly about the period in which he knew her, and she commented that it must be mostly about drinking. He initially denied it. The comment stayed with him, and he went back and reread what he had been blind to see, not just in his memoir but in his poetry in general, that much of his life revolved around drinking. She told him that she had struggled with alcoholism for most of her life and that she was now four years sober. He came to admit his own alcoholism and to begin a much improved life of sobriety. I do not know if Skoyles believes in God, but in my understanding, when lives are turned around for the better, the One who is the true author of all good deeds is responsible. This season after Pentecost is a wonderful time for us to be more fully aware of the Holy Spirit acting around us, not just for the faithful, but for all: God sends rain "on the righteous and the unrighteous" (Matt 5:45). As Skoyles says about his friend, she turned my wine into water.[2]

Apparently serving a drink of water can be a very big deal, especially if it comes with being known more deeply than you imagined possible. Jesus says to the woman, "You are right in saying 'I have no husband'; for you have had five husbands, and the one you have now is not your husband." She is amazed that he knows. They talk and she says, "He told me everything I have ever done." He knows not just what sins she has done in her time, but also what sins have been committed against her, the abuse she has suffered, the scorn she has received, the grief she has endured, the loneliness she has borne, the deep pain she knows of being on the outside. The only thing better than being known for who you are is being loved as you are. She is most amazed that in knowing her completely, Jesus does not turn from her, but he singles her out for honor. He pronounces she will be a "true worshipper" who will worship "in spirit and in truth" and that God "seeks such as these"—such as her, such as you

---

1. (Sag Harbor, NY: Permanent, 2014).

2. John Skoyles, "How My Wine Turned to Water," *New York Times*, June 22, 2014, New York edition, Sunday Review, 8.

and me—to offer worship! Not only does Jesus tell her who she is, he tells her who he is, and that is the biggest gift of all. When she half-guesses and says "I know that Messiah is coming," he replies, "I am he, the one who is speaking to you."

Is not that the deepest longing in all of us, to be known and loved, to hear the words, "I am he, the one who is speaking to you," and to have the reality of God made present? Offering a cup of living water is a very big deal. It is too big a deal for us to do on our own. We cannot offer the cup of water by ourselves. It is Jesus who offers the living water, for the living water is himself, the one who is true life. All we have to do is become like Liz, become one of the outsiders, dare to be rejected: she rushes around calling folks over to Jesus' table, inviting them to his table, and introducing them to him. Invite anyone who is willing, "Come and see someone who told me everything I have ever done!" Some may laugh and some may scorn. Invite them any way that will be hospitable, invitationally welcoming, respectful of who they are, and loving of whose they truly are. Tell them what has happened to you. Tell them about a love that has never let go of you.

When we offer a cup of water to others, often we are the ones who receive. Liz was not thirsty, Jesus was, but when he asks her for a drink, he ends up offering her living water. We have a student at our college from Ghana, whom I will call Jeremy. He developed facial cancer, and Jim and Sharone on different occasions were among those who went to visit him in his apartment and in hospital. Jim went to visit in the days before the surgery, and Jeremy took him to another apartment in the building. "I have a surprise for you. Now I am going to show you how we pray Ghanian style." Jim was amazed: there was singing and dancing and ululating. Jim said, "You could feel the palpable presence of God in that room. I thought I was going to pray for him, and they ended up praying for me." Sharone had a similar experience. She went after his surgery, which proved remarkably successful, and found herself being asked by Jeremy what she would say to someone who was dying. She was wondering what she would say, but Jeremy gave her instruction about what to say to the dying. He even gave her a dog-eared copy of a pamphlet he had marked up. "Take this and read it; it will help you," he said. When driving away with her husband, she said, "I thought I was going there to comfort him, and he ended up ministering to me."

Sometimes we offer a cup of water just in being present to others in their need— the ministry of presence. Sometimes we offer a cup of water with prayer, sometimes it is with Scripture, sometimes it is with a good deed, and sometimes it is with just a drink of water. However we do it, in so doing in Jesus' name, he will make himself known. He is the living water. He is the living water poured out for us on the cross. He makes himself known through our giving of ourselves to one another, even now, even here.

ANNOTATED BIBLIOGRAPHY

Augustine. *Confessions*. Oxford World's Classics. Translated by Henry Chadwick. New York: Oxford University Press, 2009. This autobiographical work is a devotional classic. Readers are allowed to follow Augustine's journey to conversion through questions of sin, astrology, Manicheism, paganism, and God. Significant insight is offered on a theological understanding of the human plight, the nature of God, and the relation of humans to God.

Bantum, Brian. *Redeeming Mulatto: A Theology of Race and Christian Hybridity*. Waco: Baylor University Press, 2010. *Redeeming Mulatto* explores the intersection of race, discipleship and identity. Considering race as a form of discipleship, or distorted discipleship, Bantum explores how race shapes everyone's life, including those who are rendered "interracial," "in-between," or "neither/nor," and how they must navigate this space. Bantum thinks a reconsideration of the enfleshed Word as occupying a neither/nor existence ultimately draws all who confess Christ into a disruptive and liberating mode of discipleship.

Barclay, John M. G., and Simon Gathercole, eds. *Divine and Human Agency in Paul and His Cultural Environment*. Early Christianity in Context. Library of New Testament Studies 335. London: T. & T. Clark, 2006. This collection of essays by an international team of biblical scholars is perhaps the most direct effort to wrestle with the topic, at least regarding Paul's letters and the intellectual culture surrounding him. The essays attempt to make sense of Paul's thought without either removing it from or dissolving it into debates within Judaism in his time. The discussions emerge from a conviction that the topic has not been sufficiently treated since the beginning of the new perspective on Paul.

Bartholomew, C. G., and R. P. O'Dowd. *Old Testament Wisdom Literature: A Theological Introduction*. Downers Grove, IL: InterVarsity, 2011. This is the most accessible and helpful introduction to Wisdom literature available today. The emphasis is on the literary and especially the theological meaning of Proverbs, Job, and Ecclesiastes. Significantly, there is a chapter on the wisdom of Jesus.

Block, Daniel I. *For the Glory of God. Recovering a Biblical Theology of Worship*. Grand Rapids: Baker Academic, 2014. Block examines worship in the OT and establishes its key principles and practices. He develops a theology of worship rooted in the Bible and relevant to today's church and argues that worship is a response to the gift of God's revelation.

Bobzien, Susanne. *Determinism and Freedom in Stoic Philosophy*. Oxford: Clarendon, 1998. This book describes the Stoic theory of causal determination and how it was related to ideas of freedom and moral responsibility. Bobzien identifies arguments by which Stoic philosophers defended their views in conversation with competing philosophies of the time. This allows a more complete picture of the larger Greco-Roman intellectual climate in which Christianity emerged.

Boda, Mark J., Tremper Longman, and Christian G. Rață, eds. *The Words Of The Wise Are Like Goads: Engaging Qohelet in the 21st Century*. Winona Lake, IN: Eisenbrauns, 2013. This book has contributions by twenty-one experts on the book of Ecclesiastes that give up-to-date discussions of the book of Ecclesiastes from a linguistic, literary, historical, and theological point of view.

Borchert, Gerald L. *Worship in the New Testament: Divine Mystery and Human Response.* St. Louis: Chalice, 2008. Borchert defines worship as human response to the mystery of God in Christ revealed in the canonical writings. He explores the NT texts to show what each book tells us about worship and argues that these texts have much to contribute to living worship that affects individual and corporate discipleship, both within the church and throughout life.

Bowald, Mark Alan. *Rendering the Word in Theological Hermeneutics: Mapping Divine and Human Agency.* Aldershot, England: Ashgate, 2007. Within the field of theological hermeneutics there is need for discussion of the role that divine and human agency play in the composition of the biblical text and its interpretation. Bowald discusses the role divine agency plays in the process of human readings of the text and treats in depth the hermeneutics of George Lindbeck, Kevin Vanhoozer, Stephen Fowl, Karl Barth, and others.

Brown, Alexandra R. *The Cross and Human Transformation: Paul's Apocalyptic Word in 1 Corinthians.* Minneapolis: Fortress, 1995. Brown argues that Paul uses the word of the cross to liberate and transform the Christians in Corinth. This liberation from the old world's enslavement allows Christians to live lives of reconciliation as they are transformed to share the mind of Christ in response to the will of God.

Brown, William P. *Character in Crisis: A Fresh Approach to the Wisdom Literature of the Old Testament.* Grand Rapids: Eerdmans, 1996. Brown sees the Wisdom literature as a tool for our moral formation. His literary and theological analysis provides an interesting emphasis on the importance of Wisdom literature for the community and not just for the individual.

Butin, Philip W. *Revelation, Redemption, and Response: Calvin's Trinitarian Understanding of the Divine-Human Relationship.* Oxford: Oxford University Press, 1995. This reexamination of traditional readings of Calvin's theology argues that Calvin's understanding of the divine-human relationship is consistently grounded in the life of the Trinity. This provides the theological basis for Calvin's doctrinal work, including his writing on human response to God.

Calvin, Jean. *Institutes of the Christian Religion.* Edited by John T. McNeill. Translated by Ford Lewis Battles. Library of Christian Classics 20 and 21. Philadelphia: Westminster, 1960. Obviously Calvin's *Institutes* needs to be in such a bibliography, both for its careful discussion of the sovereignty of God and its impact.

Carson, D. A. *Divine Sovereignty and Human Responsibility: Biblical Perspectives in Tension.* Atlanta: John Knox, 1981; Repr. Eugene, OR: Wipf and Stock, 2002. Carson explores the tension between God's sovereignty and human response in the OT, intertestamental literature, and John's Gospel. This is a valuable discussion, one that considers the implications of this tension for other fundamental questions of theology and which concludes with reflection on how this tension affects mission and ministry in the contemporary world.

Carson, D. A., Peter T. O'Brien, and Mark A. Seifrid, eds. *Justification and Variegated Nomism: Volume I: The Complexities of Second Temple Judaism.* Wissenschaftliche Untersuchungen zum Neuen Testament 2.140. Tübingen: Mohr Siebeck, 2001. This volume evaluates E. P. Sanders' description of covenantal nomism through a detailed examination of available literature from Second Temple Judaism. The authors offer valuable critique of Sanders's work, emphasizing the complexity of Second Temple Judaism in an effort to establish a more nuanced understanding of this context.

————. *Justification and Variegated Nomism: Volume II: The Paradoxes of Paul.* Wissenschaftliche Untersuchungen zum Neuen Testament 2.181. Tübingen: Mohr-Siebeck, 2004. This volume reexamines the new perspective on Paul in light of the previous volume's evaluation of E. P. Sanders's work on Second Temple Judaism. The authors, while often appreciative of the contributions of the new perspective, argue in a variety of ways for corrections to positions that have become dominant in recent decades.

Cassian, John. *John Cassian, the Conferences.* Translated by Boniface Ramsey. New York: Paulist, 1997. John Cassian was a noted Christian monk and theologian whose interest in Egyptian monastic movements brought a greater diversity of practices and ideas to the movement in his time. Cassian's *Conferences* interacts with second- and third-century monks who responded to the divine by viewing quite literally Christ's instruction to take up their cross and give up their possessions. Cassian addresses the theology of self-denial as a way of life for a monk and has influenced future monastic movements with his work in disciplining the self and caring for the integrity of the heart.

Celsor, Scott. "The Human Response in the Creation and Formation of Faith: A Narrative Analysis of John 12:20–50 and Its Application to the Doctrine of Justification." *Horizons in Biblical Theology* 30 (2008) 115–35. Celsor argues that John's Gospel can speak to the tension still found between Lutheran and Roman Catholic understandings of the role of human response in justification. The gift of God's grace empowers and demands human response, but this response is not possible apart from God's initiative. The testimony of the Gospel of John counterbalances the Pauline epistles in important ways.

Chartier, Gary. *The Analogy of Love: Divine and Human Love at the Center of Christian Theology.* Exeter, UK: Imprint Academic, 2007. Chartier argues for an integrated theological method developed around the core themes of God's love and human love. Human love is a necessary response intertwined with the love of God at the heart of Christian theology.

Churchill, Timothy W. R. *Divine Initiative and the Christology of the Damascus Road Encounter.* Eugene, OR: Pickwick Publications, 2010. The Damascus Road experience is the first recorded post-ascension appearance by Jesus, and it is thus important in the discussion of Christology and the divine initiative. This book examines epiphany texts in the OT and other ancient Jewish literature, which leads to two categories for understanding the appearance of God, angels, and other heavenly beings: divine initiative and divine response.

Coffey, John. *Exodus and Liberation: Deliverance Politics from John Calvin to Martin Luther King Jr.* New York: Oxford University Press, 2014. *Exodus and Liberation* is an excellent examination of how the themes of exodus and deliverance are invoked throughout Christian history. The author demonstrates how cultural context has such a vital impact in the interpretation of biblical texts and offers a fascinating account of Christian responses to the Exodus narratives.

Duff, Jeremy, and Joanna Collicutt McGrath. *Meeting Jesus: Human Responses to a Yearning God.* London: SPCK, 2006. The authors explore encounter with God by reflecting on four parables from Luke's Gospel. The book uses both theology and contemporary psychology to discuss how humans respond to a God who longs for reconciliation with his lost people.

Dunn, James D. G. *The Theology of Paul the Apostle*. Grand Rapids: Eerdmans, 1998. This major work attempts to lay out the whole of Paul's theology as revealed in the canonical sources. While the role of human response in Paul's thought is discussed throughout, the eighth chapter's discussion of the life of believers is particularly relevant to questions of human response to God's initiative.

Duvall, J. Scott, and J. Daniel Hays. *Living God's Word: Discovering Our Place in the Great Story of Scripture*. Grand Rapids: Zondervan, 2012. Duvall and Hays present the large narrative framework of the Old and New Testaments in a way that invites readers into the narrative through participation in what God is doing in and through the Scriptures. The authors' goal is to motivate and enable meaningful discipleship in response to God's saving work in history.

Edwards, Jonathan. *Freedom of the Will*. New Haven, CT: Yale University Press, 1957. Written in 1754 by one of the leading philosophers and theologians in America at the time, Jonathon Edwards discusses the differing views of Calvinists and Arminians. Questions of free will, sin, and the knowledge of God are discussed, especially in relation to what is desirous, good, or evil.

Eigo, Francis A., ed. *Contemporary Spirituality: Responding to the Divine Initiative*. Proceedings of the Theology Institute of Villanova University. Villanova, PA: Villanova University Press, 1983. This volume explores different ways of understanding response to the divine initiative. Contributions include essays on Jewish responses, Jesus' response, and Christian responses. The essays offer windows into continuities and discontinuities between responses from related traditions both ancient and modern.

Ellis, Robert R. "Divine Gift and Human Response: An Old Testament Model of Stewardship." *Southwestern Journal of Theology* 37.2 (1995) 4–14. God's gifts to people in the OT call for stewardship. Proper management of the resources in creation is a way of acknowledging God's sovereignty and expressing gratitude. Stewardship, then, is a key human response to the creative initiative of God.

Engberg-Pedersen, Troels. "Gift-Giving and Friendship: Seneca and Paul in Romans 1–8 on the Logic of God's Χάρις and Its Human Response." *Harvard Theological Review* 101 (2008) 15–44. Engberg-Pedersen argues that our modern conception of gift-giving does not align with Paul's ideas about covenant and gift. Instead, we must read Paul through the lens of the ancient system described by Seneca. This provides an important hermeneutical key to unlock Paul's discussion of God's action and human response.

———. *Paul and the Stoics*. Louisville: Westminster John Knox, 2000. Engberg-Pedersen argues that Paul's theology was influenced in significant ways by Stoicism, particularly its approach to ethics. Scholars must recognize the influence of both Judaic and Hellenistic thought in order to reach a full and accurate understanding of Paul's theology. Engberg-Pedersen attempts to correct the dichotomous thinking that has distorted interpretation of Paul.

Erasmus, Desiderius, and Martin Luther. *Discourse on Free Will*. Translated by Ernst F. Winter. Bloomsbury Revelations. London: Bloomsbury, 2013. This exchange between two giant figures in Christian history is the background for nearly five centuries of conversation in the Western church about the human will's ability to respond to God. This is a particularly important text for understanding Protestant ideas about humanity and the will.

Fernandez, Eleazar S. *Reimagining the Human: Theological Anthropology in Response to Systemic Evil*. St. Louis: Chalice, 2004. Fernandez explores how human response to

God's action in creation is affected by systemic evils. Idolatry is at the heart of these evils, driving us away from the proper response to the gift of the image of God.

Ford, David F. "Divine Initiative, Human Response, and Wisdom: Interpreting 1 Corinthians Chapters 1–3." Pages 145–64 in *Shaping Theology: Engagements in a Religious and Secular World*. Challenges in Contemporary Theology. Malden, MA: Blackwell, 2007. Ford argues that much scholarship in the fields of theology and biblical studies, particularly in relation to questions of divine initiative and human response, has been too limited in its horizons. He suggests a "wisdom" interpretation of Scripture that he believes will allow theologians and biblical scholars to engage more fruitfully by taking seriously Scripture, doctrinal tradition, and contemporary life.

Fretheim, Terence E. "Divine Dependence upon the Human: An Old Testament Perspective." *Ex Auditu* 13 (1997) 1–13. This article examines OT texts that describe a prominent role for human response in God's work of creation and redemption. Fretheim suggests that these texts portray God as working so closely with humanity that God's plans can in some sense be described as dependent on human response.

Gathercole, Simon J. *Where is Boasting? Early Jewish Soteriology and Paul's Response in Romans 1–5*. Grand Rapids: Eerdmans, 2002. Gathercole challenges key conclusions of the new perspective on Paul. He focuses on the relationship of Torah observance and final judgment in early Jewish writing. He then interprets the first five chapters of Romans in light of this background, arguing that Paul is in fact rejecting a Jewish perspective about obedience to the law and final vindication.

Gaventa, Beverly Roberts, ed. *Apocalyptic Paul: Cosmos and Anthropos in Romans 5–8*. Waco: Baylor University Press, 2013. This collection of essays by NT scholars explores the implications of God's cosmic work for humanity and creation as presented in Romans 5–8. The essays treat the relationship between Paul's rhetoric on Law, righteousness, and the self along with the connection between grace and obedience.

———. *Our Mother Saint Paul*. Louisville: Westminster John Knox, 2007. Gaventa examines the use of maternal language in the letters of Paul. This language has not been treated sufficiently, but it can lead to helpful insights on how humans are to relate to each other and the divine and how the larger cosmic understanding of the gospel fits with feminine language and apostolic ministry.

George, Timothy. *Amazing Grace: God's Pursuit, Our Response*. 2nd ed. Wheaton, IL: Crossway, 2011. George analyzes historic controversies about the nature of God's grace and human response, mostly those dealing with classic Reformed theology. This book was originally used in many Southern Baptist Convention congregations to study these questions.

Gregory of Nyssa. *The Life of Moses*. Translated by Abraham J. Malherbe and Everett Ferguson. New York: Paulist, 1978. Gregory of Nyssa's *Life of Moses* is a spiritual classic that sees Moses as an allegory of Christian discipleship. Even more, Moses is an allegory of Christian transformation and what it looks like to be conformed into the image of Christ.

Hick, John. *An Interpretation of Religion: Human Responses to the Transcendent*. New Haven, CT: Yale University Press, 1989. Hick advocates for religious pluralism that represents authentic human response to a universe than cannot be fully understood. He argues that the human response of religion is deeply culturally conditioned. This is one philosophical explanation of human religious response across the boundaries of faith communities.

Joyce, Paul. *Divine Initiative and Human Response in Ezekiel.* Journal for the Study of the Old Testament Supplement Series 51. Sheffield, UK: JSOT, 1989. Joyce explores the tensions in Ezekiel between Israel's responsibility before God and God's promise to act to make Israel obedient. To understand Ezekiel correctly we must recognize the theocentricity of the book, particularly the focus on vindication of God's name.

Kaminsky, Joel S. *Corporate Responsibility in the Hebrew Bible.* Journal for the Study of the Old Testament Supplement Series 196. Sheffield, UK: JSOT, 1995. Kaminsky attempts to clarify the relationship between the individual and the community in ancient Israel. He is particularly interested in how God holds individuals and groups responsible for actions. This discussion is important for understanding individual and corporate responsibility for responding to God's initiative.

Kessler, John. *Old Testament Theology: Divine Call and Human Response.* Waco, TX: Baylor University Press, 2013. This text provides an overview of OT theology with an emphasis on the relationship between God and humanity. Kessler focuses on responses to God's initiative by his people. In addition to examining the OT texts, he also looks briefly at the NT and reflects on the Bible's significance for the identity of the people of God today.

Lapsley, Jacqueline E. *Can These Bones Live? The Problem of the Moral Self in the Book of Ezekiel.* Berlin: Walter de Gruyter, 2000. Lapsley argues that, in Ezekiel's understanding, identity is given to a person. Right action follows from knowledge of that identity. Appropriate human activity, then, is a response to God's initiative in bestowing identity upon his people.

Long, Thomas G. *What Shall We Say: Evil, Suffering and the Crisis of Faith.* Grand Rapids: Eerdmans, 2011. Long reviews the origins and history of the theodicy problem and enlists the help of major thinkers throughout the centuries to work through the issue. What is our human response to all the evil, natural disasters, war, and other devastating events? Questions on how to respond through our preaching are explored.

Longman III, Tremper. *The Book of Ecclesiastes.* New International Commentary on the Old Testament. Grand Rapids: Eerdmans, 1997. As in his paper in this volume, Longman argues Ecclesiastes is a book that contains two voices, not just one. In the body of the book "the Teacher" concludes that life is without ultimate meaning, while in the frame (1:1–11; 12:8–14) a second wise man tells his son the "Teacher's" message is true "under the sun," but one should not live there but should fear God, obey the commandments, and live in the light of the coming judgment. That is the proper human response to the divine initiative.

_____. *Proverbs.* Baker Commentary on the Old Testament Wisdom and Psalms. Grand Rapids: Baker Academic, 2006. This commentary focuses on the theological meaning of the book of Proverbs. Wisdom is more than a practical category or even an ethical category. In the frequent admonition to fear the Lord the sages alert us to the proper human response to the divine initiative. The divine initiative itself is connected to the figure of Woman Wisdom who represents Yahweh's wisdom and ultimately Yahweh himself. The commentary offers a Christotelic reading that explores how the NT associates Jesus with the figure of Woman Wisdom.

_____. *Job.* Baker Commentary on the Old Testament Wisdom and Psalms. Grand Rapids: Baker Academic, 2012. Job features the "fear of God" as the proper response to the divine initiative. This commentary focuses on the literary shape and theological message of the book. The divine initiative is seen primarily in the Yahweh speeches at the end. Job, while appropriately complaining to God about his pain, responds to the divine initiative at the end by repentance and suffering in silence.

Luther, Martin. *The Bondage of the Will*. Translated by J. I. Packer and O. R. Johnston. Grand Rapids: Baker Academic, 2012. This book brings to light one issue of dissent between the Roman Catholic Church and the early reformers. The subject matter of this book is what Luther says is the, "hinge on which the whole gospel turns." The text presents Luther's main argument in the debate with Erasmus, which is that salvation is not received through works of the law or any human merit but only through the gift of grace received through faith in Jesus Christ who through his work on the cross redeemed us.

Mackintosh, H. R. *The Divine Initiative*. London: Student Christian Movement, 1921. Based on a 1921 lecture series, this small book is organized into sections exploring humanity's need for God, God's initiative in relation to humanity, and human response to that initiative.

Malherbe, Abraham J. *Paul and the Popular Philosophers*. Minneapolis: Fortress, 1989. Malherbe examines the possible influence on Paul's thought from a variety of popular philosophical traditions in the ancient world. Because most of these philosophies were focused on the moral life, it is particularly enlightening to determine what influence they had on Paul's treatment of human life in response to God.

Martyn, J. Louis. *Theological Issues in the Letters of Paul*. Nashville, TN: Abingdon, 1997. Martyn emphasizes the apocalyptic themes in Paul's writings and challenges the usual stance of understanding Paul in isolation. He treats covenant, cross, and new creation in Paul's writings and in relation to views of humanity, both those of Paul and his contemporaries, especially the "competitors."

Maston, Jason. *Divine and Human Agency in Second Temple Judaism and Paul: A Comparative Study*. Wissenschaftliche Untersuchungen zum Neuen Testament 2.297. Tübingen: Mohr-Siebeck, 2010. Maston breaks away from recent scholarship that holds that both Paul and Second Temple Judaism thought salvation was through grace alone and not through works of obedience. Maston shows there was a range of opinions about human and divine actions and their relationship to each other within Jewish schools of thought. Using Romans 7–9, Maston places Paul within this spectrum of views and demonstrates with old Jewish texts the lack of a single view of salvation for all.

Myers, Benjamin. "From Faithfulness to Faith in the Theology of Karl Barth." In *The Faith of Jesus Christ: Exegetical, Biblical, and Theological Studies*, edited by Michael F. Bird and Preston M. Sprinkle, 291–308. Peabody, MA: Hendrickson, 2009. The chapter by Benjamin Myers examines the debate on the interpretation of *pistis Christou*, whether Paul was talking about the faith in Christ, or the faithfulness of Christ. Myers brings the theological perspectives of Karl Barth to the debate to center the discussion on Paul's theological concerns.

Oakes, Peter. *Reading Romans in Pompeii: Paul's Letter at Ground Level*. Minneapolis: Fortress, 2009. Peter Oakes uses both biblical studies and archeological finds to take the reader into the lives of Paul and his audience. Oakes examines what the human response and understanding would be from various people in society during the first century in Pompeii.

Runzo, Joseph, Nancy M. Martin, and Arvind Sharma, eds. *Human Rights and Responsibilities in the World Religions*. Library of Global Ethics and Religion 4. Oxford: Oneworld, 2003. This book is a broad exploration of how different religious traditions approach the ideas of human rights and responsibilities. While not focused on a Christian approach to humanity's response to God's initiative, it provides a useful interfaith context to important aspects of this topic.

Sacks, Jonathan. "Divine Initiative, Human Initiative." In *To Heal a Fractured World: The Ethics of Responsibility*, 148–61. New York: Schocken, 2005. Sacks argues that the narrative of Israel's relationship with God, from Genesis to today, reveals a movement from divine initiative to human activity as God shifts from controlling to empowering. In Sacks' understanding God both initiates and empowers, with humanity given great responsibility for the completion of God's work.

Shields, Martin A. *The End of Wisdom: A Reappraisal of the Historical and Canonical Function of Ecclesiastes*. Winona Lake, IN: Eisenbrauns, 2006. This is one of the more interesting and insightful studies of Ecclesiastes in recent years. Shields sees in Qohelet an advocate of an off-base wisdom movement of his day that is criticized by the second wise man who speaks in the epilogue.

Sprinkle, Preston M. *Paul and Judaism Revisited: A Study of Divine and Human Agency in Salvation*. Downers Grove, IL: InterVarsity, 2013. Sprinkle offers a way through the impasse he believes exists in Pauline studies. He argues that the key to interpreting Paul's understanding of divine agency, human agency, and the Jewish Law is found in two key OT paradigms. He proposes a new, more nuanced way to articulate both Paul's continuity and discontinuity with his Jewish community's theological conclusions.

Steensland, Brian, and Phillip Goff, eds. *The New Evangelical Social Engagement*. New York: Oxford University Press, 2014. This collection of essays examines the human response today in the evangelical church. The introduction tracks the history of the evangelical movement and its interactions with politics and civic engagements and acknowledges the presence of both conservative and progressive roots to this movement. The essays that follow describe the important work that the evangelical church has done and chart the future of contemporary evangelicalism.

Stewart, Alexander. "James, Soteriology, and Synergism." *Tyndale Bulletin* 61 (2010) 293–310. Beginning with a discussion of soteriological synergism in James 2:14–26, Stewart interprets the difficult passages in James within the context of the whole book and argues that the holistic human response described is the necessary and appropriate response to God's activity.

Swinton, John. *Dementia: Living in the Memories of God*. Grand Rapids: Eerdmans, 2012. John Swinton compassionately engages the question of the human response in dementia. The book offers two main questions: (1) Who are we when we cannot remember? and (2) When we cannot remember God, what does it mean to love God and be loved by God? Swinton offers theological and pastoral responses to these questions.

Talbert, Charles H., and Jason A. Whitlark. *Getting "Saved": The Whole Story of Salvation in the New Testament*. Grand Rapids: Eerdmans, 2011. The introduction and eight of the twelve essays are by Talbert and Whitlark, with four others contributing one essay each. Each part of the NT canon is treated, and three of the essays explicitly treat divine enablement. The essays focus on the role of the faithfulness of believers in salvation and show a particular interest in the implications of recent studies on Paul and ancient Judaism.

Te Velde, Rudi A. *Participation and Substantiality in Thomas Aquinas*. Leiden: Brill, 1995. Te Velde offers a detailed interpretation of Thomas Aquinas and his understanding of a God-centered reality. Attention is given to Aquinas's views on creation, the reality of being finite beings, and our total dependency on God. Aquinas's focus on the concept of participation of being and how we participate with others and God is a main focal point.

Theissen, Gerd. *Psychological Aspects of Pauline Theology*. Translated by John P. Galvin. Philadelphia: Fortress, 1987. Combining psychology, history, and theology, Theissen exegetes the writings of Paul and argues that faith in Jesus allows previously unconscious aspects of life to move into consciousness. This enables behavior that would not previously have been possible and provides a lens through which Theissen understands human response to God's activity in Christ.

Thomas à Kempis. *The Imitation of Christ*. Translated by Joseph Tylenda. Wilmington, DE: Vintage, 1998. This devotional classic is focused on providing direction for the spiritual life. The book is divided into four sections: Helpful Counsels of the Spiritual Life, Directives for the Interior Life, On Interior Consolation, and On the Blessed Sacrament. Thomas is concerned to teach the follower of Christ to renounce evil and the ways of the world and to embrace the truths of the faith.

Tiessen, Terrance. *Providence and Prayer: How Does God Work in the World?* Downers Grove, IL: InterVarsity, 2000. Tiessen lays out several models for understanding the interplay between human prayer and God's providence. He believes that the theology of providence many Christians confess is inconsistent with their practice of faith. He examines options and proposes a model that fits his theological belief about divine providence and the human act of prayer.

Valentin, Benjamin. *Theological Cartographies: Mapping the Encounter with God, Humanity, and Christ*. Louisville: Westminster John Knox, 2015. Christian theology contains three central doctrines: God, humanity, and Christ. In this book Valentin outlines each doctrine and traces their history in Scripture and in the Christian community. He compares and contrasts present-day understandings with historical understandings and notes where each doctrine engages the others.

Vanhoozer, Kevin J. *Faith Speaking Understanding: Performing the Drama of Doctrine*. Louisville: Westminster John Knox, 2014. Vanhoozer presents the need and reality that our faith in God is not solely about cognitive belief but is also about our actions and words in everyday life. With faith understood on analogy with the theater, discipleship happens through the performance of Christian doctrine in the church. We are then to take that performance and integrate it into our daily lives, where we acknowledge God and participate with God in the working of the Spirit in the world.

Williams, Rowan. *Being Christian: Baptism, Bible, Eucharist, Prayer*. Grand Rapids: Eerdmans, 2014. In this short book Williams argues that, despite great differences in Christian thought and practice, there are key elements of the life of discipleship that have remained important for the vast majority of Christians throughout time and place. Williams believes that these unifying responses to God's actions in history ground the life of faithful discipleship.

Witherington, Ben. *Jesus the Sage: The Pilgrimage of Wisdom*. Minneapolis: Fortress, 1996. Witherington's study of NT wisdom is quite helpful for understanding the biblical witness to wisdom. Jesus is the ultimate wise man and the very embodiment of God's wisdom. This book looks at the wisdom tradition from Israel, how Jesus fits with and moves beyond that tradition, and how Jesus can speak as a prophetic sage outside of the dominant culture.

Wyschogrod, Michael. *The Body of Faith: God in the People Israel*. San Francisco: Harper & Row, 1989. Wyschogrod offers a beautiful interpretation of Israel's identity and how we may understand Israel's existence and persistent presence in the world, not simply as another ethnic or racial group but as the embodiment of God's promise to be present with what God creates.

NORTH PARK THEOLOGICAL SEMINARY SYMPOSIUM ON THE THEOLOGICAL INTERPRETATION OF SCRIPTURE

SEPTEMBER 25–SEPTEMBER 27, 2014

Encounter with God: The Human Response to the Divine Initiative

PRESENTERS

Brian Bantum
Associate Professor of Theology, Seattle Pacific University

Beverly Roberts Gaventa
Distinguished Professor of New Testament, Baylor University

Jodie Boyer Hatlem
Teaching Fellow of the Louisville Institute in Theology, North Park Theological Seminary

Cheryl Bridges Johns
Robert E. Fisher Professor of Spiritual Renewal and Formation, Pentecostal Theological Seminary

Robert K. Johnston
Professor of Theology and Culture, Fuller Theological Seminary

Paul C. H. Lim
Associate Professor of the History of Christianity, Associate Professor of Religious Studies, Divinity School and College of Arts and Science, Vanderbilt University

Tremper Longman III
Robert H. Gundry Professor of Biblical Studies, Westmont College

John E. Phelan Jr.
Senior Professor of Theological Studies, North Park Theological Seminary

Paul Scott Wilson
> Professor of Homiletics, Emmanuel College, University of Toronto

RESPONDENTS

Andy Alexis-Baker
> Ph.D. Candidate, Marquette University

James K. Bruckner
> Professor of Old Testament, North Park Theological Seminary

Rebekah A. Eklund
> Assistant Professor of Theology, Loyola University Maryland

David W. Kersten
> Dean of the Seminary, North Park Theological Seminary

Nicholas Perrin
> Franklin S. Dyrness Professor of Biblical Studies, Wheaton Graduate School

Geoff Twigg
> Adjunct Professor, North Park Theological Seminary, Pastor of Worship and Adult Ministries, Elizabethtown Brethren in Christ Church, Pennsylvania

Jonathan Wilson
> Ph.D. Candidate, Lutheran School of Theology, Pastor, Evangelical Covenant Church of Elgin, Illinois

Paul Scott Wilson
> Professor of Homiletics, Emmanuel College, University of Toronto

Made in the USA
Middletown, DE
17 September 2022

10594312R00106